Bronx Ecology

ABOUT ISLAND PRESS

Island Press is the only nonprofit organization in the United States whose principal purpose is the publication of books on environmental issues and natural resource management. We provide solutions-oriented information to professionals, public officials, business and community leaders, and concerned citizens who are shaping responses to environmental problems.

In 2002, Island Press celebrates its eighteenth anniversary as the leading provider of timely and practical books that take a multidisciplinary approach to critical environmental concerns. Our growing list of titles reflects our commitment to bringing the best of an expanding body of literature to the environmental community throughout North America and the world.

Support for Island Press is provided by The Nathan Cummings Foundation, Geraldine R. Dodge Foundation, Doris Duke Charitable Foundation, Educational Foundation of America, The Charles Engelhard Foundation, The Ford Foundation, The George Gund Foundation, The Vira I. Heinz Endowment, The William and Flora Hewlett Foundation, Henry Luce Foundation, The John D. and Catherine T. MacArthur Foundation, The Andrew W. Mellon Foundation, The Moriah Fund, The Curtis and Edith Munson Foundation, National Fish and Wildlife Foundation, The New-Land Foundation, Oak Foundation, The Overbrook Foundation, The David and Lucile Packard Foundation, The Pew Charitable Trusts, The Rockefeller Foundation, The Winslow Foundation, and other generous donors.

The opinions expressed in this book are those of the author(s) and do not necessarily reflect the views of these foundations.

ABOUT THE NATURAL RESOURCES DEFENSE COUNCIL

The Natural Resources Defense Council (NRDC) is a nonprofit environmental research and advocacy organization with more than 550,000 members. Since 1970, NRDC scientists and attorneys have been working to protect the world's natural resources and improve the quality of the human environment. NRDC has offices in New York; Washington, DC; Los Angeles; and San Francisco. More information is available at www.nrdc.org.

BRONX ECOLOGY

BLUEPRINT FOR A
NEW ENVIRONMENTALISM

Allen Hershkowitz

Foreword and Original Designs by
Maya Lin

ISLAND PRESS
Washington • Covelo • London

ISLAND PRESS is a trademark of The Center for Resource Economics.

Library of Congress Cataloging-in-Publication Data

Hershkowitz, Allen.
Bronx ecology : blueprint for a new environmentalism / Allen Hershkowitz.
p.   cm.
Includes bibliographical references and index.
ISBN 1–55963–864–8
1. Industrial ecology—New York (State)—New York.
2. Wastepaper—Recycling—New York (State)—New York.   I. Title.
TS161.H46   2002
363.7'0525'09747275—dc21
2002010629

British Cataloguing-in-Publication Data available.

Book design by Brighid Willson

Printed on recycled, acid-free paper

Manufactured in the United States of America
02 03 04 05 06 07 08 09   8 7 6 5 4 3 2 1

For Dylan, Lea, and Connor
and, especially, for Meg

If you have built castles in the air, your work need not be lost;
that is where they should be. Now put the foundations under them . . .

—Henry David Thoreau

CONTENTS

Foreword, by Maya Lin   xi

Acknowledgments   xv

INTRODUCTION

The Hopes behind the Bronx Community
Paper Company   1

The Seeds of Discontent 6 • The Rise and Fall of the National
Recycling Act 8 • A New Beginning 15 • The BCPC 17

1. A New Blueprint: The Practical Side
of Idealism   27

Why Government-Dependent Advocacy Is Inadequate 30 •
The Prevailing Green Strategies 37 • An Industrial-Ecological
Approach 40 • Eco-Realism 46 • Conclusion 51

2. The First Step: Choosing a Target   57

A Dreadful Record of Damaging Impacts 59 • The Enormous
Surge in Paper Consumption 61 • Upstream Burdens 62 •
The Problems with Tree Plantations 72 • Downstream
Impacts 76 • The Influence of Government Subsidies 77 •
Conclusion 80

3. The Keys to a Better Ecological Bottom Line: Raw Materials and Siting   87

Using Recycled Raw Materials 89 • Why a Brownfield Site Makes Sense 96 • The Challenge of Infrastructure Issues 102 • Conclusion 117

4. Confronting the Technical and Economic Facts   121

The High Cost of Brownfields 122 • Cleanup 124 • Permitting and Zoning 129 • Construction-Labor Costs 146 • Managing Water 151 • Coping with Energy Expenses 159 • The Difficulties of Using Recycled Raw Materials 162 • Conclusion   167

Designing the BCPC

INTRODUCTION
Working with Maya Lin

CONCEPT DESIGN

COLLAGES

---

5. Clearing the Social Market   171

Understanding the Social Forces Shaping Market Possibilities 172 • The Challenge from Existing Businesses 174 • The Difficulties of Working with Community Groups 176 • The Interests of Local Political Leadership 178 • Litigation Intimidation from Construction Companies 183 • The Impediments That Color Dealing with Unions 185 • Dealing with the Culture of Business 188 • Old-Guard Resistance to Environmentalists in Business 191 • Conclusion 193

6. Getting Practical: Implementing Industrial
   Ecology   197
   Guidelines for the New Industrial Developer 197 • Understanding
   Systemic Barriers to Sustainability 205 • Building Bridges:
   The Power of Collaboration 209 • Conclusion 212

7. Forming Partnerships: Moving Past the
   Roadblocks   215
   Creating a Development Partnership 220 • Choosing
   Construction and Engineering Partners 225 • Working with
   Investment-Banking Firms 228 • Encouraging Community
   and Environmental-Group Participation 232 • Fostering
   Mutual Respect among Collaborators 245 • Conclusion 248

8. Getting Started: What Is to Be Done?   251
   What Environmentalists Can Do 257 • Allies Who Can
   Help 261 • Establishing Mutual Respect and Trust   266

Index   269

FOREWORD

When Allen Hershkowitz first approached me in 1993 to become involved in a project that would bring a large-scale paper-recycling plant to an abandoned industrial site just outside Manhattan in the South Bronx, I was only too glad to be involved, not solely from my interests as a designer but also from my concerns as an environmentalist.

His idea that recycling paper should be brought nearer to the source was groundbreaking. We would no longer mine virgin forests for paper mills in rural America, but harvest the urban forests that modern times have created, in cities where we generate more than enough wastepaper to take the place of our virgin forests. It was a precedent-setting dream that connected an environmental group, NRDC, with a community-action group, Banana Kelly, with government and unions and numerous paper companies throughout an almost eight-year process during which the Bronx Community Paper Company, the BCPC, took shape. The journey the BCPC took, from an abandoned rail yard in the South Bronx to paper mills from Maine to Sweden—where Allen and I and a few other coura-geous and hopeful souls traveled to learn, and to teach—is the story told here.

Allen always had faith that good design needed to be a strong part of the equation. I attempted to create a design that would showcase the recy-cling process—educate visitors about the importance of recycling, create a sense of community for the workers at the plant, and create a building that would give a sense of identity to the project. But I also felt I had a responsibility to not jeopardize the project with additional design costs.

Even if design were not a factor, the plant would mean so much to the community and to the environment.

The BCPC was an idea that perhaps was ahead of its time—at least in this country, where, sadly, the price of milk is higher than that of gasoline and it is cheaper to sprawl out in rural America than rebuild parts of our inner-city landscapes. But it was important to put forth the idea as a possibility: an idea that *should* happen. While we worked on this project, sky-high returns on technology stocks seemed like such a sure bet that no one was even considering investments in something like a real factory, regardless of the social and environmental vision behind it. And the politics of New York City at the time made certain the BCPC couldn't overcome that. It certainly wasn't for lack of effort.

Sometimes, as tools for us to learn from, ideas on paper are as important as physical structures. When the Municipal Art Society produced its 1997 show *Designing Industrial Ecology: The Bronx Community Paper Company* in its main gallery at Rockefeller Center during Christmastime, it was both to present the project and to educate people on what was possible.

We came surprisingly close to realizing a project that would have been an amazing collaboration between environmentalists, community, industry, and design. The idea that Allen put forth and that this book chronicles has been—and remains—of interest to numerous countries, city officials, designers, and international agencies across the world—in Europe, in Asia, and in dozens of cities throughout the United States. To me, we built an idea, one so fully formed that I look forward to when it can give fruit. This book is a guide for that time.

MAYA LIN
New York City, 2002

ACKNOWLEDGMENTS

Many people provided assistance to me during my eight-year effort to develop a recycled-paper mill in the South Bronx, and during the two years I spent writing this book about it. A few others, also acknowledged, provided valuable guidance, information, or inspiration. In all cases, these fine people, colleagues, and friends alike are blameless and the errors that may have crept into this work are mine and mine alone.

Thanks especially to my extraordinary colleagues at the Natural Resources Defense Council (NRDC): John Adams, Frances Beinecke, Eric Goldstein, and Patricia Sullivan. Working alongside these remarkable people is among the greatest privileges in my life.

Thanks especially also to my NRDC co-workers and trustees Sarah Chasis, Tom Cochran, Bill DeWind, Mark Izeman, Robert F. Kennedy Jr., Maya Lin, Joel Reynolds, Jonathan F. P. Rose, Larry Rockefeller, Jacob Scherr, Greg Wetstone, and Fritz Schwarz.

At Island Press, thanks to my gifted and committed editors and book-development team, particularly Todd Baldwin: I couldn't have hoped for a more thoughtful, hardworking, and collegial editor, whom I'm now delighted to consider a friend. Thanks so much to Michele Wolf—a most remarkable person—Randy Baldini, Donica Collier, Cecilia González, Amelia Durand, Krista Fisher, Sam Dorrance, James Nuzum, Taryn Roeder, Chuck Savitt, and Brighid Willson.

I owe huge professional and personal debts—and have a great admiration for—Per Batelson, Rick Campbell, and Rich Schrader, all of whom helped me conceptualize the Bronx Community Paper Company

(BCPC) project, compassionately implement its development, and sort through the many complex issues that arose almost every day we worked on it.

Thanks as well to all my NRDC colleagues and trustees, with whom I am truly blessed to be able to work each day. They assisted me—or consoled me—during the BCPC development effort and the drafting of this book. I owe a special thanks to Dan Saccardi, who helped research data; prepare tables, diagrams, and charts; check footnotes; maintain files; and contribute to editing this text. Without him this would have been a much less accurate and enjoyable endeavor. Thanks also to Robert Borque, Liz Barrett-Brown, Mitch Bernard, Henry Breck, Jennifer Burns, Ralph Cavanagh, Thomas Chu, Anjanette DeCarlo, Bob Denham, Robert Ferguson, Mike Finnegan, Bob Fisher, Ashok Gupta, Kate Heaton, Ari Hershowitz, Gerry Hauxhurst, Rich Kassel, Kit Kennedy, Chuck Koob, Ruben Kraiem, Brian Lake, Jonathan Larson, Nancy Marks, Tim Martin, Maribel Marin, Alan Metrick, Peter Morton, John Murray, Mary Nichols, Alex Perera, Juliet Rogers, Lynne Shevlin, Lisa Speer, Johanna Wald, Rob Watson, George Woodwell, and Sami Yassa.

Thanks to friends and philanthropic supporters of this work: Peggy Ayers, the Robert Sterling Clark Foundation; Marianne Lais Ginsburg, The German Marshall Fund of the United States; Lynn and Jerry Babicka, Diane Allison, and Beth Scribner Boyland, the Educational Foundation of America; Hooper Brooks and Ed Skloot, the Surdna Foundation; Matt Davidson, Joan Davidson, Charles Hamilton, and Henry Ng, the J. M. Kaplan Fund; Carol Guyer and Anne Romasco, the James C. Penney Foundation; Jeff Olsen, the Ford Foundation; Juliette Gimon, the Flora Family Foundation; Frank and June Larkin, the Edward John Noble Foundation; Mary McCormick, the Fund for the City of New York; Anita Miller, the Comprehensive Community Revitalization Project; the Overhill Foundation; Josh Reichert and Kathy Wagner, The Pew Charitable Trusts; and Jill Bullitt, Boca Lupo Fund.

Thanks to friends, BCPC supporters, and other colleagues: Hans and Carla Schultz, Len Formato, Michael Totten, Jill Lancelott, Terry Agriss, Bob Balder, Jim Black, John Cahill, Ed Campbell, John Cavanagh, Mary Ceasar, Marian Chertow, Randy Coburn, Ed Costikian, Chris Choa and HLW, Eric Deutsch, Gavin Donohue, Dan Donovan, John Dyson,

Thomas Falconer, Will Ferretti, Joe Fiteni, Tony Garel, Francesco Galesi, Marilyn Gelber, Mike Gerrard, Marty Gold, Jody Golub, Al Gore, Irving Gotbaum, Victor Gotbaum, Jim Haggerty, Oscar Andrew and Jennifer Hammerstein, Susan Henry, John Holusha, David Hotson, Rick Jacobs, Karl and Margarita Kempe, Susan Kinsella, Tapio Korpeinen, Anthony Lacavalla, Robert Lange, Mike Lee, Andrew Levine, Mark Levinson, Laurie and Lauron Lewis, Reid Lifset, Phil Lippincott, Emily Lloyd, Charlie Ludlow, Sharon Matola, Katie McGinty, Ron McHugh, Brian McLaughlin, Jim McNutt, Alan Milton, Ross Moskowitz, Torbjorn Nilsson, Vidar Nilsson, George Pataki, Hans Pettersson, Fred Prins, Bruce Pulver, Barbara Pyle, Tony Riccio, Rex Richardson, Barry Schneider, Phil Sears, Brendan Sexton, Ron Wallace, Bob Ward, Chris Ward, Carl Weisbrod, Lennart Westberg, and John Wissman.

Thanks as well to Matt Arnold, Marshall Berman, E. O. Wilson, Paul Hawken, Bill McDonough, Bill Browning, Marcus Kollar, Amory Lovins, Jacqueline Aloisi de Larderel, Surya Chandak, Helmut Schneuer, Phil Shabecoff, Dahlia Zaidel, Eran Zaidel, Lis Harris, and Martin Washburn.

And above all, thanks to Dylan, Lea, Connor, and Meg, and to Helen, Leon, Suzanne, and Michael. Words cannot convey my gratitude and affection.

It may be said there exists no limit to the blindness of interest and selfish habit.

—Charles Darwin

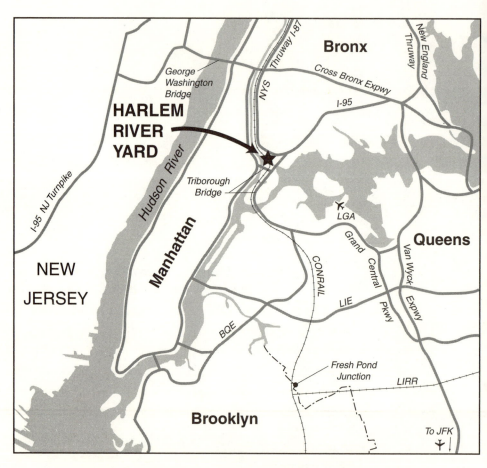

Location in New York City of the Harlem River Rail Yard, site of
the Bronx Community Paper Company.

Introduction

The Hopes behind the
Bronx Community Paper Company

> I tackled one job after the other for which I was not
> qualified. I had a self-confidence that was scandalous.
> I didn't appreciate all the possible dangers
> and things that could go wrong.
>
> —Ernst Mayr

IN 1992 I DECIDED to develop a world-scale recycled-paper mill in New York City at an abandoned rail yard—a brownfield, as former industrial sites are known—in the city's poorest zip code, in the South Bronx. It was a project designed to marry environmental remediation and economic development. Although I initially intended the project to be large enough to have a meaningful ecological and market impact, the project's scale and complexity grew well beyond anything I had originally imagined. At an anticipated cost that would ultimately have exceeded $500 million, its facilities were to include an integrated recycled-paper mill, a wastepaper de-inking plant, a newsprint paper-making machine, a wastepaper sorting plant, and a steam boiler. (See mill site plan on pages 2 and 3.) If it had been completed, the Bronx Community Paper Company (BCPC) project would have helped remedy many environmental problems—described later in this text—and produced 2,200 jobs during construction (for 22 months) and more than 400 full-time, permanent jobs. Just before the project met an untimely

1

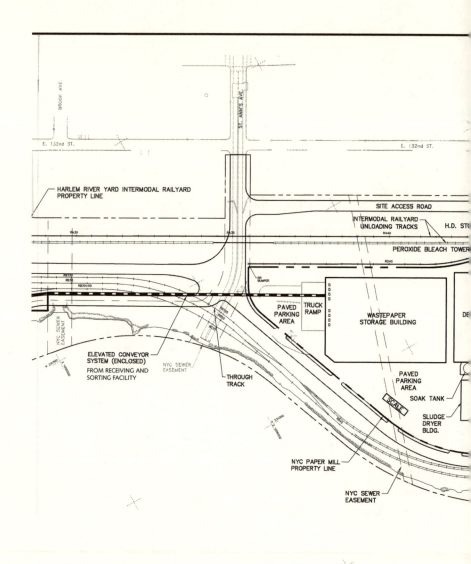

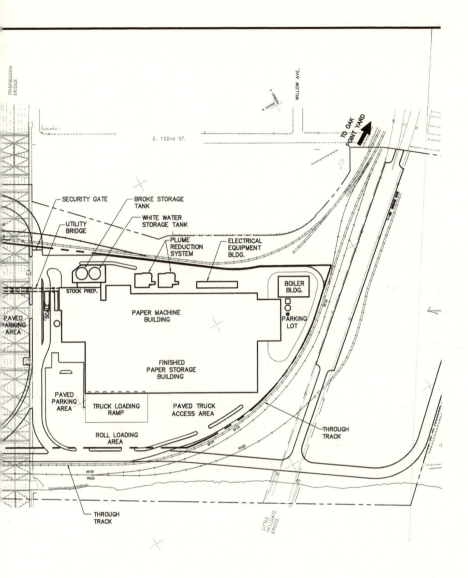

DRAFT

IT IS A VIOLATION OF THE PROFESSIONAL LICENSE LAW FOR
ANY PERSON TO ALTER THIS DRAWING IN ANY WAY, UNLESS
ACTING UNDER THE DIRECTION OF A LICENSED PROFESSIONAL
ENGINEER. THE ALTERING ENGINEER SHALL AFFIX HIS SEAL
AND THE NOTATION "ALTERED BY" FOLLOWED BY HIS SIGNATURE
AND DATE OF ALTERATION.

demise, it was recognized by President Bill Clinton—and throughout the industrialized and developing world by many other politicians, environmentalists, developers, and cultural observers—as a model for future development. Even America's most prominent critic of recycling, *New York Times* columnist John Tierney, wrote that my "dream of building a mill in the Bronx for recycled newsprint was nothing if not appealing. It evoked a certain admiration even from his [my] professional enemies, a group I [John Tierney] joined in 1996 by writing an article for the New York Times Magazine titled 'Recycling Is Garbage.'"[1]

I wasn't a visionary. I was just committed to getting something done. I had been involved in professional environmental-advocacy work since 1982, specializing for most of that time on issues related to solid-waste management, recycling, sustainable development, medical wastes, industrial ecology, and sludge management. As a member of the Natural Resources Defense Council's (NRDC's) senior staff since 1989, I had worked to promote recycling and reduce landfilling domestically, and I had also worked alongside environmentalists from around the world to prevent first-world nations from dumping hazardous wastes into less developed countries. To someone like myself, unschooled in the challenges and intricacies of industrial development—indeed, unschooled in any type of development—building a recycled-paper mill in New York City seemed like not only a feasible but a reasonable thing to do.

Wastepaper was—and remains—among New York City's top three exports. Of the approximately 36,000 tons of commercial and residential waste discarded in the city each day, a whopping 12,600 tons of it is paper.[2] The city is nothing less than a Saudi Arabia of wastepaper. Its annual production of cellulose (the raw material used to manufacture paper) is remarkable, equaling anywhere from between one half to the total amount of virgin cellulose in the entire Brazilian rain forest, a tropical forest that is by itself almost as large as the entire continental United States.[3] Moreover, the New York City metropolitan area hosts the world's strongest urban market for finished-paper products, serving some of the world's busiest law firms, the world's largest securities industry, and a huge publishing market that includes the *New York Times,* the *Wall Street Journal,* the New York *Daily News,* the *New York Post, El Diario,* the *Village Voice,* and hundreds of local, regional, and trade presses. The 1.5 million tons of newsprint consumed in the New York City metropolitan area each year is by itself more than the 1.2 million tons consumed annually by all of Canada. The New York City area alone consumes nearly 12 percent of the entire United States newsprint market, which annually uses 12.7 million tons of newsprint.[4] With this in mind, I couldn't understand why paper companies weren't clamoring to develop an in-city recycled-paper mill to take advantage of this plentiful supply of environmentally superior raw materials.

I was also moved to build a recycled-paper mill because of the decline in manufacturing jobs in New York City. Between 1995 and 2000, during the greatest economic boom in the city's history—and one of the greatest economic expansions in United States' history—manufacturing jobs actually declined by 11.8 percent.[5] Although broadening employment opportunities and alleviating poverty are generally not the focus of environmental groups, they are essential attributes of a truly sustainable society. As Mohammed Valli Moosa, minister of environmental affairs and tourism in South Africa, has remarked: "The single most important threat to sustainable development globally is poverty and the widening gap between the rich and the desperately poor. This is not only a threat to poor nations but also to wealthy nations, as the instability, conflict, disease and environmental degradation associated with poverty threaten the overall status of our planet."[6] Unfortunately, current international business trends are working in exactly the opposite direction. According to Joseph E. Stiglitz, winner of the Nobel Prize in economics, "Globalization has distorted the allocation of resources . . . [B]asic, and even obvious, principles often seem contradicted. One might have thought that money would flow from rich countries to the poor countires; but year after year, exactly the opposite occurs. One might have thought that the rich countries, being far more capable of bearing the risks of volatility in interest rates and exchange rates, would largely bear those risks when they lend money to the poor nations. Yet the poor are left to bear the burdens."[7]

At the time I was working to develop the recycled-paper mill in the Bronx, unemployment in New York City consistently exceeded 6 percent, averaging more than 2 percent above the national rate. In the South Bronx community hosting the mill, the single poorest 1990 census track in the city, unemployment hovered at the incredibly high 20 percent level.

(Since the early 1990s the citywide rate has continued to climb, and as of this writing it is 7.6 percent, 8.8 percent in the Bronx.)[8] This impoverishment makes it difficult for families to keep their children well nourished, safe, and properly clothed, and difficult for them to prevent or repair environmental hazards in and around their homes—making them more susceptible to public-health risks. And in New York City, as in Boston, Chicago, Denver, Kansas City, and other cities where manufacturing jobs have been declining, homelessness remains at record levels. Between 1997 and 2001—precisely the time the Bronx mill was originally intended to begin producing hundreds of permanent jobs—homelessness increased 50 percent in New York City.[9]

My initial vision for the mill was simple and seemed logical: It should remedy economic and environmental problems, not merely be "less bad" than other mills. The mill would take some of the enormous amount of newspapers and magazines New Yorkers throw away each day and manufacture new newsprint from it. Environmental problems in New York City were already serious, and although developing a recycling mill that added fewer burdens might have been an improvement over building a paper mill that used virgin resources, that would not have been accomplishment enough. My aim was to ecologically and economically improve the location where the mill would be sited. However, in pursuing the BCPC, I was also pursuing a larger set of goals, one informed by several decades of frustrated efforts to rectify industrial and social ills by more traditional means.

THE SEEDS OF DISCONTENT

Throughout the late 1980s and early 1990s, I directed NRDC's solid waste management project.[10] The job involved research and congressional, legislative, and regulatory lobbying, often in coalition with representatives of cities, counties, states, and other environmentalists. Among the legislative and regulatory initiatives we fought to enact were those designed to encourage consumer-products companies to reduce the potentially toxic, nonrecyclable waste designed into the products and packaging you and I purchase every day. One way we attempted to do this was by promoting legislation and regulations that would stimulate broader markets for recycled materials. If manufacturers had to use recycled packaging instead of virgin-based resources, they themselves would then have to deal with the dangerous and pricey-to-dispose-of toxics they had designed into their goods, so they would have an incentive to reduce their use of them. Also, if they had to take back their priced-to-dispose-of packaging—as the Europeans require—they would be encouraged to reduce the wastes going to costly incinerators and landfills. Because less packaging means less material, manufacturers would invariably produce less pollution in creating each unit of product. We in the environmental community believed that our various legislative and regulatory efforts would have created significant environmental and economic value, and that the public strongly supported us.

It's important to remember that the 1980s was the decade when municipal solid-waste management matured as an environmental issue, worthy of federal policy makers' attention. Federal and state regulations had caused the closing of thousands of open dumps and landfills throughout the United States. With landfill space at a premium, waste-disposal costs spiked so high that some communities' leaders said they had to budget more for garbage disposal than they did to maintain their education, police, or fire departments. Community battles about siting new landfills became fierce, and the term *NIMBY*—not in my backyard—gained currency. As an alternative to landfilling, equipment vendors, financiers, and engineering consulting firms teamed up to sell many community leaders on the idea of building expensive and environmentally problematic waste-incineration schemes, which, like landfills, also led to politically divisive local siting battles, affecting communities in virtually every state in the nation.

In the late 1980s, incineration of solid waste was restricted in New York City because of public opposition based on its resource wastefulness and documented environmental hazards. At the same time, political and regulatory pressure was mounting to close the city's last remaining landfill, the gargantuan environmental nightmare known as Fresh Kills, on Staten Island. In 1986 the *Mobro* barge sailed around the Americas looking to off-load a ship full of New York City garbage. The daily media attention focused on the *Mobro* gave the solid-waste issue national visibility, as did new political battles about interstate waste transport, medical-waste debris washing up on beaches, ever-greater amounts of packaging, and growing waste-disposal rates. Other volatile public-health issues related to poor waste-management practices included dioxin-spewing hospital and apartment-house incinerators, spectacular waste-tire fires, and revelations that highly toxic materials increasingly saturate everyday consumer products.

During this time frame, research reports from Europe and Japan confirmed that the United States was unusually wasteful. Those countries had higher levels of recycling, lower levels of per-capita (and per-GDP) waste generation, and greater controls—if not outright moratoriums—on waste incineration. According to a report issued by the Congressional Research Service (CRS) in 1991, "both Japan and the European Community appear to generate at least one-fourth less [waste] on a per capita basis. Once generated, European and Japanese packaging is far more likely to be recycled. Of the 18 countries for which glass recycling data were available . . . the United States ranked last. . . . The United States' rate of paper recycling also lags most of Europe and Japan: of the 18 countries, the United States ranked 15th."[11] In other words, it was possible to be economically successful and produce less waste, and there were better ways to get rid of the waste. Other countries had proven they could do it. Why shouldn't we?

THE RISE AND FALL OF THE NATIONAL RECYCLING ACT

By 1988 it became clear that although garbage management was a local problem, it had both national and global dimensions, including policies related to interstate commerce and international trade. In response to pressure from state and local governments and activists, Congress seemed ready to consider drafting a National Recycling Act to help develop recycling markets. I joined NRDC that year to lead the organization's effort to help draft that statute.

It would be hard to overstate the complexity of getting a meaningful, environmentally progressive bill adopted by both houses of Congress and signed into law by the president. I worked on the national-recycling bill for more than four years and, as part of that process, led perhaps two

dozen research tours to Japan and Europe—and many others throughout
the United States—to educate members of Congress and other federal,
state, and local officials about recycling and other waste-management
practices. One of the congressional fact-finding trips I led included,
among others, Senator Max Baucus (D-Montana), then chairman of the
Senate Environment Committee, and Representative Al Swift (D-Wash-
ington State), then chairman of the House Subcommittee on Transportation and Hazardous Materials, the subcommittee that governed waste
recycling; members of their staffs also attended. After that trip, I continued to work with these congresspeople and their staffs to draft provisions
of a recycling bill, vet them with other members to ensure their political
feasibility, work with scientists and economists to ensure that the provisions would have the desired effect, then redraft the legislation, and so on.

By early 1992, after four years of work, our coalition of pro-recycling
advocates and our handful of congressional supporters had what seemed
at the time to be an environmentally progressive draft National Recycling
Act ready for markup in the House of Representatives. Among other provisions, the draft bill contained a requirement for a deposit on beverage
containers—an environment-friendly policy whose effectiveness, obvious
to anyone living in a bottle-bill state, was substantiated by data compiled
from around the world by the CRS that showed container deposits to be
the most successful means of recovering packaging.[12] (The ten states in
the United States that now have a beverage-container–deposit requirement account for the collection of more than 90 percent of all plastic bot-
tles recovered in America.)[13] Modeled on laws in force in Europe, the
draft National Recycling Act required a commitment to recycle from
those manufacturers whose products and packaging made up a substantial portion of any community's costly waste stream. It provided incentives for municipalities to direct noncombustible and toxic materials away
from incinerators. And, to further enhance recycling markets, it required
that manufacturers of consumer products, including those that distribute
paper and plastics packaging, use at least a minimum amount of recycled
content in lieu of virgin materials.

As laborious as it was to draft the bill and build political support for
it, this was easy compared with markup. Markup is when a subcommittee or a full committee of members of Congress get together to review and

amend a bill before it is reported out for wider consideration in the House or Senate chambers. At this stage, access to committee members and their staffs by lobbyists and experts, who suggest and draft legislative language while the process unfolds, greatly influences the outcome of the legislation.

During any given year only about 10 percent of the House and Senate can be considered firm friends of the environmental community. By an overwhelming margin, most members of Congress are more supportive of the industrial sector, especially those industries that employ people in their districts and states and, even more especially, those industries that financially support their political campaigns. Of course, industry lobbyists who financially support members of Congress get disproportionate access to the member and his or her staff. Commenting on how he might try to influence some of the majority of U.S. senators still holding out against commonsense—and ecologically urgent—automobile–fuel-efficiency standards, an environmentally inclined chief executive officer of one of the world's largest firms reported to a few of my colleagues and me at NRDC that "for $5,000 you get a breakfast with a senator, for $10,000 you get a lunch, for $25,000 you get to have a long dinner with them. If you don't give them any money, they don't want to hear from you."[14] (Though the required mileage increase would have been modest, the ecologically overdue initiative to enhance fuel-efficiency standards again failed to pass the Senate in 2002.)

What the environmental community experienced during the day the National Recycling Act was marked up did nothing but confirm my view that most members of Congress are indirect employees of private capital interests. It exemplifies what environmentalists are up against when we rely on Congress to enact ecological reforms.

On June 6, 1992, when I showed up at 7:30 A.M. at the hearing room for the House Committee on Energy and Commerce in the Rayburn Office Building for a markup that was going to begin at 10 A.M., I was handed a slip by the House security guard with number 189 on it and told to get on line. Industry lobbyists routinely pay per-hour place holders to show up at 6 A.M. and get good spots on line for them when they want to attend such committee meetings for which seats are scarce. I could not justify spending NRDC members' funds on the luxury of not having to get up before dawn and wait in line, so I showed up early and waited. Ten minutes before the committee-room door officially opened, the industry lobbyists showed up and replaced their sleepy place holders in line.

Industry can always afford to hire many more lobbyists than the environmental community can hire. By around 9:30 there were at least 450 people in the hall of the Rayburn Building, all on line to get into the House Energy and Commerce Committee room—in which there are no more than about 150 seats—and not six of us were from environmental groups. One staff member working for Senator Jim Jeffords (I-Vermont), a proponent of deposits on beverage containers, told me he estimated that Coca-Cola alone had forty lobbyists working on the bill to sabotage any bottle-deposit or recycled-plastic–content provision. A subcommittee of the full Committee on Energy and Commerce, called the Subcommittee on Transportation and Hazardous Materials, was considering our recycling bill. Since I was number 189 to get in, I finally decided to walk over to the office of the subcommittee chairman, who was then Representative Swift, to ask if he would walk me into the Commerce Committee room through a back door used by the chairman, so I could be assured of getting a seat. Because I had worked closely with Representative Swift for four years on the bill and we had traveled to Europe together to visit recycling plants, he smiled, took out his ever-present cigar, patted me on the back, and readily agreed to walk me into the committee room through the chairman's entrance.

When I entered the Commerce Committee room, it was already two-thirds filled with industry lobbyists, who had had their own congressional allies walk them in earlier. So much for equal access to democracy. By the time the doors opened at 10 A.M., only two other environmentalists besides me had gotten in.

During markup, we got hammered.

Industry representatives had spent weeks coordinating with the staffs of supportive members of Congress and working up draft amendments for them to take into the markup, for members to attach to the draft bill. Then, during the actual markup, the staffs of pro-industry congresspeople—in this case, and typically, most of the committee—methodically strategized with their industry friends and trade-association supporters, communicating through the passing of notes or quiet voices about how to subvert any environmental provision they viewed as threatening to their narrow industry interest. Among the amendments they introduced that we opposed:

- an amendment that classified incineration of plastics as "recycling" for regulatory-compliance purposes;

- an amendment that eliminated the distinction between post-consumer wastepaper (the paper you and I discard every day and which needs stronger recycling markets so it isn't wasted in landfills or incinerators) and pre-consumer wastepaper (industrial scraps that are always recovered at the mill and have a low likelihood of winding up at a landfill or an incinerator);

- an amendment that allowed the administrator of the Environmental Protection Agency (EPA) to override local zoning ordinances to facilitate the siting of waste incinerators;

- an amendment that eliminated provisions in the bill that would have required deposits on containers;

- an amendment that gave industry broad control over environmental labeling on consumer-goods packaging; and

- an amendment that eliminated minimum post-consumer recycled-content standards.

Logrolling, a term familiar to anyone who has taken an elementary political-science course, is the "you-scratch-my-back, I'll-scratch-yours" way of the world in Congress. On that markup day for the draft National Recycling Act, pro–paper-industry congresspeople obviously agreed beforehand to combine forces and trade votes with pro–plastics-industry congresspeople, and anti–container-deposit congresspeople traded votes with pro-incineration congresspeople. Before you knew it, literally within a matter of hours, virtually all the progressive provisions in the draft National Recycling Act that had been painstakingly researched and assembled during the previous four years had effectively been sabotaged.

In fact, the bill's provisions were now worse than had the draft just been diluted through the deletion of pro-recycling provisions. The new provisions would have actively undermined environmental progress, and recycling in particular, had they actually become law. With incineration of plastics defined as recycling, the corrupted recycling bill would have ensured that a closed-loop recovery of plastics along with all the fossil-fuel–saving, resource-conserving, pollution-reducing benefits of true recycling would have literally gone up in smoke. The corrupted bill would have allowed industry to single-handedly control labeling of a product's environmental attributes; thus, consumers who selectively buy products with the environment in mind would have no independent ecological information to guide them. And the corrupted bill would have allowed the routine industrial process of reintroducing paper-mill production scraps—not the post-consumer paper you and I separate for recycling but pre-consumer industrial waste—back into the paper-production process to be labeled as recycling. As a consequence, municipal governments would not benefit from any new market-development expansion for the wastepaper they collect from our homes, virgin-timber production would continue to be encouraged, and consumers would be misled as to what the "recycled paper" they were buying was actually made of. All of these ecology-subverting provisions threatened to make their way into the draft National Recycling Act that the subcommittee was considering reporting out to the full House.

By the time the subcommittee was ready to vote, our mission was clear. We had to kill the bill. Our coalition of environmental groups issued a damning press release to the members of the Subcommittee on Transportation and Hazardous Materials and their staff, along with a threat to release it to the national media and to the press in their home districts. The release said that any member who voted for this bill was voting against recycling in America, the most popular of all environmental activities. It attacked the subcommittee members for drafting an anti-environmental bill, on the heels of the twentieth anniversary of Earth Day, that would not only set back recycling but would also cede control over environmental labeling to industry.

Congressional subcommittee members were in a bind. Given the great popular support for recycling, no action on the bill was better than voting in favor of it—however beneficial this would be for the House members' industrial clients—if this would label these congresspeople as anti-recycling. In response to our threats to send our press release to the media, the bill was never even reported out of markup, infuriating Al Swift, who wanted something, anything, to show for his four years of effort on it. He resigned from Congress shortly after that legislative debacle.

The National Recycling Act was history. Because industry wrested control of the bill away from environmental scientists, economists, and recycling advocates, within a few short hours we were forced to sacrifice years of hard work. Industry was relieved; some lobbyists were overtly jubilant as they left the Commerce Committee room after the once–environmentally valuable bill had died.

Unlike in Europe and Japan, no requirements to recycle municipal wastes would become federal law in the United States. To this day, no national law mandating recycling exists, even though local officials from cities throughout the United States continue to beg for recycling market assistance. What they find is an industry-controlled veto over any meaningful approach initiated by the few environmental advocates in Congress who intermittently try to advance this cause.

Former President Bill Clinton's 1993 Executive Order 12873,[15] requiring the executive branch to buy recycled paper, was drafted largely in response to the inability of Congress to act on recycling. It was written by environmental advocates the president had appointed—at the behest of then–Vice President Al Gore—to his Council of Environmental Quality and applies only to the executive branch of government. Alas, even with environmental advocates leading the charge within the White House for this pro-recycling executive order, I still watched from up close as a storm of opposition was unleashed inside the West Wing from lobbyists representing the virgin-based–paper industry. These lobbyists included the president's former secretary, from when he had served as governor in Arkansas. She had been hired by the American Forest and Paper Association (then known as the American Paper Institute) to help force a series of compromises on the original draft by relying on pro-business allies within the Office of Management and Budget and the White House Council on Economic Advisors. Even senators, including Senate Majority Leader George Mitchell (D-Maine), who was politically indebted to the big paper-industry producers in his state, weighed in on behalf of their virgin-paper–industry supporters, although the executive order dealt only with procurement by the executive branch.

A NEW BEGINNING

Disillusioned with our national lawmaking process as the dominant means to advance environmental objectives, I returned to NRDC's New York City office, looked out of my office window, and recalled a small recycled-paper mill I had visited a year earlier in Gemmrigheim, a small German town. The mill seemed to be a good neighbor, used no chlorine bleaching, and produced good jobs. As I stared at the city's downtown skyline in 1992 it occurred to me that perhaps my best option for promoting recycling markets in a meaningful way—indeed, perhaps my only option given industry's disproportionate control of government—was to build a paper mill myself, a mill that could serve as a real-world model confirming that environmental remediation and economic development could work in a mutually supportive fashion.

Although many years of recycling research and work with government officials had built up to this decision, the thought dawned on me suddenly, like the sun coming forth from behind a cloud. It illuminated a narrow path, but a path nonetheless. Many reasons for trying to build a recycled-paper mill rushed through my mind: I knew so many pro-recycling people in business—surely they could help. The sanitation commissioner in New York City was desperate to find markets for the recyclable materials her department was collecting—surely she would be supportive. New York City residents throw out a forest's worth of wastepaper each year, and so many newspapers, publishers, law firms, printers, and other consumers of paper were concentrated here—surely such a mill could make economic sense. And if environmentalists or community groups were to own part of it, as I had hoped, it might provide progressive forces with the economic clout to compete in the legislator-purchasing process, because meaningful campaign-finance reform remained (and remains) an unrealized dream. I even envisioned that it could be made into a beautiful addition to the often ugly cityscape that characterizes so many poor communities. Perhaps equally important, developing a mill in New York City would help keep me away from the legislator auction in Washington, D.C.

I walked downstairs to my colleague Eric Goldstein's office. Eric, the senior attorney at NRDC who coordinates our urban program's work, is an uncompromising environmental strategist, deservedly among the most influential environmental advocates in New York State. His major role in drafting and forcing the government to adopt the law that eliminated toxic lead from gasoline was praised in a *New York Times* editorial, which hangs framed on his office wall. (In a rare personal reference by the *Times*'s editorial board, Eric was singled out in the editorial for his effective advocacy work on the law.)[16] In 1992 Eric's strategic vision, when I first discussed developing this mill with him, was traditional and fierce: Litigate and regulate industrial bastards until they cleaned up their act or went out of business. When I walked into his office and announced, "We're going to build a recycled-paper mill," he looked up from his desk and said in a kindly and skeptical tone, "We don't build mills. And where would you put it anyway? We don't choose sites. Forget it."

If I had thought there were other likely-to-be-effective options to expand recycling markets, I probably would have taken Eric's initial advice and forgotten this idea. But at the time, following our legislative defeat in Washington, I saw no other advocacy path that made as much sense to me. To the extent that recycling mills had been developed in the past, they were invariably located as add-on technologies at remote virgin-resource–based mills. This increased their transportation impacts—by increasing the miles that have to be traveled to deliver the product, and the energy use and pollution that go along with that—and the mills did not substantially compete with high-quality grades in the virgin-paper market. I envisioned developing a recycled-paper mill that would diversify the range of paper grades that used recycled wastepaper. Typically, most recycling mills made tissues, delivery cartons, and cereal and shoe boxes, but very little higher-quality paper. Most magazine-grade paper and newsprint—on which newspapers are printed—contain little post-consumer recycled content.

Also, quite frankly, I was personally frustrated with the adversarial relationships that had characterized so much of my lobbying work. I was excited about the idea of building bridges with traditional adversaries, of getting to know more people in industry and working with them, of bringing their formidable resources and profit motive to our cause. After all, most of the people I spent time with personally were not professional environmental advocates but people in the private sector, and they personally seemed well-informed and sympathetic to environmentalists' objectives.

It took a few months, the encouragement of a former Greenpeace paper-industry activist that I had hired as a consultant, and a ten-day fact-finding trip to Sweden with Eric and a dozen New York City officials, financiers, grassroots environmentalists, and community leaders, but I ultimately convinced Eric Goldstein and, with that, most of my colleagues at NRDC that developing a model recycled-paper mill, designed to advance the still-vague concept of "sustainable communities," was something we should attempt to do. Though Eric never compromised his litigation schedule, his eventual enthusiasm for what the BCPC project was designed to accomplish underscores that even the most uncompromising environmentalist can add direct market intervention to the traditional toolbox that emphasizes litigation and regulation.

THE BCPC

As I've established, the BCPC's explicit purpose was to advance a variety of environmental objectives while bringing hundreds of new, livable-wage manufacturing jobs to New York City's poorest 1990 census tract. Before the BCPC effort, no "world-scale"—large enough to have a meaningful market impact on global prices and production levels—industrial-development project sought to test the concept of "community-based" sustainable development, or the viability of a industrial-ecology project on that scale, in any real-world context. Located in a New York State Economic Development Zone, as well as New York City's Federal Empowerment Zone, the BCPC evolved into the largest private-sector manufacturing venture ever attempted in New York City.

This book explains the larger notion behind the mill, as well as some of the many obstacles we faced trying to develop it. For now it is worth noting that the BCPC had a number of innovative features:

- *Recycling.* By using 400,000 tons of recycled wastepaper as its raw material, the BCPC was designed to advance the market for recycled, 100 percent post-consumer, totally chlorine-free paper. Locally, the project was designed to increase the availability of paper-recycling facilities in New York State. In doing so, the BCPC would confirm the viability of recycling as a solid-waste management option for a city that, in the 1980s, had proposed building five large waste incinerators at a cost of more than $3 billion.

- *Forestry.* The BCPC was designed to be world-scale, large enough to eliminate the market for harvesting more than 5 million trees annually, saving 16,000 acres of forest habitat each year. The BCPC would manufacture only newsprint, a largely imported commodity now manufactured using mostly virgin timber. It was designed to assist local publishers make the transition to using newsprint manufactured from recycled paper.

- *Brownfield reclamation.* The BCPC helped make an abandoned rail yard and brownfield site economically productive after a quarter century of disuse. Because the BCPC project signed a lease for the site, funds were released by the state and the private sector to clean it up. This included the removal of six underground storage tanks, lead, asbestos, volatile organic compounds (VOCs), polyaromatic-hydro-carbons (PAHs), and other debris.

- *Rail-freight development.* Along with the New York State Department of Transportation, the site's landlord, and a private developer, the BCPC planned to provide financial backing and market support for public- and private-sector investments into new rail-freight capacity. This represented the first private-sector investments in rail transportation infrastructure in New York City in more than forty years.

- *Community participation.* The project team—the team that ultimately formed the BCPC—accepted the South Bronx location after being invited in by a local community-development corporation (CDC). The development group carried out a best-efforts public outreach and dialogue process (more than 220 public or governmental meetings on the BCPC were conducted during its first 30 months, 122 of these in the Bronx). The project was endorsed by virtually every local elected official and received letters of support from two dozen local civic organizations, including housing groups, senior-citizens groups, and community-development groups. It was unanimously supported in a resolution issued on its behalf by the New York City Central Labor Council.

- *Reclaimed water use.* The BCPC was planned to advance the use of reclaimed sewage-treatment–plant wastewater. The project was designed to rely on treated effluent for more than 80 percent of its water needs and, in so doing, help establish a new water-rate classification for New York City that would have been one third the price of freshwater. This economically and environmentally superior approach was intended to show how other brownfield-redevelopment initiatives could be made more viable. Also, the use of cleaned effluent instead of freshwater would have been an important signal to upstate New Yorkers, showing that New York City developers can do more to conserve upstate watershed resources.

- *Advancing air-quality assessments in low-income areas.* The project helped promote a better understanding of local air-quality characteristics in its host community, the South Bronx. The project's environmental consultants performed the first small-particles assessment (known as a PM_{10} analysis) ever for a development project in New York City. (Today, we would have performed a $PM_{2.5}$ analysis, to study even finer particles.) We assessed the joint impact of pollution sources that were stationary (nontransportation related, such as factories and other buildings) and mobile (transportation related, such as trucks and cars), and we combined these predicted impacts with known "background concentrations" (i.e., the amount of pollutants already in the air from all sources we breathe every day). We envisioned developing, with some of the proceeds from financing, a Community Health Institute (CHI) that could help identify and characterize air-emission sources in the South Bronx and ways to reduce them, identify new uses for lower-cost recovered wastewater, and craft strategies to overcome the obstacles to the redevelopment of brownfields.

- *Air-pollution control and energy efficiency.* The BCPC was designed to advance the use of sophisticated air-pollution–control technology and industrial-energy efficiency. Plans anticipated the installation of advanced selective-catalytic-reduction–denitrification (de-NO$_x$) equipment (the first use ever in New York City) and also incorporated advances in energy-efficiency strategies for paper mills—such as energy recovery from vented steam plumes—not yet used in the U.S. paper industry.

- *Design.* Maya Lin, designer of the Vietnam Veterans Memorial in Washington, D.C., the Women's Table at Yale University, and the Civil Rights Memorial in Montgomery, Alabama, among other notable monuments, was the BCPC's facility designer. The *New York Times* listed her design of the BCPC mill as among New York City's most notable architectural highlights for 1998, and a catalog published by the Bronx Museum of the Arts—where the BCPC's design was exhibited—said "it may turn out to be the most impressive public artwork created in the Bronx."[17] (See digitally created photo of the mill below.)

Digitially created image of Maya Lin's mill design, viewed from the south.

- *Community projects.* As an outgrowth of our collaboration with a local community-development corporation, the BCPC was designed to fund a variety of off-site facilities and programs that would provide enhanced environmental oversight of the project as well as improve social services in the surrounding South Bronx neighborhood.

Though a few colleagues in the local New York City environmental world were initially skeptical, as NRDC's Eric Goldstein was, about gaining community support for choosing a site and nervous about collaborating with industry, I was greatly encouraged by the initial response I received from a broad array of city and state officials, community groups, and financial and industrial interests.

Of course, it never occurred to me that those supportive public officials would move on to other jobs, that community groups were not always the bastions of virtue my progressive inclinations had led me to presume, and that the friendly faces in industry who had wanted to work with me on the mill would change jobs. Nor did I have any idea how complicated it was to obtain a city contract, and we needed many. Being preoccupied with the environmental, social, economic, and even the aesthetic ideas I had for the mill, I never dwelled on the areas in which I was lacking expertise. And I was unfamiliar with the many and diverse political and market barriers that need to be overcome in order to design, develop, finance, build, and profitably operate a cost-competitive industrial project. It was in fact my outright ignorance of industrial financing and complicated project-development issues that allowed me to work so blissfully hard developing the BCPC. Yet despite the obstacles, the project came within a few months and a few signatures of groundbreaking.

But, ultimately, it didn't get there. It is difficult to give just one reason why.[18] My perspective is that although the technical, economic, and competitive barriers to the BCPC described throughout this book made it a more difficult-to-develop than usual endeavor, those barriers would have been overcome had our project team not suffered three decisive nontechnical blows.

First, and perhaps most important, the BCPC's project team and the government officials with whom we were working—including the governor of New York State—lost confidence in our community-group partner after the *New York Post* reported that the group's executive director, Yolanda Rivera, had become more interested in personal gain than in the project's broader benefits and objectives. According to the *Post*,[19] her staff had charged her with misusing the community group's funds for personal expenses. A second *Post* article reported that her friend Aureo Cardona had obtained a $1 million "consulting" contract with her group for work on the BCPC project, although based on my experience in the project he never actually did work on it. These revelations, coming just months before our anticipated financial closing, made it impossible for us to ask for continued support from the highly visible government officials who controlled tax-exempt financing and other technical and economic benefits for which the project might qualify. As far as they were concerned, after the *New York Post* articles appeared, and a state investigation into the group's finances commenced,[20] our community-group partner had the word *corruption* stamped prominently on it, and the officials wanted no part of it.

Second, the BCPC project's need for a wastepaper contract with New York City ultimately ran afoul of the political interests of then-mayor Rudolph Giuliani. As the project approached fruition, a number of companies that would have been adversely affected by the BCPC—firms such as Waste Management, BFI (now Allied Waste Industries), and Visy Paper, which were then exporting or using the city's wastepaper—made large political donations to the mayor, and their political friends lobbied the mayor to stop our project from getting the city, state, and private-sector support we needed. Moreover, if successful, the South Bronx location of the project was likely to generate plaudits to the Bronx borough president, Fernando Ferrer, who was an archrival[21] of the mayor and a mayoral candidate himself. Given their rivalry, the last thing Mayor Giuliani wanted was to lend any stature to Ferrer. In addition, in early 2000, when the BCPC project sought to finalize its wastepaper, water-supply, and economic-development contracts with New York City and needed the mayor's approval to do so, Mayor Giuliani was still contemplating a run for the U.S. Senate. His opponent at the time was Hillary Rodham Clinton. Her husband, President Clinton, and his vice president, Al

Gore, had both written favorably about the BCPC project—the vice president had traveled to New York City to praise it, and the president had written favorably about it in a book[22] as well as in a handwritten memo to White House staff, reproduced in a *New York Times* article,[23] indicating he wanted to attend its groundbreaking. So Giuliani may have viewed the BCPC's potential success as something Mrs. Clinton would support and that would be favorable to her interests, and New York City's famously competitive former mayor wouldn't allow that.

Finally, and as discussed later in this book, it is not uncommon for some firms, such as construction companies, to try to litigate their way into a large project. After all, if a business can get a judge to believe it is entitled to even a small—say, 5 or 10 percent—piece of a $600 million construction project, that still amounts to $30 million to $60 million worth of business. Consequently, some executives at construction firms working in New York City feel it is worth the hundred thousand dollars or so they might have to spend to litigate their way into a project. Thus, late in our project a small construction firm that claimed that we had at one time given it some construction rights sued NRDC and other participants in the project. Although the complaint was specious and was ultimately dropped, its threat, an $80 million claim, was enough to force NRDC in 1999 to cede its coordinating role for the BCPC to the project's for-profit partners. Without our advocacy skills—coordinating the complexities of permitting, water acquisition, wastepaper supply, acquiring environmental subsidies, community relations, and many other issues with which we had a decade-long familiarity—and facing the factors previously mentioned, the BCPC failed to achieve financing in June 2000.

Did that make the project a failure? Veteran environmental observer Philip Shabecoff wrote in 2000, when the project looked as if it might be built, that "Even if the [BCPC] project ultimately does not succeed, it can be seen as the beginning of a learning process for entrepreneurial environmentalism, a pathway to a new approach in the 21st century."[24] Likewise, former President Clinton observed that "the Bronx Community Paper Company teaches us that we have the power, if we muster the will, creativity, and cooperation, to recover lost pieces of America's environment, return them to good health, protect other lands and resources from being destroyed, and even create environmentally friendly jobs in the process."[25]

Without failures through attempts at innovation it is much harder to make any future headway. As Victor Hugo put it, "Often the losing of a battle leads to the winning of progress."[26] As it turned out, I learned first-hand that undertaking an ambitious, socially progressive effort and failing offers many lessons from which we gain valuable experience and, hopefully, some wisdom. The BCPC endeavor taught me great lessons about the many barriers to sustainable industrial development. It is my conviction that these lessons, recounted in the chapters that follow, have wide applicability for environmental advocates working in all fields throughout the world. Although a few of these lessons are somewhat technical, I present them in some detail. I make no apology for this. I have seen too many recycling advocates who know so little of the technical challenges of industrial development and manufacturing that they undermine their ability to be effective advocates. We must understand industrial design and processes as well as we understand their ecological impacts if we are to make informed industrial decisions. And if we don't make the decisions, corporate officials will make them for us.

Environmentalists are not in the business of writing laws. Nor are we in the business of suing corporations. Rather, we are in the business of reducing pollution, protecting habitat, and conserving resources. We are in the business of promoting sustainability, and everything we do must be focused on that objective. Passing a law or taking a corporation to court may sometimes be effective tools to help us accomplish our primary business goal, but these tools should not be confused as *being* our business goal. What we are trying to do when we use these tools is to legislate or litigate advances in ecologically favorable industrial, economic, political, and social behavior. While regulatory and judicial approaches to environmental and social reform remain essential to pursue, and were especially essential in the past to control gross pollution impacts, these approaches by themselves are now inadequate if we want to overcome pervasive market barriers and heal our global ecosystem problems. Large-scale industrial ecology—getting ecologically sophisticated industries off the ground—is our next task.

NOTES

1. John Tierney, "Paper Profits That Failed to Materialize," *New York Times,* 1 August 2000, p. B1.

2. Department of Sanitation, City of New York, *Comprehensive Solid Waste Management Plan, Draft Modification* (May 2000), Table 2.1-1 and Appendix 1.2-2 "RFEI." Approximately 35 percent of the waste stream discarded in New York City is paper, not including bathroom tissue discharged to the sewage system.

3. According to 2001 calculations by NRDC. At least two other institutions—New York University and the Regional Plan Association—have concluded that New York City actually hosts *more* cellulose per acre than the Brazilian rain forest. Regardless of which data one accepts, New York City still arguably hosts the most concentrated supply of wastepaper of any city on Earth. It *is* the Saudi Arabia of wastepaper.

4. Data provided by Central National-Gottesman, 4 February 2002.

5. Calculated from data provided by James Brown, labor market analyst, New York State Department of Labor, 16 April 2002.

6. Quoted in the agenda for the United Nations Environment Programme's 7th International High-Level Seminar on Cleaner Production, Prague, 29–30 April 2002, p. 5.

7. Joseph E. Stiglitz, "A Fair Deal for the World," *New York Review of Books,* 23 May 2002, p. 24.

8. New York State Department of Labor, Division of Research and Statistics, 16 April 2002.

9. Pam Belluck, "New Wave of the Homeless Floods Cities' Shelters," *New York Times,* 18 December 2001, p. A1.

10. I continue to hold this position.

11. James E. McCarthy, *Report for Congress: Recycling and Reducing Packaging Waste: How the United States Compares to Other Countries* (Washington, D.C.: Congressional Research Service, 8 November 1991), p. 3.

12. Ibid., p. 2.

13. In May 2002, Hawaii became the eleventh state to adopt a container deposit law, but it has not yet been implemented, so no data on the effectiveness of its recovery rate are available.

14. The discussion took place on 7 March 2002 in New York City.

15. In 1998 Executive Order 12873 was replaced by the more comprehensive "Greening the Government" Executive Order 13101.

16. *New York Times,* 27 August 1982, editorial page.

17. Distinguished professor Marshall Berman, "Views from the Burning Bridge," *Urban Mythologies: The Bronx Represented Since the 1960s,* catalog for an exhibit at the Bronx Museum of the Arts, 8 April–15 September 1999, p. 82.

18. For the most in-depth and savvy treatment analyzing the issues that prevented the BCPC from being financed and built, see the forthcoming book by Lis Harris, *Tilting at Mills* (Boston: Houghton Mifflin, 2003).

19. Allen Salkin, "Charity Big Axes Aide Who Called in FBI," *New York Post,* 16 May 1999, p. 20, and "Charity Chief's Pal May Get $1M: His Cut of Bronx Paper-Mill Project," *New York Post,* 17 May 1999, p. 19.

20. As of this writing, that investigation is still ongoing.

21. Such was the animosity between Giuliani and Ferrer that at the inauguration of Michael Bloomberg, who succeeded Giuliani as mayor of New York City, Ferrer was the only person on the dais of public officials to remain sitting when all in attendance were asked to stand and express their thanks for Giuliani's universally admired "Man of the Year" response to the aftermath of the World Trade Center attack.

22. William Jefferson Clinton, *Between Hope and History: Meeting America's Challenges for the 21st Century* (New York: Random House, 1996), pp. 102–5.

23. Don Van Natta Jr., "Mill Sought by Bronx Is Blocked; Railroad Buff Delays a Project in Train Yard," *New York Times,* 27 August 1995, p. A31.

24. Philip Shabecoff, *Earth Rising: American Environmentalism in the 21st Century* (Washington, D.C.: Island Press, 2001), p. 108.

25. Clinton, *Between Hope and History,* p. 103.

26. Victor Hugo, *Les Misérables,* first published 1862, translation copyright: The Folio Society, 1976 (London: Penguin Classics), p. 314.

1. A New Blueprint: The Practical Side of Idealism

> Those who serve life adapt to changes as they act.
> Changes arise from the times, those who know
> the times do not behave in fixed ways.
>
> —Lao-tzu

COMMERCE AND INDUSTRY are global, but every factory exists in some species' backyard. Thus, at the same time that global problems have become more complicated, transnational, and severe, the need to invest in and build *local* industrial corrections has taken on a greater ecological urgency. As the National Research Council's Board on Sustainable Development has observed, "Developing an integrated and *place-based* understanding of . . . [ecological] threats and the options for dealing with them is a central challenge for promoting a transition toward sustainability." It should be nothing less than an international "priority."[1]

Climate change, the destabilization of atmospheric chemistry, the proliferation of hazardous and nonhazardous wastes, contamination of freshwater resources, habitat destruction, biodiversity loss, fisheries depletion, and deforestation are occurring on a global scale. These problems now plague communities in ever more remote regions and have become more technically and socially complex to remedy. But the strategies traditionally used by environmental advocates to encourage more sustainable industrial practices—legislation, regulation, land purchases, and consumer action—while still critical to intensify and while effective in some (generally more affluent) regions and for some problems, are now inadequate to the more severe, complex, trans-boundary task of protecting the environment on a global scale. The task is complicated by the fact that the global environmental problems we face are themselves a consequence of local, fragmented, and industry-specific "rational" business decisions.

There are those within the environmental community who take this to mean that advocates must constructively engage with industry in order to reform it. Yet, in practice, despite its open-minded, progressive veneer, the environmental movement has been quite rigid and adversarial when it comes to relations with the captains of industry. Given the severe and sometimes deadly public-health threats and habitat destruction that industry has historically caused—so much of it affecting humanity's most sensitive and vulnerable population subgroups, children and the poor, and so much of it based on nothing more than pure greed—the antipollution, preservationist focus of environmentalists has understandably morphed into a general and disdainful anti-industrial worldview. But the focus on stopping or merely regulating bad practices, however essential it remains, has practical limits. Stopping a bad industrial practice, however infrequently successful that important act is, does not ipso facto result in a good remedy taking its place. Aside from the political challenges of enacting effective and timely legislation and maintaining a vigilant environmental-enforcement regime, it is not clear that government has the managerial or technical tools, or the political will, to redirect the global economy—currently on a path that will soon overrun much of the Earth's remaining natural ecosystems—toward more sustainable practices.

If the sustainable economy does not yet exist, it needs to be built, and—unless our governing ideology takes an unlikely shift to the left—it will ultimately have to be built and owned not by the government but by the private sector, primarily transnational industries. Whether we like it or not, these industries will continue to determine the course of the global economy. If we authentically want to reshape industrial practices, we should openly acknowledge that without influencing industry more directly, we cannot realize the potential of promising new approaches such as industrial ecology. Likewise, without cultivating capital—through collaboration with investment bankers and other sectors in the global financial community—we will not be able to meaningfully develop industrial alternatives to the destructive status quo.

More than a change in the worldview of environmentalists will be required. Businesses, too, must change and come to recognize that a rich, resilient environment provides the basis for all of life's activities, including commerce. Neither commerce nor culture is possible without a chemically stable atmosphere, biologically productive oceans, living forests, a healthy food web, fertile land, naturally replenishing clean-water cycles, and the processing of wastes by microorganisms in our soil, water, and air. Ultimately, natural systems and natural resources provide the basis for all economic value.[2] Besides its dire effect on public health, resident species, and our spiritual life, undermining our planet's environmental health also tends to make it more difficult for many businesses to profit or plan for the future.

Although environmentalists may tend to be idealists, there is, as Emerson suggested, a practical side to idealism[3] that is often ignored by progressive reformers. This strain within the movement is often called market-based environmentalism. Under its aegis, a number of strategies and initiatives have been pursued. Until now, however, unfortunately, with very few exceptions, market-based approaches to environmental advocacy have positioned the environmental community as a supplicant, begging for scraps of progress at the industrial table.[4] Working with McDonald's to modify the disposable styrene packaging for its hamburgers or with Starbucks to redesign its disposable coffee cups provided useful but narrow ecological benefits. More fundamental ecological and social impacts of the products' use or manufacture are left unresolved. For example, the impacts of industrial farming; the marketing of nutritionally derelict foods to children; habitat destruction; conversion of tropical forests; highway-dependent, sprawl-inducing marketing strategies; the impact of chemical fertilizers and pesticides on natural habitat; the depletion of freshwater resources and nonrenewable resources; and the dangerous disparity in well-being between rich and poor have, with very rare exceptions, been left largely untouched by most market-based collaborations initiated to date. New means of addressing these critically important issues must be found.

WHY GOVERNMENT-DEPENDENT ADVOCACY
IS INADEQUATE

Government regulations can't keep up with the pace of the economy's evolution or its damages to our ecosystems. There are many reasons for this, beginning with the fact that, in legislative as well as in regulators' offices, environmentalists have assumed the position of supplicant, begging an invariably small group of potentially receptive government officials to mobilize other potential supporters in government—and there are always only a few of them—to pass a law or draft a regulation that will stop bad commercial practices or, much less frequently, promote good investments. Yes, it is indisputably true that, in the most industrially advanced nations, this approach has, after thirty years, achieved some meaningful successes in reducing gross pollution impacts. As the Organisation of Economic Cooperation and Development (OECD) has confirmed, since the 1970s government "regulations and restrictions have been particularly successful in reducing industrial pollution, cleaning up the worst polluted surface waters, and reducing the levels of some air pollutants. . . ."[5]

But the pace of legislative and regulatory action and the demands of ecological sustainability do not proceed in tandem. While regulations have attended to many of the "low-hanging fruit" pollution impacts (i.e., those most easy to correct), dealing with the worsening pace of global deforestation, climate change, loss of biodiversity, urban air quality, and the growing burdens of municipal-waste generation have become less amenable to resolution by government regulations. I estimate that between 30 billion and 50 billion tons of wastes from all sources[6] are generated annually worldwide, and the amount generated each year is steadily increasing. The United States alone generates between 12 billion and 14 billion tons. That means that during the next decade the world will have to manage approximately 300 billion to 500 billion tons of wastes, a situation an EPA advisory board anticipates will be "environmentally disastrous."[7] Can we really expect any one state's regulations—or even trans-boundary regulations collaboratively enacted by an international agency or a regional group of states, which is of course very unlikely to happen—to effectively address this problem in a timely, economically equitable, and ecologically beneficial way? To quote again from the

OECD: "The problems of the future are likely to be more complex, and their resolution will require more difficult trade-offs and greater international cooperation" beyond the reach of traditional regulatory approaches.[8] Obviously, there is no natural—or man-made—law that says the United Nations or the U.S. Congress (or the EPA or another body) must respond promptly and effectively as global biodiversity is undermined, forests are destroyed, and fisheries are depleted, or as the chemistry and temperature of the atmosphere is altered.

Government action is limited by technical compromises and constrained and shaped by ecologically and economically arbitrary political jurisdictions. For example, the nesting and migration route of the endangered scarlet macaw traverses the political boundaries of Belize and Guatemala, two biologically diverse Central American rain-forest countries that are often on the verge of war with each other. These countries do not cooperate to protect their vast trove of biological treasures (including human settlements near their borders). While the macaw's habitat is protected in Guatemala, in Belize its nesting region is under assault from a hydroelectric-dam project being vigorously—and, some have argued, illegally—pushed by a Canadian energy company, Fortis, Inc., with the support of the Belizean government. The troubling political and economic boundaries that frame this threatening ecological situation are, from the perspective of the macaw's survival, irrelevant. The astoundingly beautiful, spiritually revered, and biologically valuable bird, which has existed and been worshiped by indigenous cultures for millennia, will soon become another of the many casualties caused by politically and environmentally uncooperative—in this case, unstable—relationships between states.

Sometimes a balkanized approach to policy making is in fact a good thing, since it tends to prevent a centralized, remote, and one-size-fits-all government bureaucracy from omnipotently deciding what is best for each and every region on Earth. But the fact remains that resolving the most serious ecological problems requires adherence to sound scientific, financial, and engineering truths that aren't limited by fragmented political maps and politically driven scientific compromises. Quite the contrary, advancing sustainability is thoroughly dependent on a respect for the facts. On the other hand, the legislative arena—or international political forums, a prince's palace, or a dictator's residence—is not a place where determining the truth is the principal objective, whether defined as good engineering, sound economics, or honest biological assessments based on the latest life-sciences data. Here are two of the more obvious ones: (1) While scientists would classify CO_2 as a pollutant contributing to global climate-change problems and the destabilization of atmospheric chemistry, politicians in the United States and elsewhere feel free to ignore the science at hand and have consistently resisted classifying CO_2 as a pollutant; and (2) during a debate in the U.S. Senate about the technological options available to car manufacturers to very modestly enhance fuel efficiency, Senator Christopher S. Bond (R-Missouri) said—idiotically, from the perspective of transportation engineers—that "stiffer mileage requirements would make golf carts the dominant means of transportation."[9] This nonsensical argument won the day, buttressed with hefty financial payments from the auto industry, and the Senate refused to enact an increase in fuel efficiency standards.

Rejection of biological, technical, and economic facts in favor of political expediency has been standard operating procedure in Congress and other legislative assemblies for decades—indeed, for centuries. Alas, even before a member of Congress introduces a bill for consideration by a subcommittee, it has already been compromised by anticipated considerations of what might be *politically* acceptable to the legislative body as a whole. Whether or not advancing a piecemeal compromise is *scientifically* adequate to resolve the environmental problem under consideration is always secondary to the political realities underlying the legislative process. As a result, tobacco remains an unregulated drug, hazardous oil and gas wastes have not been regulated as the hazardous wastes they actually are, and arsenic in water systems throughout the United States has been deemed "acceptable" by the government at concentrations that scientists know to be unhealthy.

What's more, the international nature of ecological problems, as well as the international nature of investments, absent international environmental laws and democratically organized administrative structures, further compromises the effectiveness of environmental strategies based on litigation or regulations within any particular nation-state.

Of course, getting the science right is only half the battle. Equally critical are the social and economic issues. And while government can theoretically integrate policies designed to alleviate social as well as ecological problems, it almost never has. More often than not, legislation—pushed by single-issue advocates—focuses on one fragmented environmental issue at a time, ignoring integrated social values like creating jobs in poor communities to build the kind of social capital needed to sustain environmental remedies. Consequently, even when government regulations incorporate accurate and seemingly comprehensive information for a single environmental issue, this still results in ecologically and socially fragmented—and usually inadequate—policies. By contrast, environmentalist-led efforts to help coffee growers in Central America earn livable wages and operate more ecologically—to cite one of the better-known examples of market-based environmental advocacy that integrates livable-wages issues into its objectives—reduces the fragmentation of social and environmental issues. So do the non–government-dependent efforts of environmentalists to save the fisheries industry, to promote jobs in waste-recycling businesses, and promote sustainable agriculture, which all try to integrate considerations of sustainable livelihoods with ecological issues.

But even in a perfect world, in which legislators would take both scientific and social issues seriously and recognize the need to manage them in tandem, the limits of the legislative process would remain inherent and abundant. By the time a bill gets through a subcommittee—for environmental laws this small step itself usually takes years, if it happens at all—it is substantially changed from what it was when it was introduced. I learned this quite clearly during markup of the National Recycling Act. By the time it gets through full committee, if it ever does, and full-chamber debate, which is even less likely to occur, any environmental bill is compromised again and again and again. If politics permit it, the same compromising process must then get repeated in the other legislative chamber, where a different version of the original bill ultimately emerges, if it emerges at all. The two versions of the bill must then get reconciled in a bicameral conference-committee meeting. During negotiations in conference-committee, the president's and vice president's offices also weigh in.[10] Before the president is advised to sign it, of course, the bill can be—and usually is—subjected to more technical compromises for political reasons at the White House Office of Management and Budget (OMB) and other more obscure White House agencies like the Office of Information and Regulatory Affairs (OIRA), the U.S. Trade Representative (USTR), the National Economic Council (NEC), the Council of Economic Advisors (CEA), and the Domestic Policy Council (DPC), not to mention the vice president's office, all of which, like the House and the Senate, are also heavily influenced by lobbyists for industrial polluters.

Even when a bill is signed and enacted as law, the governmental process of compromising the science related to public health and ecology is far from over. Before a newly enacted law can be implemented by the affected industry, it must still go through regulatory rule making, itself a multiyear process, where its provisions are further compromised by industry lobbyists or other representatives of the business interests that the evolving legislation would impact. Often these lobbyists have no engineering or scientific training related to environmental sciences, and they certainly have little sympathy for the social issues related to promoting sustainable communities. After all, how can people who are ruthlessly focused on performing one task—influencing government to benefit industrial clients—develop a concern for all of life's diverse necessities, including the needs of other species? A lobbyist's only expertise is in being a paid spokesperson able to slow down or otherwise derail regulatory implementation of federal—or state—environmental laws. They also have the power of the purse, and through the bevy of money-channeling vehicles available to large financial contributors, they can and do make our elected representatives dependent on their largesse.

After the Environmental Protection Agency, the Department of the Interior, or any other relevant agency finally designs its regulation (often a decade-long endeavor), it must then again go back to the White House for review by the OMB, to determine its "cost-effectiveness"—which means whatever any influential government official in charge at the time, or his or her business-interest master, decides it should mean—before it can be issued. Then, perhaps, it might become enforceable, unless it is challenged in court to delay it or change it, as frequently happens.[11]

Once a regulation emerges from this lengthy, scientifically corrupted process and is promulgated, industry must implement it. (See Figure 1.1.) Usually this is carried out by means of a multiyear, often decade-long,

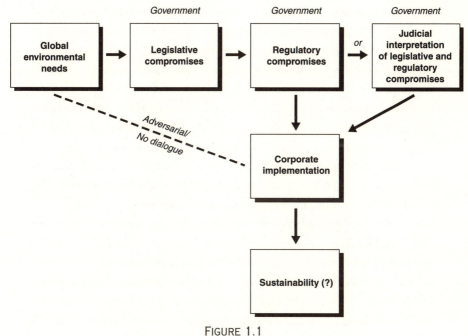

FIGURE 1.1

The Traditional Government-Mediated Advocacy Paradigm
to Promote Sustainability

phase-in. And, of course, the motivations of industrialists implementing government regulations are usually fundamentally opposed to the original spirit or ecological need behind the regulation. For environmentalists, clearly, implementation is supposed to protect biological diversity, public health, and/or habitat, or promote some other environmental value. By contrast, implementation of environmental regulations by corporations is invariably viewed merely as a compliance issue, to be achieved at the least possible cost, not as a call to usher in a new era of sustainability.

This scientifically compromised adversarial approach today remains the dominant one employed to address environmental problems. In fact, very often business interests don't even need to subvert environmental intensions in the legislative chamber to get what they want: They literally draft pro-polluter government policy for the president to mandate as an executive order. Recently it was reported that trade groups for world's oil and gas industries, the American Petroleum Institute and the American

Gas Association, each drafted executive orders for President George W. Bush to proclaim and sign, which he did with virtually no changes from the original text offered by these business interests. The trade groups' wish list was simply reprinted as written on White House stationery. These orders promoted the use of polluting fossil fuels, downplayed conservation, subverted oversight by citizens, and encouraged oil and gas exploration in some of the world's most ecologically fragile areas, including designated wilderness areas. Other proposed regulations—drafted by business interests and adopted by the executive branch without bothering with congressional battles—undermined public-health protections in the Clean Air Act in order to perpetuate a reliance on polluting fossil fuels.[12]

But the weakness of relying heavily on the legislative arena, or the executive branch, to advance environmental reform is only half of the problem. Just as deadly as the reliance on government-mediated action is the fact that environmentalists' work in legislative, regulatory, and international arenas is now primarily defensive, focused predominantly on trying to stop industry-financed and ideologically driven attempts to *roll back* important environmental legislation and past regulatory advances.[13] Not surprisingly, global and local ecosystem problems continue to escalate. Although gross attacks designed to roll back or avoid environmental regulations confirm that, to protect past successes, we need to intensify our presence in the governmental process, it is nevertheless true that this ecologically slow, intellectually corrupt approach is terribly insufficient.

Perhaps even more troubling than the corruption of ostensibly democratic institutions in the United States has been the emergence of unaccountable and ever more powerful international forums established under treaties such as NAFTA and the World Trade Organization. These organizations were created by corporate officials and their paid political hacks who sold out our democratic heritage—and hopes—by crassly designing these entities without even pretending to incorporate the most rudimentary democratic structures or to provide access to their environmental—and social—policy-making proceedings. Not one of the officials of these incredibly important global-regulatory bodies is in any way popularly elected, even though their policy-making influence is almost as great as or greater than that of any head of state—because they are subject to virtually no political checks and balances. In fact, the structures of these multilateral agreements were devised specifically to exclude democratic input on critical policy issues, particularly from consumer groups, environmentalists, and workers who, by seeking to defend a long-standing local way of life and preserve values other than the accumulation of wealth, have been stigmatized with the label *protectionist*.[14] The growing influence of these politically remote international bodies is by itself a powerful argument for environmentalists to establish greater influence over industrial production, investment, and other financial decisions.

THE PREVAILING GREEN STRATEGIES

Of course, green strategy to advance sustainability has not focused exclusively on litigation and government regulation. One well-known tactic environmentalists have used to soften humankind's impact on the planet has been to encourage individuals, families, and government to reduce consumption. The idea that living simply is a path to spiritual and intellectual enlightenment is found among humanity's earliest writings. A prayer in Proverbs states, "Give me neither poverty nor wealth, but only enough," and Socrates wrote, among many references to this issue, "Men are to be esteemed for their virtue, not their wealth." Through the centuries, based on philosophy or religious practice, many people have celebrated the value of what Wordsworth called "plain living and high thinking."[15] But it wasn't until the mid-nineteenth century and later, in the writings of Emerson, Thoreau, Muir, and Veblen, that reducing consumption was explicitly enunciated as a strategy not only to spiritual enlightenment but to counter industry's ugly and threatening ecological impacts. In 1980 economist Robert Heilbroner expressed it this way: "Whether we are unable to sustain growth or unable to tolerate it, there can be no doubt that a radically different future beckons. In either eventuality it seems beyond dispute that the present orientation of society must change. In place of the long-established encouragement of industrial production must come its careful restriction and long-term diminution within society. In place of prodigalities of consumption must come new frugal attitudes."[16] More recently, limiting consumption as a means of reducing industrial impacts became a basic philosophical premise of environmentalism when this was incorporated into the Agenda 21 treaty convention adopted in 1992 at the United Nations Convention on the Environment and Development (UNCED) in Rio de Janeiro.

Alas, people want what they want. By almost any measure, exhortations to reduce consumption have failed: Available data indicate that both individual and government consumption have increased dramatically in the last two centuries, especially in the last twenty years, and these trends are expected to continue and, in all likelihood, to accelerate. Between 1980 and 1999, private consumption increased by 46 percent and government consumption by 21 percent in the thirty most industrialized countries, those that make up the OECD.[17] According to the Worldwatch Institute, "Only population growth rivals high consumption as a cause of ecological decline, and at least population growth is now viewed as a problem by many governments and citizens of the world. Consumption, in contrast, is almost universally seen as good—indeed, increasing it is the primary goal of national economic policy."[18]

If we can't get people to reduce consumption, perhaps we can at least turn them into environmentally smarter consumers. Believing that industrial processes mirror consumer preferences,[19] environmental activists have logically suggested a strategy that focuses on changing consumers' consciousness about the products they buy, so they are more environmentally aware. The most authoritative expression of this—and arguably the most market influencing as well—was President Clinton's Executive Orders 12873, signed in 1993, and 13101, signed in 1998. These orders—which I helped craft and vigorously defend as they moved through many antagonistic, paper-industry–influenced White House agencies until they wound up on the president's desk—were ultimately signed only because Vice President Al Gore personally intervened. They set guidelines for environmentally oriented procurement by the federal government's executive branch, principally by strengthening the commitment of its many agencies to using recycled-content products. Because of these executive orders, the amount of recycled paper purchased by the federal government—about 300,000 tons each year—increased by 98 percent between 1993 and 1999, the last year, as of this writing, for which data are available. This has helped to reduce the inane dumping of valuable paper products into landfills, cut emissions of greenhouse gases, reduced pollution discharges into our waterways, and worked to reduce the conversion of green spaces that otherwise would have fallen to harvesting or mining. By increasing the purchase of recycled goods, the federal government is helping to broaden markets for these products and helping as well to make them more price competitive for all consumers. In a very real way, these executive orders have helped boost the market for a few slightly greener products, making them more accessible at more competitive prices.

Perhaps the most attractive suggestion for how citizens should influence the market comes from Wendell Berry, the reigning prose poet of the environmental movement. Giving voice to one of the most cherished of all environmental ideas, that of local self-reliance, Berry urges us to

> develop and put into practice the idea of a local economy—something growing numbers of people are now doing. . . . [S]horten the distance between producers and consumers. . . . [L]earn to use the consumer economies of local towns and cities to preserve the livelihoods of local farm families and farm communities. . . . [U]se the local economy to give consumers an influence over the kind and quality of their food, and to preserve and enhance the local landscapes. . . . [G]ive everybody in the local community a direct, long-term interest in the prosperity, health, and beauty of their homeland. . . . A viable community . . . protects its own production capacities.[20]

But despite Berry's smart and hopeful poetry, campaigns by most environmental groups, and a few people in government dedicated to shifting local development and the consumer movement toward self-reliant economies and recycling, remote global production systems and megacity sprawl are spreading faster than ever: More than half of the population of the planet now lives in and around cities. Food travels greater distances than ever (though contrary to popular belief, most is still consumed in the country in which it is produced). Increases in recycling have grown too slowly—and shifts by transnational corporations working in the developing world away from the use of more sustainably obtained raw materials, such as nonwood products and agricultural wastes for paper production, have been too rapid—to stem the life-threatening ecological impacts caused by the global expansion of timber harvesting, industrial agriculture, and forestry.

Thus, in spite of broad public support for the concept of local self-reliance and the widespread practice of recycling, environmental concerns don't play a large role in consumer decisions, whether people are buying food, paper, household cleaners, paints, furniture, carpet, or cars. Market research has confirmed that consumer decisions are based almost exclusively on price, performance, and style. As Reg Modlin, the director of environment and energy planning at DaimlerChrysler, observed, "Customers aren't going to choose to pay more money for an environmentally sensitive product."[21] While a few very committed—often affluent—environmentally oriented consumers might regularly do this, don't bet your child's future on the hope that billions of consumers will set aside their interest in low prices or in being part of the latest fashion trend because of concerns about the environment. Emma Rothschild, director of the Centre for History and Economics at King's College, Cambridge, England, notes that it is emotions, rather than an intellectual understanding of our ecological plight, that motivates consumers: "Economic life is . . . a matter of sentiment . . . the desire to be attended to, and taken notice of. . . . Sentiments are the objective of economic striving, and they are also the adjunct of economic exchange." To buttress her view, she quotes no less an authority than Adam Smith, who wrote in the *Theory of Moral Sentiments* that "[i]t is chiefly from this regard to the sentiments of mankind, that we pursue riches and avoid poverty."[22] Complicating the informed-consumer approach to ecological reform is the fact that in almost all cases, information about a product's life-cycle environmental impacts are rarely known outside the industry—indeed, often industry itself doesn't pursue the studies needed to know these impacts—and virtually never appear as information on labels or in advertisements that might be useful to environmentally interested consumers. As Klaus Töpfer, executive director of the United Nations Environment Programme (UNEP), wrote, we're not even sure what sustainable consumption might look like: "One of the reasons for the slow uptake of the sustainable-consumption challenge has been a lack of clarity, understanding, and confidence around the question of sustainable consumption. *What is 'sustainable consumption'? How do the various aspects fit together? Isn't it about just having less?*"[23]

AN INDUSTRIAL-ECOLOGICAL APPROACH

Until that faraway idealistic time when consumers, businesses, government-procurement officials, and industrial designers all become enlightened, committed, and consistent environmentally oriented purchasers, the most realistic way to husband resources and preserve the biologically complex ecosystems that make up our natural capital—to redesign, in effect, our industrial systems—is to actually develop ecologically smarter factories and businesses.

My blueprint for the BCPC emerged in part from my interest in industrial ecology, which involves studying the flows of materials and energy in industrial and consumer activities to assess their effects on the environment, and also involves an analysis of how economic, political, regulatory, and social factors affect the flow, use, and transformation of resources. By designing industrial facilities from the start with industrial ecology in mind, production facilities are more likely to work in harmony with natural biological systems and promote sustainability.

The field of industrial ecology emerged in the late 1980s when environmental scientists and engineers worked to ecologically refine and financially promote recycling businesses and safer waste management generally. Specifically, industrial ecology evolved from three antecedent attempts by environmentalists to assess how industry could be reformed to promote "closing the loop"—recovering all wastes for productive uses—and, in so doing, reduce the amount of materials winding up as residues that couldn't be recycled. These three attempts to help promote sustainable business practices are: (1) the design-for-recycling movement, (2) the product-policy movement, and (3) life-cycle assessments.

The Resource Conservation and Recovery Act (RCRA) is America's solid-waste–management act, and it was first enacted in 1976.[24] Though it is, predictably, a very weak statute in ecological terms—nowhere does it require any type of recycling—it did mandate the closure of the thousands of polluting, dangerous open dumps that had been widely relied upon for waste disposal by communities throughout America. The closure of these dumps in the late 1970s and early 1980s caused cities and counties to seek alternative waste-treatment and disposal options, including the development of new landfills and incinerators. Americans—and people the world over—protested the siting of these wasteful and environmentally risky technologies and clamored instead for the development of recycling programs.

However, as battles against incinerators and landfills raged in the early 1980s, it became clear that many consumer products and packaging couldn't be recycled—were essentially being forced to go to incinerators or landfills—because they were not designed by their manufacturers with waste impacts in mind. As a result, a design-for-recycling movement emerged. This movement emphasized making products more recyclable by limiting the use of toxic and composite materials that add costs to recycling—or make it impossible entirely. Among the types of packaging and products raising these concerns were multiplastic and metal products and packaging composites that can't be separated for recycling (e.g., aseptic packaging, aka juice boxes), plasticized metalicized bags (potato-chip bags), paper coated with plastics and heavy metal inks, cadmium-coated plastic auto bumpers, mercury lighting switches, heavy metals in stabilizers, and coloring agents in plastics, to name only a few.

The design-for-recycling movement evolved into a field that became known as product policy as it became clear that certain nonrecyclable products and packaging also needed to be redesigned because of the dangerous, costly impacts they generated when they were sent to an incinerator or a landfill because no recycling market existed. Mercury in batteries or in lighting ballasts, chlorine in bleached paper, and cadmium yellow in lead-saturated plastic packaging are examples of products that form hazardous air emissions after microbial methanagens decompose them at a landfill; when they are incinerated and converted into dioxins; or, after the hydrocarbons are burnt off, produce heavy-metal air emissions and residue for incinerator operators—usually funded by taxpayers—to deal with.

It soon became clear that to comprehensively address the issue of product policy it was necessary to analyze more than just the downstream (waste-disposal) impacts and look upstream as well—at the entire supply chain feeding a production process and at the production process itself. Thus, the field of product policy gave birth to the analytical tool known as life-cycle assessments (LCAs). LCAs were designed to help reveal an industry's, a factory's, or a product's upstream and downstream environmental impacts by listing, describing, and quantifying the energy and materials it uses, and the wastes it creates.[25] A key component of any LCA—indeed, perhaps its single most important purpose—is pinpointing the industrial action and redesign needed to reduce any ecological burden it identifies. Unfortunately, a glaring weakness of LCAs is the way they have been used by industry: While the use of resources is quantifiable, less frequently assessed are the hard-to-quantify habitat and biodiversity impacts that industrial processes engender. Hence, the work involved in refining LCAs led to the field of industrial ecology, which focuses not only on analyzing and enhancing material flows and energy use, but on reducing life-sciences–habitat, biodiversity–ecological impacts as well.

In the last decade interest in industrial ecology has grown enormously. Though it still remains on the margins of industrial behavior (and is occasionally bogged down in intellectually tantalizing but obscure philosophical debates), the field of industrial ecology has energized thinking about how we make and use consumer products. This thinking goes on in arcane-sounding disciplines like material-flow analysis and life-cycle assessments, ecological footprints, supply-chain management, ecologically integrated urban planning, ecological design, downcycling, nanotechnology, biomimicry, and pollution prevention.[26] But in fact it has instigated a few—albeit very few—real-world projects that will indisputably serve as models for generations to come.

Unfortunately for the world, no industrial-ecology project besides the BCPC has ever been initiated on a scale large enough to have a meaningful impact on any industry's market or its ecological footprint. Perhaps the most notable example of an industrial-ecology initiative other than the BCPC with potentially large benefits is the eco-industrial park in Kalundborg, Denmark, which evolved out of a local waste-exchange network over a period of more than a decade. The industrial symbiosis in the Kalundborg district evolved out of a network of cooperation between five industrial enterprises and the municipality of Kalundborg. The five enterprises—the Asnæs Power Station, the plasterboard manufacturer GYPROC, the pharmaceutical and biotechnology company Novo Nordisk/Novozymes, the soil-cleanup company A/S Bioteknisk Jordrens, and the STATOIL refinery—trade residual by-products because the "waste" of each process is a valuable raw material to one or more of the others. The result is a reduction of resource consumption, waste generation, and other environmental impacts. The five business partners also gain financially from the cooperation because all contracts within the symbiosis are based on sound commercial principles.

Another emerging and innovative industrial-ecology model worth watching is the effort to develop an eco-industrial park in Santa Perpètua de Mogoda, a city near Barcelona. The city hosts a number of neighboring "industrial estates," and in 1998 the municipality sought to convert two of them (Can Roca and Urvasa) into an eco-park. Together these industrial estates host more than one hundred diverse small enterprises, and most of them employ fewer than fifty workers each. As of this writing, the project is still at a planning and analytical stage. Should it succeed at establishing an industrial symbiosis involving land-sharing, waste-exchanging, energy, and worker-transport collaborations, it could prove to be a valuable model.

Despite these two inspiring examples and the enormous promise industrial ecology holds to transform future industrial behavior, to date most industrial ecology has focused on the *analysis* of material flows, energy use, and product life cycles at a few existing facilities. This is, of course, extremely valuable work and, given the origins of the industrial-ecology movement—evolving from the work of farsighted industrial engineers who were focused on improving the life-cycle profile of products—such an engineering-focused approach is understandable. But actually the primary obstacles to these kinds of projects are not the engineering problems.

It's important to recognize that manufacturing processes exist within a larger social context. Consumption and waste are not only a function of industrial design but are also largely a matter of cultural norms and perhaps more important, affluence. Although environmentalists have been largely unsuccessful in reducing consumption, we have been tremendously successful in making recycling an important cultural value. In a sense, recycling is the fundamental social component underlying industrial ecology, and the fields of industrial ecology, product policy, and life-cycle assessments emerged from the analytical work related to efforts to promote and facilitate recycling almost twenty years ago. Recycling is the industrial and *social* process by which we turn the wastes of one activity (product consumption) into the raw material feedstocks of another activity (product manufacture). Recycling is among the most basic activities in the natural world, and every vision of sustainability includes recycling as a fundamental, essential component.

Yet, while more of us recycle than ever before—it is indisputably the most widely practiced environmental activity on Earth—the fact remains that markets for recycled products have been limited, by cost factors but additionally by infrastructure, ecologically perverse subsidies promoting virgin-resources exploitation, permitting issues, and general indifference on the part of corporate America, which is much more concerned with the bottom line than with developing new products, processes, and marketing strategies to benefit the environment. It is this disjunction—between the cultural values that support recycling and other innovative, environmentally responsive technologies, and the corporate values and government policies that discourage it—that industrial ecology must overcome.

My experience struggling with barriers that stymie world-scale commercialization of innovative environmental technologies suggests that the social and political obstacles are as important as—if not more important than—the technical barriers. These challenges include industrial-development tasks such as acquiring early-stage financing, finding a suitable site, navigating through the industrial regulatory permitting process, coordinating teams of precision engineering firms and construction companies (which are all wedded to nonsustainable practices), managing law firms, gaining legal savvy, designing a marketable financial structure, adding production capacity to an industry that wants to keep supplies limited and prices high, obtaining government-to–private-sector contracts, educating urban politicians about factories that are typically rural endeavors, negotiating with laborers, obtaining industrial subsidies, acquiring water, figuring out how to compete successfully in a global market. These are industrial-development matters that, frankly, environmentalists, politicians, community groups, and even industrial ecologists in general know very little about.

But it is in precisely these development tasks that environmentalists can most effectively influence industrial impacts. The routine determinations of corporate decision makers and financial institutions are environmental and social policy making of the first order, though they are rarely evaluated or regulated that way. As Figure 1.2, which follows, indicates, financial institutions and the markets they dominate are at the heart of almost every economic decision by governments, corporations, and households. Consequently, one important objective that pro-sustainability reformers must embrace includes getting CEOs and MBAs to think

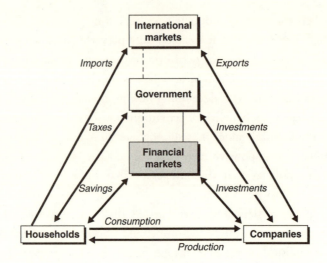

FIGURE 1.2

The Role of Financial Markets in a Political Economic System. *Source:* Marcel
Jeucken, *Sustainable Finance and Banking: The Financial Sector and the Future
of the Planet* (London: Earthscan Publications Ltd., 2001), p. 55.

more like environmentalists, and getting environmentalists to think more
like CEOs and MBAs.

ECO-REALISM

Barry Commoner, a grandfather of the modern environmental movement, correctly observed more than thirty years ago that the worst environmental impacts occur at production (manufacturing) facilities and
during the processes manufacturers rely on to acquire raw materials.[27]
More recently, this assessment was reinforced by Klaus Töpfer, executive
director of the United Nations Environment Programme, when he estimated that "95 percent of environmental impacts occur at the production
stage, during the use of industrial equipment."[28] To reduce the impacts of
production, Commoner wrote, industrial "technologies need to be
redesigned to conform as closely as possible to ecological requirements."
To more effectively get companies to carry out this redesign of technol-

ogy, he claimed, environmentalists must increase their influence over the "means of production"—manufacturing plants and the supply chains that feed them—by beginning to serve on the boards of directors of large industrial corporations.[29]

More than thirty years after Commoner suggested having environmentalists serve on the boards of corporations to increase our influence over production decisions, few activists embrace that approach, and few corporations allow it. As my colleague Ralph Cavanagh, a winner of the prestigious Heinz Environmental Prize, put it to me when we shared thoughts about this approach, "You seem to favor putting people like me and you on corporate boards. . . . I encourage you to reconsider; while I agree with everything you say about all the other things that we need to be doing, I think we should AVOID board seats; the public appearance of a conflict goes on to diminish the effectiveness of the constructive partnerships that you and I favor. NRDC bends over backward to avoid having any financial interests that are tied in any way to the companies that its advocacy addresses, and I think that's also the right policy for NRDC employees. . . . My concern is the appearance or reality of our own advocacy decisions being influenced in some way by personal financial interests. It would not have been good had you or I been on Enron's board, for example."[30]

My own feeling is that while avoiding participation on corporate boards may be a philosophically noble stance, I don't think future generations will appreciate it as they suffer through the worsening ecological consequences that this absence of collaboration and added influence perpetuates. The Earth doesn't benefit from these symbolic gestures, and the well-being of future generations requires that we increase our influence over environmentally destructive institutions wherever possible and to the greatest degree possible.

It is hard to imagine that any environmentalist could have done worse on the boards of Enron, WorldCom, ImClone, Global Crossing, Waste Management, Arthur Andersen, and other firms than did the career businesspeople who served there. Indeed, perhaps some of the unethical behavior of these business executives and lax oversight by their self-serving boards would have been prevented if more ethically minded, vigilant, and hardworking environmentalists had served on their boards. Perhaps putting environmentalists, human-rights workers, advocates for children, and other social reformers on the boards of transnational corporations is precisely what is needed to restore confidence in the business sector. After all, an essential part of an environmentalist's day-to-day work is oversight and prevention of a company's misdeeds. Why must we assume that serving on corporate boards will corrupt environmentalists? Can we not instead assume that the ethically powerful, vigilant, and intelligent influence of environmentalists will instead prevail and add integrity to corporate boards? And why is it logical to presume that environmentalists will advance their cause with less vigor if they were paid better wages? Does it make sense to reward polluters who destroy sacred lands and traditional cultures more than we reward ecologists? Moreover, why is it logical to allow corporate officials to sit on the boards of environmental groups, which they do, in substantial numbers—and in so doing give these businessmen influence over the work of advocates—while we virtuously prevent ourselves from joining the boards of industry? Some of the activities of the firms these officials represent would not successfully withstand an environmental or human-rights evaluation by the very groups on whose boards they serve. This only reflects a more sober truth: The reach of industrialism is expanding, even as its burdens on the planet are increasing.

As an example of the potential benefit of getting environmentalists on corporate boards, I cite the following: When I served on the board of the BCPC, a financial expert advised us early on to avoid New York City's high-tax environment by incorporating the project in Delaware or "even better," he said, "offshore." I adamantly opposed this idea, and I was able to get the bottom-line–motivated businesspeople on the BCPC's board to reject this approach: I insisted it was unethical to do business in New York City, to be located in New York City, and to rely on the services, workers, and infrastructure of the city but pay lower taxes elsewhere just because we had the legal right to do so. I felt it was wrong to ask a community to support your business plans, to ask for government subsidies and tax breaks, and then try to avoid paying the taxes that finance community needs and the ability of government to supply those services and subsidies. By contrast, corporations without ethical environmentalists or community representatives on the board are more likely to use offshore tax havens to avoid their financial and social obligations to host communities and the U.S. government.[31] This example—and a two-decade-long career spent among professional environmentalists—indicates to me that having environmentalists on corporate boards would more likely have a salutary effect than result in these participants' selling out. But one thing is certain: Without environmentalists on corporate boards, environmentally oriented businesspeople will have a much harder time advancing sensible environmental improvements, and businesspeople will typically never pursue these without our involvement.

I believe, however, that environmentalists serving on the boards of corporations isn't enough: We must strive to become the developers and owners of corporations so we can effectively outcompete those firms now imposing the worst ecological damage.

Climate change; habitat destruction; biodiversity loss and floods resulting from increasing deforestation in Asia, Latin America, Africa, and the southeastern United States; and water shortages in the Pacific Northwest and elsewhere—these ecological problems are real trends, not figments of our imagination. They mean that new manufacturing facilities need to be built that use less energy and less water, emit fewer pollutants, and rely on renewable resources or recycled materials like reclaimed wood, agricultural wastes, or recovered wastepaper. But most industrial decision makers are not inclined to fight for developing new factories based on the principles of industrial ecology. Therefore, environmentalists must ourselves be realistic about what needs to be done: We must cause ecologically superior factories to be built. This demands the kind of executive decision making that is only in the hands of corporate officials. Environmentalists must gain access to this power. This is a matter of principle and idealism. But it is also the environmental equivalent of realpolitik. It is eco-realism, if you will, a central tenet of my blueprint for a new environmentalism, and the distillation, into a word, of the impetus for the BCPC.

It is the manufacturing sector that creates the biggest environmental burdens, but most green development today—to the extent it has advanced at all—is focused primarily in the residential–land-use and commercial–real-estate sectors. Despite wide-ranging discussions about the value of market-based advocacy as a strategy to correct polluting, habitat-destroying industries, in fact this approach is not yet even close to effectively reforming large-scale manufacturing sectors. It is accurate to say that green development today has only a marginal impact on a very few commercial buildings, and on a very few housing subdivisions—mostly in more affluent towns in affluent nations—and has an even smaller marginal effect on global industry.[32] From the perspective of ecological sustainability, the data relating to waste generation, resource consumption, habitat destruction, and pollution impacts in most regions on the planet show worsening trends.[33]

These trends will begin to reverse only when environmentalists become more effectively involved with industrial business as developers, financiers, and owners rather than supplicants. Taking on these roles—rather than just talking about them or begging a few government officials to influence the businesspeople now in these positions—is the future work of environmentalists, of eco-realists. If we do these things, we should expect that social benefits beyond ecological improvements will emerge. Philanthropic benefactors, foundations, and other supporters of environmental causes will receive greater value for their investments if environmental groups begin to leverage their funding to initiate, in addition to new regulations, the development of new industrial-ecology projects. For example, with less than $2 million in philanthropic support for the development of the BCPC, we helped raise an additional $6 million in private-sector and government support during the project's development phase and, in turn, craft that into a $500 million–plus investment that would have produced thousands of temporary jobs, hundreds of permanent jobs, and a wide range of environmental benefits for generations, not dependent on sporadic government enforcement or financing.

With environmentalists more in charge of industrial business development and operations, their employees and communities might be freed from some of the alienating contradictions that now define most relationships between workers, their companies, and the ecological impacts of their work. Writing in the *Harvard Business Review* on the few firms that have incorporated environmental issues into their business model, Paul Hawken, Amory Lovins, and Hunter Lovins have noted, "Perhaps the biggest payoff of the resulting new [ecologically oriented] business models is . . . aligning corporate values with those of customers, host communities and workers, not the reverse. Removing contradictions between what people do at work and what they want for their kids when they go home liberates extraordinary latent creativity trapped in stale employee and customer relationships."[34] Whether a meaningful liberation of "latent creativity" would actually take place—certainly other factors besides the environmental profile of one's job affect human potential—aligning the tasks of industrial employees with environmental remediation certainly has a better chance of reconciling their work and personal goals than does work that depends on despoiling their neighborhoods, habitat, and the planet.

Another important benefit that might logically emerge if environmentalists more substantially controlled industrial business decisions: A reduction in the damaging influence of environmentally hostile political contributions. If industry operated more in line with ecological principles because environmentalists were more influential business decision makers, subsidies that support industrial activities would more likely favor ecological interests.

CONCLUSION

Private corporate interests are the most powerful economic and political force on Earth. In rare circumstances, with effective pressure, a given corporation or a given CEO may be benign, or even helpful, in the quest for a better, more ecologically enduring world. But the collective global impact of this unprecedented and largely unaccountable force is a destructive one. It is so destructive that a great many, if not the majority, of the scientists who study human impacts on Earth regard it as threatening to our very survival. The force is so powerful that, even when it wants to, government has proven incapable of restraining it, and consumers have proven unable to resist its temptations in the marketplace. As much as environmentalism has protected our communities and wild places in the past, it must also now face an unsettling fact: We have effectively reached the limits of what we can accomplish through legislation and the education of consumers. We need a new plan of attack.

Executing the blueprint proffered by this book is a tall order, and may seem an impossible objective. The BCPC, after all, was never built. But it did bring world-scale industrial ecology out of the realm of the impossible and breathtakingly close to reality. My hope for the BCPC was always that it would be a blueprint for other developers to follow, to spawn other efforts, other initiatives for other manufacturing plants and industries, the collective effect of which would be to redefine what it means to do business in the twenty-first century. As urgent as are the realities of our global environmental straits, the rise of industrial ecology can't happen overnight. To travel ten thousand miles, we must begin with the first step. Likewise, the transformation of the industrial economy must be taken one step at a time.

NOTES

1. Board on Sustainable Development, National Research Council, *Our Common Journey: A Transition Toward Sustainability* (Washington, D.C.: National Academy Press, 1999), pp. 8 and 10, emphasis added.

2. For an excellent discussion of this perspective see Ernest A. Lowe, John L. Warren, and Stephen R. Moran, *Discovering Industrial Ecology: An Executive Briefing and Source Book* (Columbus, Ohio: Battelle Press, 1997).

3. See Robert D. Richardson Jr., *Emerson: The Mind on Fire* (Berkeley, California: University of California Press, 1995), p. 271.

4. My distinguished colleague Ralph Cavanagh suggests that a compelling counterexample to my general argument is the work that won our NRDC colleague David Goldstein the Leo Szilard Award for Physics in the Public Interest. David and a handful of other environmental activists instigated what the National Research Council has labeled one of the last half-century's more remarkable technology achievements in the energy efficiency field, which since 1974 has resulted in reducing the average electricity consumption of refrigerators by more than two thirds, even as average unit sizes increased, performance improved, and ozone-depleting chlorofluorocarbons and hydrogen chlorofluorocarbons (HCFCs) were removed. This market-based advocacy work has had very broad and beneficial ecological and economic implications.

5. *OECD Environmental Outlook* (Paris: OECD, 2001), p. 21.

6. Examples include mining wastes, municipal wastes, hazardous wastes, agricultural wastes, food-processing residues, radioactive wastes, refinery wastes, oil- and gas-industry wastes, cement-kiln dust, incinerator ash,

utility wastes, construction and demolition debris, sludge, etc. The global-waste–generation tonnage estimates are my own, based on various statistical sources and field research. Waste-generation data are often unreliable. Data for the United States and other OECD countries, based on commercial and government estimates, tend to be more accurate than middle-income and developing-world data. Since the United States is reliably estimated to generate between 12 and 14 billion tons each year, I believe the higher global-waste–generation rate—50 billion tons annually—is more likely the accurate estimate. Otherwise, the United States by itself would account for more than one third of the global-waste–generation rate, a percentage I believe is too high.

7. National Advisory Council for Environmental Policy and Technology, cited in *Solid Waste Report,* 32, no. 47 (30 November 2001), p. 369.

8. *OECD Environmental Outlook,* p. 21 and Table 1, p. 20.

9. Quoted in David E. Rosenbaum, "Senate Deletes Higher Mileage Standard in Energy Bill," *New York Times,* 14 March 2002, p. A28.

10. For a comprehensive discussion of the political give-and-take—and corruption of policy substance—involved in the legislative process, see Eric Redman, *The Dance of Legislation* (Seattle: University of Washington Press, 2001).

11. For just one of the many examples that could be cited of how long this process can drag on, see John J. Fialka, "EPA Wants Review by Supreme Court in Smog-Rules Case," *Wall Street Journal,* 1 November 1999, p. A8.

12. Don Van Natta Jr. and Neela Banerjee, "Bush Energy Paper Followed Industry Push," *New York Times,* 27 March 2002, p. A20, and Don Van Natta Jr. and Neela Banerjee, "Review Shows Energy Industry's Recommendations to Bush Ended Up Being National Policy," *New York Times,* 28 March 2002, p. A18.

13. For one of the best summaries of how widespread this rollback assault has been under President George W. Bush, see Robert Perks et al., *Rewriting the Rules: The Bush Administration's Unseen Assault on the Environment* (New York: NRDC, 2001).

14. Wendell Berry, rejecting the negative connotation implied by this globalist epithet, has written "It is a protectionism that is just and sound, because it protects local producers. . . ." See Wendell Berry, "The Idea of a Local Economy," *Harper's,* April 2002, p. 20.

15. See David E. Shi, *The Simple Life: Plain Living and High Thinking in American Culture* (New York: Oxford University Press, 1985).

16. Robert Heilbroner, *An Inquiry into the Human Prospect* (New York: Norton, 1980), p. 110.

17. *OECD Environmental Indicators: Towards Sustainable Development* (Paris: OECD, 2001), p. 77–78.

18. Alan Durning, *How Much Is Enough?* (New York: Norton, 1992), p. 21.

19. Some have argued that it is not consumer preferences that drive industry but, instead, industrial planning and advertising that determine what consumers want. I find much merit in that argument, though admittedly it may now be a chicken-and-egg debate. For the first and most persuasive discussion of this perspective, see J. K Galbraith, *The New Industrial State* (Boston: Houghton Mifflin, 1972).

20. Berry, "The Idea of a Local Economy," p. 19.

21. Steve Liesman, "Car Wars," *Wall Street Journal,* 19 October 1999, p. B1.

22. Emma Rothschild, *Economic Sentiments* (Cambridge, Massachusetts: Harvard University Press, 2001), pp. 8–9.

23. United Nations Environment Programme, *Consumption Opportunities: Strategies for Change* (Geneva: UNEP, 2001), p. 3, emphasis in original.

24. *Resource Conservation and Recovery Act of 1976* (RCRA), Public Law 94-580; 7 USC 1010 et seq, 40 CFR 280 and 281.

25. See, for example, *A Technical Framework for Life-Cycle Assessment* (Washington, D.C.: SETAC Foundation for Environmental Education Inc. and Society of Environmental Toxicology and Chemistry, 1991).

26. For an almost encyclopedic summary of the many areas of work ongoing in the field of industrial ecology—both practical and philosophical—see the abstracts from the inaugural meeting of the International Society for Industrial Ecology, which can be found at http://www.yale.edu/is4ie/images/abstractbook_leiden.pdf. See also past issues of the *Journal of Industrial Ecology,* which can be found at http://mitpress.mit.edu/JIE.

27. Barry Commoner, *The Closing Circle* (New York: Knopf, 1971), p. vi.

28. Klaus Töpfer, executive director United Nations Environment Programme, keynote address *UNEP's 7th International High Level Seminar on Cleaner Production,* Prague, 29–30 April 2002.

29. Commoner, *The Closing Circle,* p. 283.

30. Ralph Cavanagh, NRDC senior attorney and codirector of NRDC's energy program, personal communication, 31 December 2001, excerpted with permission.

31. For an extensive discussion of this, see David Cay Johnston, "United States Corporations Are Using Bermuda to Slash Tax Bills," *New York Times,* 18 February 2002, p. A1.

32. According to Ralph Cavanagh, appliance–energy-efficiency data in OECD countries are the notable exception; more heartening: Energy

intensity and carbon intensity per unit of production are down substantially over the past thirty years.

33. OECD *Environmental Indicators: Towards Sustainable Development* (Paris: OECD, 2001). See tables at pp. 15–18, 21–23, 27–32, 65–66, and 77–78. Also see Edward O. Wilson, *Conserving Earth's Biodiversity*, CD-ROM (Washington, D.C.: Island Press, 2000), data provided throughout.

34. Paul Hawken, Amory Lovins, and Hunter Lovins, "Bringing the Environment Down to Earth," *Harvard Business Review*, Vol. 77, No. 6 (November–December 1999), p. 192.

2. The First Step: Choosing a Target

Despite the seemingly fathomless extent of creation,
humankind has been chipping away at its diversity, and
Earth is destined to become an impoverished planet
within a century if present trends continue.

—Edward O. Wilson

As the previous chapter pointed out, the work of industrial ecologists today must focus on remedying existing environmental problems because virtually all industries engender meaningfully adverse environmental impacts. But not all industries have equal impacts, and not all industries are equally practical targets for the kind of approach I took with the BCPC. Thus, the first step in developing a meaningfully beneficial manufacturing plant is to identify the industries in which one can make the biggest difference. This involves a kind of analysis that is rarely, if ever, undertaken in the business world today.

Why did I decide to focus on trying to reform the paper industry by building an ecologically superior paper-recycling mill? In fact, for a while I also considered developing a plastics-recycling mill. Even before I began looking comprehensively at life-cycle studies of paper and plastics, I already knew enough about these materials' adverse impacts to conclude that they each seemed like important targets for ecological reform: Paper, being the single largest component of the municipal-waste stream, dependent on disappearing and biologically essential forests, and the largest consumer of fresh water, is an industry obviously worthy of reform. Plastics production, thoroughly dependent on nonrenewable fossil fuels—coal, gas, and petroleum—was, as I knew from my previous involvement with EPA regulatory negotiations, among the most polluting and heavily subsidized industries. Plus, plastics are among the most costly materials in the municipal–solid-waste stream to dispose of, given their high-volume–to–light-weight ratio, and among the most difficult to find beneficial markets for.

To review NRDC's options—plastics or paper?—I hired a former CFO of a Fortune 500 plastics company as a consultant to perform an economic-feasibility study; meanwhile, I reviewed the life-cycle ecological impacts associated with the production and use of various plastics resins. Simultaneously, I reviewed the life-cycle ecological impacts associated with the production and use of paper products. Although the ecological need for developing plastics recycling facilities is enormous, the feasibility study I commissioned reported that the economics of a stand-alone plastics recycling mill were dissuasive, given the staggering amount of financial subsidies the U.S. government, other governments, and even international financial agencies offer the virgin-resin and fossil-fuel industries, from which plastics are manufactured. To mention just one institution's subsidies, I cite the World Bank, which in the past ten years alone, between 1992 and 2002, has provided approximately $21 *billion* in subsidies to extract, transport, and process fossil fuels,[1] which are the raw material of plastics (this is one reason why 96 percent of all plastics discarded in the United States are *not* recycled). By contrast, economic-feasibility assessments and market-related discussions with Swedish–paper-company executives interested in recycling—plus my own recollection of visiting paper-recycling mills in Europe—encouraged me to consider focusing my efforts on developing a recycled-paper mill.

But perhaps more than anything else, it was a review of the paper industry's destructive and diverse life-cycle impacts that underscored just how urgent that work would be. That review combined with the inability of government to meaningfully reform this destructive industry, more than anything else, compelled me to try and build an ecologically superior paper mill. It underscored just how absolutely essential it is to recycle paper, for municipalities to maintain paper-recycling programs, and for consumers to demand post-consumer recycled-paper products. And it confirmed the unbreakable connection between recycling and industrial ecology.

A DREADFUL RECORD OF DAMAGING IMPACTS

Despite high-minded political rhetoric celebrating our unalienable right to life, human beings are indisputably the species that is most destructive to the planet. Humans are the organisms centrally responsible for virtually all biodiversity loss on Earth—including avoidable "mass extinctions, during which a large proportion of the biota is exterminated in a very short time on a geologic scale." (These are opposed to naturally occurring "background extinctions," which affect few biota, result from naturally occurring mutations, and "have been going on since the beginning of life.")[2] And while all industries currently harm the environment in one way or another, the pulp-and-paper industry, which has relied on wood as a raw material only since the mid–nineteenth century (nonwood cellulose was used until then), may contribute to more global and local environmental problems than any other industry in the world. Perhaps no industry has forced more species into extinction, destroyed more habitats, and polluted as many streams, rivers, and lakes. It is a tragic irony of commerce that paper, perhaps the most ubiquitous and ephemeral of all consumer products, is manufactured by destroying timber forests, one of nature's most durable and biologically essential organisms.

It would be no exaggeration to argue that the paper industry—and just about all industrial activities—must change if humans and other species are to survive well beyond the twenty-first century. When it comes to the ecological impacts of the forest-products industry, and the paper-industry sector in particular, the world simply cannot afford to experience another century like the one we have just lived through. Whether through high levels of all types of recycling, scientific investigations in the emerging field of biomimicry—designing production facilities that mimic natural processes—or other advancements in engineering, linkages must be made between healthy biological processes, environmental remediation, and profitable paper production.

For the paper industry to have grown stronger over the years, habitability on Earth for hundreds of forest-based species—including forest-based human communities—was, of necessity, made weaker. While paper-production output increased twentyfold during the past century, timber-harvesting, timber-processing, and paper-bleaching technologies spit out inconceivably large discharges of hazardous wastes, toxic air emissions, greenhouse gases, and effluents into our air and almost every great river and lake on Earth, and into less great rivers and lakes as well. As the industry's appetite for virgin timber grew, so did its almost indiscriminate destruction of all types of habitat on every continent, usually regardless of who or what was affected. Sacred land revered for centuries by spiritually based indigenous communities in some of the most economically undeveloped areas on Earth has been almost routinely destroyed in the industry's unquenchable quest for raw materials. At the same time, the industry's products have become the dominant feature of the world's municipal-waste stream, filling costly and polluting landfills and incinerators throughout the globe with phenol- and heavy-metal–laden discards that have been transformed into billions of pounds of toxic organic compounds, dioxins, heavy metals, acid gases, and climate-changing chemicals. In almost every country on Earth, tax dollars that could otherwise feed, house, school, and clothe rich and poor families alike have been—and are—spent cleaning up after this rampaging, concentrated industry.

It was with this information in mind that I decided to develop an alternative environmentally benign paper mill that would not rely on virgin-wood fibers and hundreds of hazardous chemicals. I wanted to develop a model and show both industry and government officials how paper mills could become helpful stewards of life on Earth, rather than an ever-increasing threat to it. More than a third of all municipal waste managed in New York City—indeed, throughout the United States, Europe, and Japan—is wastepaper. With so much of New York City's costly and environmentally serious waste-management burden caused by discarded paper, it seemed to make sense that if New York City–based environmentalists like myself truly wanted to "think globally, and act locally," we should somehow try to tackle the paper industry and, in particular, New York City's wastepaper problem.

THE ENORMOUS SURGE IN PAPER CONSUMPTION

Consumption ultimately drives environmental impacts. Between 1950 and 1996, global consumption of paper products increased almost sixfold, from about 46 million tons to about 300 million tons; in the last three decades, global paper demand has tripled.[3] Future growth projections vary, but all of them predict substantial increases in global demand for paper products. According to the OECD, "[g]lobal production in the pulp, paper and publishing sector is expected to increase by 77% from 1995 to 2020, with production in OECD regions projected to increase by 60% and in non-OECD regions [the developing world] by 170%. . . . The sector is very capital intensive and the most rapidly growing among the wood-based industries."[4] The United Nations Food and Agriculture Organization (FAO) projects that global demand for paper will increase by an additional 30 percent in the next ten years,[5] while the International Institute for Environment and Development (IIED) estimates it could double during that same period.[6] The spectacular growth in demand for paper reflects its utility: There are more than 450 different grades of paper, with distinct functional requirements, ranging from newsprint, tissue, and writing papers to 300 special-use papers, such as filter paper, banknote paper, "Bible paper," and gasket paper.[7] (See Table 2.1.)

Although paper is consumed in every country on Earth, consumption

TABLE 2.1
The Primary Paper-Grade Classifications

Grade classification	Percent of world consumption
Communication-paper grades	41
Newsprint	13
Printing and writing	28
Household and sanitary	6
Paperboard and packaging	46
Containerboard	24
Board	14
Packaging paper and board	8
Other paper and paperboard	7
Total	**100**

Source: Pulp and Paper International, 1995.

patterns between rich and poor nations—like almost everything else between these countries—are strikingly dissimilar. The industrialized countries use 87 percent of the world's writing paper.[8] While the global average per-capita consumption of paper in 1998 was about 50 kilograms (kg), in developing countries paper consumption averaged only 12 kg per capita, less than one tenth the 152 kg per-capita average for developed countries.[9] By contrast, average per-capita consumption in the United States is 337 kg, more than double the average for developed countries, almost 7 times the average for the world as a whole, and about 28 times the average consumption of developing countries.[10] The average American annually consumes 111 times the amount of paper the average citizen in India does. And an enormous amount of the paper supposedly consumed in America is actually wasted: All businesses, including law firms and banks, and all government offices, including courts, that don't double-side print on documents and copies are among the most substantial paper-wasters. About 80 percent of the world's population consumes less than 30 kg per capita per year of paper, the amount that the World Health Organization says is required for the most rudimentary hygienic and communication needs.[11] In Africa average annual per-capita use of paper is less than 6 kg, and 26 of the 45 African countries consume less than 1 kg per person per year (36 African states consume less than 3 kg per year). Despite the rapid global increase in paper consumption in the last two decades, and an unprecedented economic expansion, per-capita consumption of paper for 23 African countries was lower in 2000 than it was in 1980.[12]

UPSTREAM BURDENS

As with all products and industrial processes, the life cycle of paper engenders "upstream" production impacts—those that occur when raw materials are acquired and processed—and "downstream" waste-disposal impacts. As mentioned earlier, life-cycle assessments (LCAs) help reveal an industry's, a factory's, or a product's upstream and downstream environmental impacts by listing, describing, and quantifying the energy and materials it uses and the wastes it creates.[13] Correctly performed, these assessments catalog impacts, including transportation-related pollution, in the raw-material acquisition stage, the transformation and production phase, during use and during disposal. Ideally, an LCA will help industrial and governmental decision makers identify and eliminate or regulate adverse environmental processes. By any measure, LCAs of paper reveal huge impacts.

Hazardous Air Emissions, Water Effluent, and Solid Wastes

Upstream, the virgin-pulp-and-paper industry is among the world's largest generators of toxic air pollutants, greenhouse gases, surface water pollution, sludge, and solid wastes. Processing rigid stands of timber into flexible, printable, smooth, glossy, or absorbent paper requires an intensive chemical and mechanical effort after a tree is harvested.

Once roads are cut and built, the forest becomes fragmented and the timber becomes accessible. The target forest is destroyed when broad swaths of trees are cut down, transported to the mill, stockpiled, debarked, chipped, "cooked"—heated, bleached and mechanically transformed—in vats of chemicals and turned into pulp, a cellulose-chemicals-and-water slurry. The pulp must then be turned into paper or dried and shipped off to another mill. Most paper can be manufactured with recycled fibers by using fewer than a dozen nonhazardous chemicals, as well as bleaching solutions that contain water and very low concentrations of nonhazardous hydrogen peroxide (at a concentration more diluted than the peroxide in your medicine cabinet).[14] In contrast, most virgin pulp and paper is made using literally hundreds of highly corrosive and hazardous chemicals, including chlorine. As the EPA has documented, this presents enormous problems in reducing pollution from virgin-paper mills, because "elimination of dioxin, furan, chlorinated phenolics, and other chlorinated organics [can] not be achieved unless all forms of chlorine-based bleaching are eliminated."[15] This is not expected to happen in the United States for quite some time, since the industry continues to strenuously fight shifting away from chlorine-based bleaching. In fact, not all of the toxic pollutants discharged in the wastewater produced by virgin-pulp-and-paper mills are currently regulated by the EPA, including various classes of dioxins and furans, some of which the agency has classified as carcinogens, and a range of chlorinated phenols.[16] Not surprisingly, the EPA has identified paper mills as a "major" source of water-borne dioxin contamination.[17]

The pulp-and-paper industry is the single largest consumer of fresh-water—"responsible for 11 percent of the total volume of water used in industrial activities in OECD countries"[18]—and, being a forest-products industry, it is directly responsible for accelerating global deforestation trends. When it destroys trees and uproots soil (the Earth's natural carbon sinks), the industry accelerates adverse climate-change impacts by causing the emission of greenhouse gases (GHGs). Indeed, the "pulp and paper industry is the third greatest industrial greenhouse gas emitter, after the chemical and steel industries"; and, unless drastic action is taken, its CO_2 emissions are projected to increase by roughly 100 percent by 2020.[19]

A 1996 assessment of the virgin-timber–based papermaking industry concluded that reducing hazardous discharges at paper mills worldwide to safe levels would cost more than $20 billion.[20] (While reducing hazardous discharges would reduce the industry's immediate public-health threats, that would not be enough to eliminate the industry's habitat destruction, water use, GHG emissions, transportation, forestry and other impacts; it would not make the industry *sustainable* [see Figures 2.1 and 2.2].) Most environmentalists associate virgin-paper mills with both the destruction of resident-species' habitat and the contamination of streams and rivers with chlorinated dioxins and other pollutants. According to the EPA, "[a]n average paper mill using standard chlorine bleaching releases about 35 tons of organochlorines *a day*, while ECF [elemental chlorine free] mills release seven to 10 tons."[21] What's more, besides the well-known, often unbearable odors associated with the industry's timber "cooking" process, which produces prodigious emissions of sulfur compounds (at "kraft" mills, causing a stench resembling rotten eggs that wafts noxiously for many miles around), virgin-timber pulp-and-paper mills are classified under U.S. federal law as generators of "significant quantities of haz-ardous air pollutants (HAPs) chlorinated and non-chlorinated." Some of these pollutants, which also include dioxins, a highly toxic category of pollutants, are "considered to be carcinogenic, and all can cause toxic health effects following exposure. In addition, most of the organic HAPs emitted from this industry are classified as volatile organic compounds

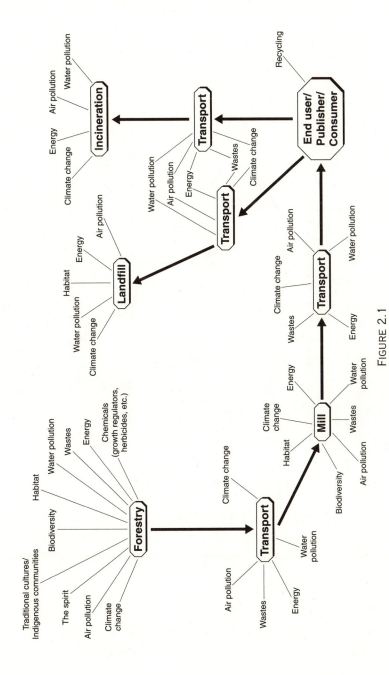

FIGURE 2.1

The Impacts Associated with Making and Disposing of Virgin-Based Paper

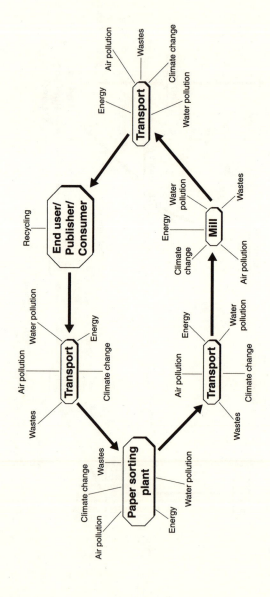

FIGURE 2.2

The Impacts Associated with Making and Disposing of Recycled-Based Paper

[VOCs], which participate in photochemical reactions in the atmosphere to produce ozone, a contributor to photochemical smog."[22]

Because it is the largest industrial water user, the paper industry generates prodigious amounts of wastewater. In the United States alone paper mills generate approximately 1,551 billion gallons of wastewater annually.[23] Water pollutants contained in these billions of gallons discharged into streams, rivers, and lakes by virgin-paper manufacturers is nothing less than a veritable toxic soup, including a wide range of hazardous and conventional pollutants as well as VOCs, including chlorinated dioxins and furans, chloroform, absorbable organic halides (AOX), methylene chloride, trichlorophenols, and pentachlorophenols.[24]

Forests and Global Biodiversity

To obtain timber, forest habitat *must be* fragmented by roads cut into the forest to get to it. According to recent research in conservation biology, habitat fragmentation "is even more devastating than we thought. Fragments are known to be inferior to intact habitat because they are more likely to lose species. New research shows fragments are also more vulnerable to hunting, fire and drought, and other kinds of ecological stress."[25] Moreover, forest fragments may be more vulnerable to airborne pollutants and may result in greater slaughter and poaching of wildlife because they "are more accessible to hunters" and are "more susceptible to damage from El Niño–Southern Oscillation Droughts." This recent research indicates that "[s]uch negative synergisms could potentially be one of the most important—and least understood—aspects of the modern environmental crisis."[26]

Natural forests are the single most important repository of terrestrial biodiversity, and the preservation of this biodiversity is clearly essential for maintaining a forest's ecological function.[27] But forests also play a social function, contributing to cultural identity, residential value, recreational and tourist value, and collective heritage. Virtually all regions on Earth suffer from industrial deforestation, and few activities threaten biodiversity as substantially as industrial logging. And as Klaus Töpfer, executive director of the United Nations Environment Programme (UNEP) has written, "Respect for biological diversity implies respect for human diversity . . . [and] both elements are fundamental to stability and durable peace on Earth."[28]

Especially in the less developed world, where most forests today are being destroyed, industrial forestry renders invisible the lives, spiritual values, and cultures of indigenous forest communities. It destroys a way of life based on the spiritual nourishment that intact forests have provided for centuries, and which has been so fundamental and enriching to the experience of being human. To quote again from Klaus Töpfer: "Deprive people of their language, culture and spiritual values and they lose all sense of direction and purpose."[29]

Forests and culture have intertwined throughout human history. But beyond the cultural losses, the disruption of forest communities also undermines the transfer of traditional knowledge about species use and forest-ecosystem management. As a result, more and more forests are being managed with a narrow commercial focus on species use, not with respect for protection of indigenous beliefs or other enriching manifestations of forest culture, which nonindigenous cultures celebrate as well.[30]

Because of the huge and increasing appetite for paper and other wood products in the United States, Europe, and Asia, the strain on global timber supplies is accelerating, and virgin-timber–based paper companies are harvesting greater quantities of wood fiber from South and Central America, Africa, and remote regions in Asia. The OECD projects a 73 percent increase in wood demand by the pulp-and-paper industry by 2020.[31] Georgia-Pacific has imported radiata chips from as far away as Chile for its mill in Bellingham, Washington, and Champion International, (now part of International Paper), has converted tropical forests to eucalyptus plantations in northern Brazil to provide pulp for its mills in the southeastern United States. Stone Container (now Smurfit-Stone) imported gamelina chips from Costa Rica for mills in North America.[32] This timber-import strategy used by the paper industry in the more developed world is clouded by the rapid growth in pulping capacity coming on-line in Latin America, which is itself now consuming most of that region's wood-fiber surplus.[33] Still, paper-pulp exports from Latin America from forests converted into plantations and from the harvesting and conversion of tropical and subtropical forests are expected to grow 70 percent between 2000 and 2010.[34]

If current industrial-logging, agricultural-conversion, and sprawl trends continue, "only 5 percent of all tropical forests will remain by mid-century."[35] Currently, less than 20 percent of the world's original forest cover remains intact, and much of what is left is threatened by commercial logging. Of the wood harvested for nonfuel uses, 42 percent is consumed by papermaking, a proportion expected to grow to more than 50 percent in the next fifty years, as the world's appetite for paper increases.[36]

Complicating an understanding of logging impacts is the fact that deforestation mapping programs often miss much of the deforestation activities that actually take place. According to a 2002 review of global forest maps by the World Resources Institute, "most recent studies show that we have underestimated the destruction" of the world's forests. "As we examined what we thought were still vast, untouched stretches of intact forests in the world, we came to the conclusion that they are fast becoming a myth."[37] Another analysis based on field surveys of wood mills and of forest burning across the Brazilian Amazon found that "logging crews severely damage 10,000 to 15,000 km² per year of forest that are not included in deforestation mapping programs. What's more, surface fires set to allow for the ecological conversion of forests into monocrop farmland burn additional large areas that are also routinely not documented."[38] In fact, field research designed to calculate annual deforestation in the Brazilian rain forest captures "less than half of the forest area that is [actually] impoverished each year, and even less during years of drought . . . potentially doubling net carbon emissions from regional land-use during severe El Niño episodes."[39]

In the continental United States, virtually no intact virgin forests remain, having already been cut down. As the OECD has confirmed, throughout the United States, "95 per cent of the originally forested [virgin] area has been cleared and logged."[40] New maps of forest cover "in the Lower 48 states [show] only 6 percent of forests are relatively undisturbed in large tracts" of at least 200 square kilometers.[41] As a consequence, "evidence concerning habitats and species [in the United States] shows that *diversity has been on the decline for many years*."[42] With the exception of very few areas in Scandinavia and Russia, no "intact"—undisturbed virgin—forests remain in Europe, and with the exception of a few remote regions in northern Canada and Alaska and very small parcels remaining in southeastern United States, no intact forests remain in all of North America.

Every region within Central and South America, Mexico, all of Africa, every region within Asia (with the possible exception of Kazakhstan), Oceania, and all of Southeast Asia has been experiencing deforestation at rates of at least 0.5 percent to >1 percent annually during the past five years. A 2002 assessment of the "Russian taiga, long thought of as an expanse of wilderness protected from human encroachment[,] . . . indicates that it now consists of fragments of wilderness, separated by logged and otherwise degraded forest."[43] Deforestation of tropical forests, according to the OECD, "is expected to continue at alarming rates over the next few decades."[44] Conservation biologists believe that tropical forests contain nearly half of all species on Earth, and non-OECD countries are expected to lose 15 percent of their remaining tropical-forested area by 2020.[45] Though we now know that estimates understate the rate of deforestation, even older assessments put the loss of tropical forests at at least 1 percent per year, an annual loss equal to an area the size of Alabama. Some estimates place the loss rate in certain less developed countries in Africa and Asia as high as 14 percent annually.[46] These tropical biomes—regions where specific flora and fauna coexist—are especially high in plant and insect diversity, and many of them have low species-population concentrations and narrow habitat ranges. A bevy of timber-industry analyses confirm that even in the United States, where the ecological impacts of industry are more regulated and visible than in Asia or Africa, "[u]nfavorable growth/drain ratios [are] clearly . . . depleting our 'forest capital.'"[47] Virtually all professional analysts of wood-fiber supply in the United States report enormous pressure on commercially available timber. And the United States is not unique: In most regions on Earth the commercially recoverable supply of timber used in the manufacture of paper is not being replaced commensurate with harvesting.

Adding urgency to our need to reverse the deforestation problem is that increasing amounts of the wood harvested for industrial use are coming from some of the most biologically rich developing countries—such as Brazil, the Democractic Republic of Congo, and Indonesia—that host the world's densest concentrations of species per acre. In the past 20 years,

80 percent of global timber harvesting and forest conversion has taken place in developing countries hosting subtropical and tropical forests between the Tropic of Cancer and the Tropic of Capricorn, an area known to conservation biologists as the latitudinal diversity gradient.[48] For evolutionary reasons, the concentration and diversity of species increase the closer they are to the equator. One reason why this is so: Biomes within the latitudinal diversity gradient experienced less dramatic temperature swings in the past 100,000 years than did other parts of the globe; consequently, a greater amount of biological niches for more diverse species evolved in this region and remained undisturbed by the glacial ice floes that affected areas in the northern and southern temperate zones. Unfortunately, logging and other forms of forest conversions have been increasing rapidly within the latitudinal diversity gradient, with the result that ever-greater numbers of species per acre of forest lost are being displaced or destroyed.

Globally, forested area in the world has declined about 6 percent during the previous twenty years.[49] However, a *global* assessment of forest conversion disguises the *local* ecological burdens imposed by industrial logging. Between 1989 and 1995, concurrent with many of the years when the BCPC was being developed in an attempt to slow pressure to harvest virgin forests, exports from the United States of southern virgin hardwood chips grew 500 percent.[50] (Flat-leaf–bearing trees are termed *hardwoods; softwoods* is the designation for needle-bearing trees.) While the southern United States contains less than one third (31 percent) of the nation's timber inventories, it is harvesting more than half (54 percent) of the nation's total timber volumes.[51] During the last decade, thousands of acres of deciduous hardwood trees were converted into rows of pinewoods in soils that have been effectively biologically sterilized due to the intensive application of herbicides and pesticides. According to the U.S. Department of Agriculture (USDA) Forest Service, monoculture tree plantations feeding the 156 chip mills in the South (110 of them built since 1990) now make up almost 40 percent of all pine stands in the southeastern United States, and within twenty years, if current trends continue, tree plantations will make up 70 percent.[52]

Because forest habitat all over the globe has been declining or disturbed, terrestrial biodiversity is declining in virtually every region on

Earth, including the United States.[53] According to one of the world's most respected conservation biologists, Harvard University professor Edward O. Wilson: "Mass extinctions are being reported with increasing frequency in every part of the world. The main cause is the destruction of natural habitats, especially tropical forests. . . . [T]he great majority of extinctions are never observed. Vast numbers of species are apparently vanishing before they can be discovered and named.[54]

THE PROBLEMS WITH TREE PLANTATIONS

Most of the world's paper supply, about 71 percent, is *not* made from timber harvested at tree farms[55] but from forest-harvested timber, from regions with ecologically valuable, biologically diverse habitat. It is inaccurate to claim, as industry apologists do, that "most of the trees used to make paper are not from virgin forests, but trees planted explicitly for manufacturing paper."[56] In the United States, where tree plantations are most prevalent, the figure is less than 20 percent.[57]

But what is so wonderful about tree plantations? According to the OECD, "through intensive production, [tree plantations] . . . have potentially negative effects on local ecosystem quality."[58] Even when trees are replanted where forests once stood, in biological terms that is a long way from "reforestation." And yet, when forested land is calculated by the paper industry and government agencies, tree plantations—like urban parks—are included, even though they hardly qualify as a forest. In Chile, as elsewhere, government policies encourage the clear-cutting of native forests that are thousands of years old to make way for plantations. As a result, "the prehistoric araucaria forests and the second oldest living trees in the world, the alerce, are in danger."[59]

Ecologically speaking, tree plantations have little resemblance to forests, and the term *reforestation,* commonly used by industry representatives to describe plantation planting after clear-cutting, is a misnomer. Forests host mixed-species, mixed-age timber in biologically active soils that protect wetlands. Dead, dying, and burnt trees—which are absent from tree plantations—are also essential components of forests, where they help create fertile soil and provide important habitat for the biologically and ecologically valuable microbial activity on which so much flora and fauna depend. Tree plantations, by contrast, are monocultural and polluted with chemicals that sterilize soils and contaminate wetlands. The ecological functions of forests, fundamental to the conservation of biodiversity, include regulation of regional water cycles and the global carbon cycle—the release and storage of carbon—as well as providing worldwide climate stability, soil protection, and habitat for animals. The OECD describes the services offered by forests as follows:

> Forests provide a range of essential environmental services as well as economic (e.g., timber, fruit and nuts) and social (e.g., recreational activities, cultural) services. Forests help to clean the atmosphere by acting as a pollutant filter: they trap solid matter and suspended aerosols, and can absorb some chemical compounds. Forests also provide a substantial CO_2 sink, countering the build-up of this greenhouse gas in the atmosphere. Forests regulate water flows, with tree roots reducing run-off and improving water infiltration into the soil. As a result, flood levels of streams can be reduced, and improved infiltration also helps to replenish groundwater.
>
> Forests also improve soil fertility. Tree roots penetrate deep into soil and add inorganic substances at the expense of parent rock. The falling leaves supply the topsoil with organic substances, which are decomposed by ground life developing in the microclimate conditions under the trees. Forests also play a vital soil protection role. Branches and leaves intercept some of the precipitation and thus diminish the effects of rainwater erosion. In mountain areas, they protect against avalanches, while in sandy areas, shelterbelts reduce wind erosion. Finally, forests host a number of species (from hundreds/ha [hectares] in tropical forests to 5 or less/ha in boreal forests).[60]

Tree plantations supply few of these services. Plantations damage biodiversity and essentially serve the same function—and impose similar ecological burdens—as do soil-eroding, habitat-destroying, herbicide-dependent industrial monocultural agricultural farms, with one important difference: Because tree plantations are not growing food to be ingested by humans, the chemicals used at these "farms" are more intensively applied, and more toxic, than those routinely used to grow food. For example, methoxychlor, just one of the many chlorinated aromatic chemicals that are "widely used"[61] as pesticides at plantations, is, according to the USDA Forest Products Laboratory (FPL), "highly toxic" and difficult to degrade; plus, it affects the development of rainbow trout, bovine embryos, mice, and other mammalian species. It persists in the environment, accumulates in aquatic microorganisms that are consumed by larger animals, and causes many water-quality problems.[62] It has been used for years by the paper industry, and its contamination threats are increasing throughout the world as plantations are spreading.

Proponents for the conversion of forests into tree plantations suggest that plantations are good because they allow new trees to soak up CO_2, thereby benefiting our fight to control climate change. The facts indicate that there is more to this ecological story than commonly reported, even when plantations are established in previously nonforested areas. Climate scientists have recently discovered that, contrary to popular belief, tree plantations don't sequester CO_2 effectively. Old growth forests are far better than tree plantations at scavenging CO_2 because in old-growth forests, carbon is locked not only into tree trunks and branches but also in the soil itself, where it can stay for centuries. When an old-growth forest is cut, not only are CO_2-absorbing (and habitat-hosting) trees lost, but much of the carbon stored in soil for centuries is also rapidly released in the form of carbon dioxide. And centuries would have to pass until newly planted trees could rebuild that reservoir of soil-stored carbon. The point of tree plantations is not ecological health. Rather, these tree farms are designed to allow for rapid reharvesting by paper companies—they are generally harvested in six- to ten-year rotations—so replenishing the original forest's reservoir of CO_2 cannot take place.[63]

The growth of plantation timber does not offset the life-cycle contribution of GHGs the paper cycle engenders. According to a life-cycle assessment of this issue, "plantations maintained to supply fibre for pulp production store larger amounts of carbon on land that previously was not forested, [but] this storage is insufficient to offset the even greater emissions from fossil fuel use in manufacture and from paper disposed in landfills. Plantation establishment does not appear to be offsetting emis sions from either energy use or landfills, let alone both of them. Production, consumption, and disposal of paper products is estimated to contribute a net addition of about 420 million tonnes in carbon dioxide equivalent units each year. . . ."[64] This amount represents 7 percent of global CO_2 emissions from all sources (and equals 14 percent of the total CO_2 emissions produced by the industrialized world and 20 percent of the total CO_2 emissions produced by the developing world).[65]

Harvesting and fragmenting forests to develop plantation trees also and obviously means the loss of habitat for resident species. In fact, tree plantations host about 90 percent fewer species than the forests that preceded them.[66] Most medicinal plants gathered in the world come from forests, and these plants are destroyed when tree plantations are established. And the development of plantations also destroys wetlands: One Duke University study found that the conversion of hardwood forests into pine plantations was responsible for half of all wetland losses in the coastal plain of North Carolina.[67]

Nature's production of soil depends on the activities of living biota, which the routine application of pesticides, herbicides, and other toxins at tree plantations are designed to kill. The fungi, microorganisms, and arthropods that decompose dead organisms and weathered rock and recycle all these nutrients into soil cannot survive the synthetic-chemical–intensive environment characteristic of tree plantations. Lichen and mosses that break down bedrock over thousands of years to create topsoil also cannot survive in a plantation's chemical-intensive environment. Soil consists of weathered rock, decaying organic matter (humus), living microorganisms, gases, and water. In the plantation environment, the living microorganisms are killed by the application of synthetic pesticides and herbicides. In biological terms there is no living soil—a growth-stimulating life-supporting nutrient—in tree plantations. Plantations not only cause biological impacts due to the routine application of pesticides, herbicides, growth regulators, and other chemicals, they also damage soil through overcultivation. Forest cover and vegetation break the fall of rain and allow it to drop gently. Without that cover soil is disrupted, resulting in erosion, flooding, or drought. Siltation from erosion can damage water systems and water habitat. Erosion of topsoil at plantations depletes the land's nutrient cycle and impairs its ability to perform water-storage functions, leading to greater runoff, siltation, and flooding of down-slope water systems.

DOWNSTREAM IMPACTS

As the single-largest product category found in household and commercial rubbish, paper is responsible for more economic and public-health burdens than any other commodity in the municipal waste stream. It would be hard to overstate the burden on the budgets of local governments that the management of municipal wastes has created throughout the world during the past two decades. Literally every OECD country and most developing nations have been struggling with the economic costs, logistical burdens, community squabbles, and dangerous health effects that managing billions of tons of municipal wastes imposes. Government advisory boards, regulatory reviews, research, and legislative initiatives designed to encourage the safe and economical management of municipal wastes have been advanced in the private sector and at every level of government—local, provincial, national, and, indeed, internationally.

Paper makes up almost 40 percent of all the household garbage generated in the United States, far and away a greater percentage than any other commodity. Sixty-six percent of all paper discarded in the United States winds up in either incinerators or landfills, imposing huge costs on municipalities, taxpayers, consumers, and the environment.[68] Paper products, especially the vast array of paper products bleached with chlorine, contribute to the production of dioxin by municipal incinerators. And of all the industrial generators of dioxin in the United States, municipal incinerators rank highest.[69] Consequently, the mismanagement of wastepaper—i.e., the combustion of wastepaper—is among the greatest contributors to global dioxin contamination.

Paper in the municipal-waste stream also creates greenhouse-gas emissions by increasing energy consumption (specifically of fossil fuels) used to transport and process municipal waste, increasing the amount of materials burned in waste incinerators—which generates GHGs such as CO_2, methane [CH_4], NO_x, and water vapors, the largest of all GHGs—and increasing the amount of materials that wind up in methane-generating landfills. Discarded paper is one of the largest contributors to methane emissions from landfills; methane, a greenhouse gas, is twenty times more potent than CO_2. Paper waste releases approximately 30 percent of its carbon as CO_2 landfill gas emissions.[70] Unfortunately, but predictably, the pulp-and-paper industry has been trying to obtain exemptions from government efforts designed to control these gases. According to the industry's *International Fact and Price Book*, "[a]t the end of last year, [1999] pulp and paper companies were lobbying hard to get exemptions on some of the proposed 'energy taxes' [i.e., government policies] that are designed to help reduce so-called greenhouse gas emissions."[71]

Thus, products manufactured by the pulp-and-paper industry generate adverse air-pollution, water-pollution, soil-contamination, and climate-change effects at virtually every stage of their life cycle. As mentioned, the manufacture, transport, use, and disposal of paper products consumes energy, including fossil fuels; these emit greenhouse gases and intensify the paper industry's adverse impact on climate change. The pulp-and-paper industry also emits non–energy-related GHG emissions from its use of chemicals and water. Paper mills contribute GHG emissions to the atmosphere, and the harvesting of trees adversely affects natural carbon storage by destroying carbon sinks that scavenge carbon dioxide from the atmosphere.

THE INFLUENCE OF GOVERNMENT SUBSIDIES

Ignoring the economic truism that an asset that is undervalued will be misused, the U.S. government, state and local governments, foreign governments, and international financing agencies have provided hundreds of billions of dollars in subsidies to the virgin-paper–production industry during the past hundred years. These subsidies are a vestige of a long-gone era when old-growth forests were plentiful, resident species were not endangered—or valued—and ecologically sound alternatives to forest-based products were few. Lobbyists for the forest-products industry are among the best connected and most influential in Washington, Ottawa, Brussels, and other political capitals, so it should come as no surprise that no comparable government programs support the environmentally superior recycling industry. To the contrary, in the United States the Internal

Revenue Service in 1998 actually eliminated a basic tax incentive for recycled-paper mills—one of the important reasons financing the BCPC became more difficult—despite the adverse upstream and downstream environmental consequences, and adverse economic consequences, that will result from this decision.

The virgin-based forest-products, mining, and energy industries have all been—and remain—huge beneficiaries of both direct and indirect government subsidies and tax breaks. Some examples of these subsidies and tax breaks include percentage-depletion allowances, which are intended to promote resource exploration; below-cost timber sales from federal lands; USDA Forest Service research donated to industry; write-offs for timber management and reforestation costs; and below-cost mining leases based on an 1872 law.[72] Among the largest subsidies—and certainly one of the most ecologically damaging because of the way it fragments habitat—is one related to the development of a transportation infrastructure designed to allow forest-products companies to acquire virgin timber from ecologically fragile areas more economically. There are approximately 369,385 miles of roads in the National Forest System that have been cut and maintained by the U.S. government for the benefit of timber companies.[73] By contrast, there are only just over 156,000 miles of interstate highways and "highways of national importance" in the entire United States.[74]

The USDA FPL was established in 1910, and until today its exclusive role has been to support and subsidize the forest-products industry with research about timber harvesting, pesticide and herbicide application, and the conversion of forests into plantations. The FPL is a government-financed appendage of a forest-products industry that is destroying biodiversity throughout the world. With funds collected from taxpayers, the government performs much of the paper industry's research. Consequently, the pulp-and-paper industry spends less than 1 percent, less than any other major industry, on research; other manufacturing industries as a whole spend 4 to 5 percent on research.[75] A review of the FPL *Research Highlights of 1999*—the most recent year for which this information exists—contains the following representative FPL studies, all tailored to benefit wood-harvesting processes and revealing the stress on larger timber forests: "Increasing the Demand for Small-Diameter Material,"

"Making the Most of Small-Diameter Western Softwoods," "Treated Wood—Does More Preservative Mean a Better Product?," "Converting Scrub Trees to Useful Composite Products," "Early Detection of Forest Health Stressors," "Updating the Standard Reference on Wood," and "Early Detection of Decay Will Extend the Service Life of Wood."[76]

Subsidies to the timber industry have historically included exemptions from environmental laws. These exemptions helped build up the virgin-resources industries by allowing them to externalize—pass on to others and in so doing keep off their financial accounting ledger—costly pollution burdens to the environment. Throughout the entire twentieth century, the U.S. paper industry was exempted from fully complying with virtually every air-, water-, and waste-pollution law that most other industries, including recycling industries, had to comply with. These are the kinds of benefits at the expense of public health and the environment an industry can obtain when it finances the campaigns and other operations of elected government officials and offers the tantalizing prospect of better paying jobs in industry to current government bureaucrats. If environmentalists owned these industries, as we need to, we would similarly own these government officials and, in so doing, we would obtain from them subsidies for ecological remedies and public-health protection, the opposite of what is now happening.

Collectively, tax breaks, subsidies, and regulatory exemptions, which first began in 1891,[77] have for decades averaged several billion dollars annually. Every level of government, as well as international agencies, provide these ecologically perverse subsidies. They have helped finance the development of a paper-manufacturing sector that relies overwhelmingly on virgin-materials extraction in ecologically sensitive regions, to the detriment of ecologically superior recycling processes. Commenting on just one year's worth of subsidies more than a decade ago (1988), an EPA study concluded that "[W]e can be quite confident that the overwhelming bias of federal tax policies and program outlays favors extractive [virgin] industries and their beneficiaries over recycled markets. . . . [F]ederal subsidies of virgin paper production undoubtedly cost the taxpayer hundreds of millions of dollars and may reduce the incentives slightly to switch from virgin to recycled paper production."[78]

Though one year's worth of subsidies may create a "slight" incentive for manufacturers to use virgin resources instead of recycled materials, the effect of more than a century's worth of subsidies has produced a much greater market distortion. Former vice president Al Gore has commented on subsidies to the paper industry in the following way: "In the case of the paper industry, for instance, taxpayers currently subsidize the manufacture of paper made from virgin timber, both as the largest single purchaser and by further subsidizing the construction of roads into national forests. In addition, the federal government pays the entire cost of managing the forest system, including many activities that exclusively benefit the timber industry. All of these policies encourage further destruction of a critical natural resource."[79]

Subsidy programs from the federal government alone that affected the U.S. virgin-timber, mineral, and energy industries averaged $3.5 billion to $6.3 billion through the early 1980s and has been $1.3 billion to $4 billion annually since that time.[80] All of these subsidies combine to make recycling and research into other alternative fibers less cost-competitive. In fact, much of the explosive growth in harvesting forests in the southeastern United States has been made possible by a single $2 billion taxpayer subsidy—under the guise of economic development—that built the Tennessee-Tombigbee Waterway, which now provides shipping access to previously landlocked forests.[81] These perverse subsidies that result in the ecological conversion of forests are obviously not limited to the United States. Government policies and subsidies supporting forest degradation exist in Canada, Scandinavia, and throughout Latin America, Asia, and Africa, and have existed for decades, resulting in the deforestation of biologically rich habitat and making environmentally superior recycling investments less cost competitive.[82] In Canada—the world's largest timber exporter—one province alone, British Columbia, "subsidizes the timber industry to the tune of $7 billion a year." In Indonesia, annual subsidies to the timber industry range from $1 billion to $3 billion each year.[83]

CONCLUSION

This chapter has outlined some of the more notable ecological impacts associated with paper production and disposal. However, words can only belittle any effort to authentically convey the sad reality, burdens, and threats that all species living around paper mills and within their supply-chain region experience each day. Viewing a clear-cut up close, living in communities subjected to the noxious odors of various sulfur gases and other toxic fumes, and suffering through the poverty that is so endemic around paper mills, is just something words cannot express. I felt palpably nauseous when I saw my first large clear-cut. I just couldn't believe what I was seeing, and I still feel ill whenever I see one. I couldn't believe my nose when I visited my first kraft sulfate mill and whiffed the vile rotten egg-like odor characteristic of those mills, which plague entire regions. But identifying an industrial problem, even regulating it out of existence, does not automatically result in the emergence of better industrial projects. And most of the problems caused by the paper industry do not derive from evil people conspiring to do harm. Rather, it is a more nefarious consequence of ordinary people acting logically in behalf of what they believe to be their own best interest within a system that is biased against ecologically sustainable investments.

One reason I had hoped to build a paper mill that would be a model for industrial ecologists throughout the world is because, in effect, the market left to its own devices—and biased with perverse subsidies—is just not yet ready to stimulate the type or scale of sustainable industrial-ecology projects the world desperately needs. And without the intervention of business savvy, realistic environmentalists, the market will remain tilted toward nonsustainable practices, and government will continue to funnel resources to actors conducting "business as usual." It is up to the environmental movement to build the superior factories that the future requires.

NOTES

1. Data provided by the Institute for Policy Studies, cited in Harper's Index, *Harper's*, May 2002, p. 11.

2. For more on this critical distinction, which is often ignored by apologists for industry's adverse impacts on biodiversity, see Ernst Mayr, *What Evolution Is* (New York: Basic Books, 2001), pp. 199–203.

3. *Toward a Sustainable Paper Cycle: An Independent Study on the Sustainability of the Pulp and Paper Industry* (London: International Institute for Environment and Development, 1996), pp. xv and 83.

4. *OECD Environmental Outlook* (Paris: OECD, 2001), p. 215.

5. *Global Forest Products Consumption, Production, Trade, and Prices: Global Forest Products Model Projections to 2010* (Rome: UN FAO Forest Policy and Planning Division, December 1998). Cited in Janet N. Abramovitz and Ashley T. Mattoon, *Paper Cuts: Recovering the Paper Landscape* (Washington, D.C.: Worldwatch Institute, 1999), p. 6.

6. Nick Robins and Sarah Roberts, "Why Rethink Paper Consumption?" *Rethinking Paper Consumption: A Discussion Paper* (London: International Institute for Environment and Development, 1996), p. 1. This can be found at http://www.iied.org/smg/pubs/rethink.html.

7. *Toward a Sustainable Paper Cycle*, p. 15.

8. Klaus Töpfer executive director United Nations Environment Programme, keynote address *UNEP's 7th International High Level Seminar on Cleaner Production*, Prague, 29–30 April 2002.

9. *Toward a Sustainable Paper Cycle*, p. 20, and Heide Matussek, ed., *International Fact and Price Book 1999* (San Francisco: Miller Freeman, 1998), p. 25.

10. NRDC, calculated from data provided in "The Nature of Paper: Trends, Patterns, and Concerns," *Rethinking Paper Consumption*, p. 32.

11. "The Nature of Paper: Trends, Patterns, and Concerns" and "Changing Paper Consumption Case Studies: India and the UK," *Rethinking Paper Consumption*, pp. 31–33 and 41.

12. Matussek, *International Fact and Price Book*, p. 25.

13. *A Technical Framework for Life-Cycle Assessment* (Washington, D.C.: SETAC Foundation for Environmental Education Inc. and Society of Environmental Toxicology and Chemistry, 1991).

14. "Bronx Community Paper Company in the Harlem River Yard: Final Environmental Impact Statement," prepared by Allee King Rosen & Fleming, New York City, April 1996, pp. i–11.

15. *Effluent Limitations and Guidelines, Pretreatment Standards, and New Source Performance Standards: Pulp, Paper and Paperboard Category; National Emission Standards for Hazardous Air Pollutants for Source Category; Pulp and Paper Production*, proposed rule, 17 December 1993, 40 CFR Parts 63 and 430, *Federal Register* 58, no. 241, p. 66103.

16. Ibid., pp. 66103–104.

17. Ibid.

18. *OECD Environmental Outlook*, p. 218.

19. Ibid., p. 218.

20. *Toward a Sustainable Paper Cycle*, p. 127.

21. Abramovitz and Mattoon, *Paper Cuts,* p. 50.

22. *National Emission Standards for Hazardous Air Pollutants for Source Category: Pulp and Paper Production,* 8 March 1996, 40 CFR Part 63, *Federal Register* 61, no. 47, pp. 9383 and passim.

23. *Effluent Limitations and Guidelines,,* pp. 66078 and passim.

24. Ibid., p. 66101.

25. "Habitat Fragmentation Can Amplify Ecological Stress," *Conservation Biology in Practice* 3, no. 1 (Winter 2002), p. 9.

26. W. F. Laurance and M. A. Cochrane, "Synergistic Effects in Fragmented Landscapes," *Conservation Biology* 15(6), pp. 1488–89. Cited in previous footnote.

27. *The State of the World's Forests* (Rome: UN FAO Forest Policy and Planning Division, December 1998, 1999), p. 8.

28. United Nations Environment Programme, *Cultural and Spiritual Values of Biodiversity* (London: Intermediate Technology Publications, 1999), p. xi.

29. For a fuller discussion of this see ibid., p. xi.

30. For an excellent discussion of this idea see Sarah A. Laird, "Forests, Culture, and Conservation," *Cultural and Spiritual Values of Biodiversity,* pp. 347 and passim.

31. *OECD Environmental Outlook,* p. 219.

32. Ralph E. Colberg, *Emerging Trends in Southern Timber Supply and Demand Relationships* (Columbus, Georgia: Decisions Support, 1996), p. 7. Paper presented at the International Woodfiber Conference, Atlanta, 14–15 May 1996.

33. Ibid.

34. Mark Payne, "Latin America Aims High for the Next Century," *Pulp and Paper International,* August 1999, in Abramovitz and Mattoon, *Paper Cuts,* p. 17.

35. Peter Ravin, Ph.D. and president, American Association for the Advancement of Science (AAAS), keynote address to the AAAS Annual Meeting, Boston, 14 February 2002.

36. Abramovitz and Mattoon, *Paper Cuts,* p. 124.

37. Jonathan Lash, World Resources Institute Global Forest Watch, quoted in press release 3 April 2002, found at http://www.enn.com/direct/display-release.asp?id=6538.

38. Daniel C. Nepstad et al., "Large-Scale Impoverishment of Amazonian Forests by Logging and Fire," *Nature* 398 (8 April 1999), pp. 505–7.

39. Ibid.

40. *Environmental Performance Reviews: United States 1996* (Paris: OECD, 1996), p. 44.

41. World Resources Institute Global Forest Watch, press release 3 April 2002.

42. *Environmental Performance Reviews,* p. 43, emphasis added.

43. World Resources Institute Global Forest Watch, press release 3 April 2002.

44. *OECD Environmental Outlook,* p. 125.

45. Ibid., p. 126.

46. Data from Edward O. Wilson, *Conserving Earth's Biodiversity,* CD-ROM (Washington, D.C.: Island Press, 2000), see "Threats to Biodiversity."

47. Colberg, *Trends in Southern Timber Supply,* p. 6.

48. Edward O. Wilson, *Conserving Earth's Biodiversity,* "Threats to Biodiversity."

49. Ibid.

50. Ted Williams, "False Forests," *Mother Jones,* May/June 2000, p. 73.

51. Ibid.

52. Ibid.

53. *Environmental Performance Reviews,* p. 43, and Wilson, *Conserving Earth's Biodiversity.*

54. E. O. Wilson, *In Search of Nature* (Washington, D.C.: Island Press, 1996), pp. 194–95.

55. *Toward a Sustainable Paper Cycle,* p. 34.

56. John Tierney, "Recycling Is Garbage," *New York Times,* 30 June 1996, section 6, p. 24.

57. Ralf Haggblom, fiber-resources senior consultant, Jaakko Pöyry, personal communications, Tarrytown, New York, 22 July and 2 December 1996, used with permission.

58. *OECD Environmental Outlook,* p. 18.

59. World Resources Institute Global Forest Watch, press release 3 April 2002.

60. *OECD Environmental Outlook,* p. 127.

61. USDA Forest Products Laboratory, *1999 Research Highlights,* p. 2.

62. Ibid.

63. Ernst-Detlef Schulze, Christian Wirth, and Martin Heimann, "Managing Forests After Kyoto," Science 289, no. 5487 (22 September 2000), pp. 2058–59.

64. *Toward a Sustainable Paper Cycle,* p. 216.

65. Calculated from data in Energy Information Administration, *Interna-*

tional Energy Annual 1999, DOE/EIA-0219(99) (Washington, D.C.: EIA, January 2001), Table H1, p. 212.

66. E. O. Wilson, personal communication, January 21, 2001, used with permission.

67. Williams, "False Forests," p. 73.

68. U.S. EPA Office of Solid Waste, *Municipal Solid Waste in the United States: 1999 Facts and Figures,* (Washington, D.C.: EPA, 2000), p. 9.

69. D. Cleverly, J. Schaum, D. Winters, and G. Schweer. *Inventory of Sources and Releases of Dioxin-Like Compounds in the United States* (Washington, D.C.: National Center for Environmental Assessment [8623D], U.S. EPA Office of Pesticides, Prevention, and Toxic Substances, 1999). Paper presented at Dioxin '99, the 19th International Symposium on Halogenated Environmental Organic Pollutants and POPs, Venice, Italy, 12–17 September 1999, p. 3.

70. J. A. Micales and K. E. Skog, "The Disposition of Forest Products in Landfills," *International Biodeterioration and Biodegradation* 39, no. 2–3 (1997), pp. 145–58.

71. Matussek, *International Fact and Price Book,* p. 26.

72. The federal government lost $126 million from logging in national forests in 1998, according to a draft report released 6 March 2001 by the USDA Forest Service. That same year the agency spent $672 million to administer timber sales that generated only $546 million in revenue. The Tongass National Forest in Alaska led the list of money losers: It cost $35.6 million to run the forest's timber program in 1998, with returns of only $6.5 million.

73. Data from the *1993 Annual Report* of the USDA Forest Service supplied by Tom Petigrew, transportation and development staff engineer, USDA Forest Service, personal communication, 7 March 1995.

74. Data supplied by Don Kestyn, transportation specialist, U.S. Department of Transportation, Washington, D.C., office, personal communication, 7 March 1995.

75. Abramovitz and Mattoon, *Paper Cuts,* p. 59.

76. USDA Forest Products Laboratory, *Research Highlights,* p. 2.

77. *Federal Disincentives: A Study of Federal Tax Subsidies and Other Programs Affecting Virgin Industries and Recycling* (Washington, D.C.: EPA, August 1994), p. 5.

78. Ibid., p. iii.

79. Al Gore, *Earth in the Balance* (New York: Houghton Mifflin, 1992), p. 198.

80. *Federal Disincentives,* p. 5.

81. Abramovitz and Mattoon, *Paper Cuts,* p. 55.

82. For more on this see, for example, Robert Repetto, *The Forest for the Trees? Government Policies and the Misuse of Forest Resources* (Washington, D.C.: World Resources Institute, 1988), pp. 8–9.

83. Abramovitz and Mattoon, *Paper Cuts,* p. 55.

3. The Keys to a Better Ecological Bottom Line: Raw Materials and Siting

> Explicit sustainability goals are required if research
> and development are to be focused on the
> most important threats and opportunities
> that humanity is likely to confront.
>
> —Board on Sustainable Development,
> National Research Council

INDUSTRIAL DEVELOPERS invariably approach the siting of a factory focused exclusively on the narrow financial and strategic needs of the firm. Financial incentives—labor, energy, and water costs—and proximity to raw materials are among the prominent factors that determine industrial siting decisions. Issues such as environmental impacts and community benefits are considered only after the siting decision has effectively been made, with the developer then trying to convince interested stakeholders—e.g., local politicians and the media, and community and environmental groups—that these crucial issues were in fact influential, if not paramount, in the siting decision. Obviously, if consideration of environmental and social sustainability issues were as influential in the siting decision as industrial developers pretend that they are, the world wouldn't be suffering from as many ecological and social burdens as it does. Because sustainability is not the motive underlying industrial development, as it should be, the environment almost always suffers when a new factory is built. This must change.

The two most important environmental decisions made by an industrial developer are (1) choosing a raw material supply and (2) choosing a location. Both of these choices shape an industrial facility's future operating attributes and options—hence, its environmental impacts—more than any other decisions an industrial developer will make. But the decisions are not causally linked: While locating at an urban brownfield makes it, in general, less costly and logistically easier for a factory to rely on recovered post-consumer recyclable materials, there is no law mandating that industries located at brownfields use them. In fact, most recycling mills are not located at brownfields but rather have been added on to existing paper mills—or steel mills, etc.—at remote green spaces, also known as greenfields. Nevertheless, it remains the case that relying on recycled raw materials and locating at a brownfield will, in combination, provide a mill with the best opportunities to advance environmental remediation and the broader objectives of sustainability.

Siting a factory at an urban brownfield—instead of at a rural greenfield—is generally the environmentally superior choice. Urban brownfield locations tend to offer more opportunities to remedy environmental problems and, at the same time, to advance meaningful social benefits. However, it is an industrial designer's choice of raw materials that influences—may actually determine—the financial and logistical viability of selecting a brownfield site. Because virgin raw materials are usually obtained from remote regions, using them will tend to discourage the siting of a factory at an urban brownfield site; clearly, it is more costly and logistically complicated to transport virgin materials from forests and mines to urban areas and process them there. Processing virgin resources virtually always requires more chemical-, energy-, and water-intensive processing technologies than does the processing of recycled materials. Consequently, trying to site virgin-based facilities at urban areas confronts even more barriers than trying to site a recycling mill there. Moreover, because virgin material-based factories typically require more energy and chemical inputs than a recycled-based factory, they are more likely to generate public-health risks. On the other hand, opting for recycled instead of virgin raw materials offers a better chance to minimize the risks and overcome barriers to brownfield redevelopment, as savings on chemicals, energy, water, and transportation costs can make brownfields cost-competitive locations.

In the future, for those many industrial processes still needing to rely on some form of virgin-materials use, industrial designers of consumer products should strive to mimic natural processes to the greatest degree feasible. For instance, spiders make waterproof threads with the strength of steel without using any combustion processes or fossil fuels. Why can't we? A leaf converts sunlight instantaneously into energy without any pollution, and a snail converts the minerals in seawater into a material harder than ceramic. Industrial ecologists must ultimately learn to do the same. Yet the field of biomimicry,[1] though promising, is not likely to be a large-scale industrial reality anytime soon. Until that occurs, increasing the use of recovered waste products in our production processes—especially municipal, agricultural, and industrial wastes—offers some of the best opportunities to promote more sustainable industrial practices. The trick is to make doing so the most cost-competitive option.

USING RECYCLED RAW MATERIALS

The key question all industrial ecologists should ask themselves is: What type of industry can I help develop that will heal an ecological problem?

Austria, Denmark, France, Germany, Japan, Korea, Norway, Spain, Sweden, Switzerland, and the Netherlands all recycle higher percentages of their wastepaper than does the United States.[2] More than nine out of every ten tons (96 percent) of all plastics discarded into garbage in the United States is not recycled. Two thirds of all wastepaper in the United States is not recycled; overall, about three out of every four tons of waste materials discarded into the U.S. municipal-waste stream are not recycled.[3] It is plain that discarding so many highly refined commodities that require resources, habitat, and energy to produce, and that cause pollution during their transformation from raw material to product, is wasteful.

As I discussed earlier in this book, my decision to launch the development of a recycled-paper mill to produce newsprint was motivated by (1) an interest in reducing some of the ecological burdens plaguing the New York City metropolitan area, (2) a desire to reduce some of the upstream ecological problems caused by the virgin-paper industry, and (3) a desire to show that ecologically valuable industrial projects can also be economically and socially developmental. Of the approximately 36,000 tons of municipal and commercial waste generated in New York City each day, almost 35 percent, about 12,000 tons a day, is wastepaper. That amounts to about 4.6 million tons of paper waste generated in New York City each year. Of that amount, only about 400,000 tons is currently recovered for recycling from residences by the city's Department of Sanitation, and about 730,000 tons is recovered for recycling from commercial establishments by private waste haulers.[4] All of the rest, approximately 3.5 millions tons annually, is shipped out to landfills or incinerators (invariably located in poor communities). In the 1980s, the New York City Department of Sanitation proposed building five large— and likely to be highly polluting—waste incinerators as an alternative to its gargantuan, highly polluting, and wasteful Fresh Kills mega-landfill, at an initial projected cost of more than $3 billion. The BCPC was designed to help respond to this polluting waste of resources and to increase the availability of paper-recycling facilities in New York, as an alternative to landfilling and incineration.

Recycling can help lessen virtually all the environmental burdens and economic costs that virgin-paper production and traditional paper-disposal engenders. Both upstream and downstream, recycling provides meaningful benefits. Indeed, for paper, metals, glass, and plastics commodities, few industrial practices provide as many advantages as does recycling.

- Recycling conserves natural resources, such as timber, water, and mineral ores, from domestic and imported sources.

- Recycling reduces the pollution that would otherwise be caused by manufacturing from virgin resources.

- Recycling saves energy.

- Recycling reduces the need for landfilling and incineration, and helps avoid the pollution produced by these technologies.

- Recycling helps reduce pressure on unmolested, still wild ecosystems.

- Recycling helps protect and expand manufacturing jobs.

- Recycling engenders a sense of community involvement and responsibility.

The environmental and economic benefits of recycling have been broadly analyzed by government and private-sector analysts in the United States and in countries throughout the world.[5] Few analysts dispute that recycling can help reduce many of the global and local environmental burdens imposed by virgin manufacturing plants, as well as the costs of administering, collecting, processing, and transporting garbage to landfills and incinerators. This is why recycling is fundamental to every vision of sustainability. Recycling even saves more energy than the combustion of wastes for energy recovery can produce. Depending on the commodity being recycled or combusted, the amount of energy saved from recycling can conserve—and free for other uses—up to 90 percent more energy than combustion. (See Table 3.1.)

Compared with producing commodities from virgin sources, recycling uses less energy. One estimate related to the benefits of using recycled instead of virgin-based magazine-grade paper (technically referred to as "coated freesheet paper") indicates that for each ton of recycled fiber that displaces a ton of virgin fiber during the manufacture of coated freesheet paper, total energy consumption by the mill is reduced by 38 percent, net greenhouse-gas emissions by 40 percent, particulate emissions by 36 percent, wastewater by 45 percent, and solid waste by 53 percent.[6] As discussed on pages 94 and 115–7, the data for the BCPC show that it would have provided even greater environmental benefits, in part because the project was located in an urban area, which reduces the transportation impacts associated with acquiring recycled raw materials and marketing finished products to local publishers.

Recycling industries use resources more efficiently than do virgin-based industries and typically produce less pollution per unit of production. For example, much less water pollution is produced per ton by paper-recycling mills than by virgin-paper mills, which are very water intensive. As I mentioned in chapter 2, the virgin-pulp and paper industry is the largest industrial process water user in the United States.[7] Some virgin-newsprint mills use twice as much water per ton of manufactured product than do recycled-paper mills. A 100 percent recycled-newsprint mill in Aylesford, England, uses and discharges less than 4,000 gallons of water per ton of manufactured product.[8] The 100 percent recycled-newsprint mill I was developing in New York City's South Bronx was

TABLE 3.1

Energy Savings and CO_2 Impacts: Recycling versus Incineration

Material/Grade	Energy savings per ton recycled				Energy generated per ton incinerated	
	Percent reduction of energy[1]	Million Btu	Equivalent in barrels of oil	Tons of CO_2 reduced	Million Btu	Equivalent in barrels of oil
Aluminum	95	196	37.2	13.8	-1.06	-0.2
Paper[2]						
Newsprint	45	20.9	3.97	-0.03	11.8	2.24
Print/Writing	35	20.8	3.95	-0.03	11.8	2.24
Linerboard	26	12.3	2.34	0.07	11.8	2.24
Boxboard	26	12.8	2.43	0.04	11.8	2.24
Glass						
Recycle	31	4.74	0.90	0.39	-0.34	-0.06
Reuse	328	50.18	9.54	3.46	NA	NA
Steel	61	14.30	2.71	1.52	-0.34	-0.06
Plastic						
Polyethylene terephthalate	57	57.9	11.0	0.985	35.9	6.8
Polyethylene	75	56.7	10.8	0.346	35.9	6.8
Polypropylene	74	53.6	10.2	1.32	38.5	7.3
Mixed municipal solid waste	NA	NA	NA	NA	10.0	1.9

Source: NRDC, 1991. Estimates derived from data supplied by the Argonne National Laboratory, U.S. Department of Energy, Franklin Associates, A-L Associates, American Iron and Steel Institute, Phillips 66, and Wellman.

[1] Relative to energy required for virgin production.

[2] Energy calculations for paper recycling count unused wood as fuel.

designed to consume about 3,800 gallons of water per ton of manufactured product, and more than 80 percent of that water was to come from a sewage-treatment plant as recovered and cleaned effluent.[9] By contrast, virgin-newsprint mills that are ten years old or older—which most mills are—use approximately 10,000 gallons of water per ton of manufactured newsprint, while the few modern mills that have been built in the past eight to ten years use 4,000 to 5,000 gallons of water per ton of manufactured newsprint, which is still more than is needed by recycled-paper mills.[10]

Overall, the recycled-paper industry is the most modern, efficient, and least polluting sector in the paper-manufacturing industry. Far from producing hazardous pollution, which is inherent in the virgin-paper–production process, modern paper-recycling mills can be designed to produce virtually no hazardous air or water pollution or hazardous wastes.[11] Also, a review of engineering designs for newsprint-recycling mills reveals that the product yield per ton of recovered paper used is in the range of 90 percent—in other words, for every hundred tons of recycled paper used as a raw material, only about ten tons does not end up as a new paper product. For virgin mills, the ratio is virtually the opposite: Two thirds of the harvested tree does not wind up as paper product. No recycled-paper mill could operate successfully, financially or otherwise, with a product yield as low as that of virgin mills, especially if the by-product generated was toxic waste—chemicals, solvents, organochlorides, liquors, and heavy metals—which requires special, extremely costly handling, treatment, and disposal in compliance with U.S. federal hazardous-waste laws. Virgin timber mills, however, have been able to get away with high-volume waste production because in the United States, and especially in the developing world, they benefit from many environmental exemptions, a huge subsidy.

Finally, the use of recycled materials reduces the pressure to destroy or convert unmolested, wild ecosystems to extract raw materials. For instance, newsprint comes primarily from softwood trees of the sort currently harvested in the southeastern United States. Not coincidentally, the region currently under the greatest pressure from industrial logging in the United States is the Southeast, a region with a biological diversity that is—or was—virtually unparalleled in North America. U.S. southeastern forests host the richest abundance of temperate

TABLE 3.2

The Impacts from the Operation of a Virgin Paper Mill Compared
with Estimated Impacts from the BCPC

Parameter	Virgin-Paper Mill	BCPC	Percent Reduction[1]
Quantity of news-print produced	220,000 metric tons (242,440 short tons)	220,000 metric tons (242,440 short tons)	NA
Brownfield remediation	No	Yes	NA
Water	6,599 gallons/ton	5,869.7 gallons/ton	11.05%
Energy usage	2.5 megawatt–hour/ton	1.2 megawatt–hour/ton	52.00%
CO_2	5,946 lb/ton	2,708.1 lb/ton	54.45%
NO_x	23.7 tons/day	.105 lb/ton	99.56%
SO_x	40.1 lb/ton	.218 lb/ton	99.46%
Volatile organic compounds (VOCs)	3.9 lb/ton	.0561 lb/ton	98.56%
Solid waste	2,413 lb/ton	644.39 lb/ton	73.30%
Particulate matter	13.2 lb/ton	.115 lb/ton	99.12%
Biochemical oxygen demand (BOD)	2.5 lb/ton	2.14 lb/ton	14.40%
Chemical oxygen demand (COD)	36.3 lb/ton	5.35 lb/ton	85.26%
Total suspended solids (TSS)	4.8 lb/ton	5.84 lb/ton	-21.67%

[1]Values for the percent reduction were calculated by taking the difference between the two mills and dividing by the value for the virgin-paper mill.
Source: NRDC, based on data supplied by S. D. Warren, MoDo Paper, Allee King Rosen & Fleming, and Rust International.

herbaceous flora in the world. Tree diversity and endemism—trees uniquely native to a region—are the highest of any eco-region in the United States, totaling 190 species with 27 endemics. If action is not taken to stop the demand for logging and other forms of ecosystem conversion, this valuable eco-region in all likelihood will not exist in the next century.[12] As indicated in Tables 3.2 and 3.3, the BCPC, by rely-

TABLE 3.3

Environmental-Impact Comparison:
The BCPC Brownfield Mill versus a Virgin Greenfield Mill

Parameter	Virgin-paper mill	BCPC
Trees harvested	5,148,000 trees/year	5,148,000 trees/year *preserved*
Forest acreage	16,860 acres harvested per year	16,860 acres *preserved* per year
Atmospheric CO_2 affected over 10-year period	–6.8 million metric tons	6.8 million metric tons
Atmospheric CO_2 affected over 49-year lifetime of the paper mill	$\geq$ 51 million metric tons	–51 million metric tons

Source: NRDC, 1998.

ing on recycled wastepaper instead of virgin timber, would have avoided the ecological conversion of habitat by almost 17,000 acres per year, and it would have reduced many other categories of pollutants typically emitted by virgin-paper mills.

Besides its environmental value, recycling is the only solid-waste–management strategy that offers the potential to generate revenue in government's otherwise losing proposition of collecting and disposing of municipal waste. Of course, as a raw-materials commodities business, recycling markets can't guarantee profits. No market does. Still, recycling industries have grown to encompass billions of dollars in competitive investments and infrastructure worldwide. And whatever the financial risks of recycling, these in no way negate its environmental benefits.

Not all production processes can easily convert to the use of recycled instead of virgin raw materials. And a certain level of virgin-materials use may always be required by the industrial sector. But a greater reliance on recycled resources—and other more benignly acquired, nontoxic, renewable raw materials such as wastepaper and agricultural wastes—is within immediate reach.

The Pluses of Producing Recycled Newsprint

When I first sought out a paper company with whom to collaborate and build a recycled-paper mill in New York City, I had in mind a mill that would manufacture a grade of paper that didn't have high-recycled content—e.g., newsprint or magazine-grade paper. It wouldn't make sense to develop a mill that would duplicate existing recycling capacity. Instead, it would be better to help develop a mill that would broaden the recycling market and, in so doing, expand both the upstream forestry benefits as well as the downstream recycling markets. To reiterate the guideline I used, the key question all industrial ecologists should ask themselves is: What type of industry can be developed that will heal an ecological problem?

Newsprint is a paper product that currently has a relatively low average recycled content, 27 percent (and an even lower average, if pre-consumer industrial scraps are factored out of the calculation).[13] More than seven out of every ten tons of newsprint manufactured in North America come from ecologically disruptive virgin-timber forests or plantation sources. A look at the type of trees used in newsprint production underscores why industrial ecologists should promote the development of mills that manufacture paper products from recycled raw materials.

Newsprint is a grade of paper currently manufactured primarily from softwood trees, and U.S. softwood *harvesting is often twice the amount of growth* in most of the large softwood-producing states, including Alabama, Arkansas, Georgia, Louisiana, Mississippi, South Carolina, and Texas.[14] According to industry analyses, there is clear evidence that for the next fifteen to twenty years southern forests will not be able to provide the softwood volumes required to meet current mill requirements without massive ecological disruptions. The trees needed to support southern mills are not in the ground and growing because softwood planting rates have not kept pace with accelerated harvest levels.

WHY A BROWNFIELD SITE MAKES SENSE

The best way to preserve habitat, prevent sprawl, and avoid many other development-related ecological disturbances is to avoid the conversion of forests and other types of greenfields that host terrestrial biodiversity.

Along with factory trawlers that strip-mine the seas of marine life, conversion and contamination of green spaces is the principal global threat to nonhuman species and the planet's limited supply of freshwater resources. The conversion of healthy habitat by industrial, agricultural, human settlements and other forms of development is accelerating throughout the globe, despite the fact that the loss of wetlands, tropical forests, and other greenspaces is the number-one threat to biodiversity worldwide. More than half of all the original water-purifying wetlands in the United States have been lost to development, and in some regions the loss of wetlands has been nothing less than astounding. In California, 91 percent of all original wetlands have been developed, and in Ohio and Illinois, 90 percent and 85 percent, respectively, of all original wetlands have been developed. Florida and New York State each have less than 25 percent of their original wetlands.[15] At the time of European settlement, there were 221 million acres of wetlands. Today, less than half that amount remains. Of all wetland types it is the forested wetlands in the United States that have experienced the greatest decline, with a net loss of 1.2 million acres between 1986 and 1997, equal to 2.4 percent of all forested wetlands that remain in the United States. For the first time in the nation's history, there are now fewer than 50 million acres of forested wetlands in the coterminous United States.[16]

I kept these facts in mind when I contemplated the best location for siting the BCPC mill. It was obvious to conclude that the most environmentally responsible site would be at a contaminated brownfield, one of the 650,000 formerly used industrial and commercial sites that blight America's landscape.[17] Numerous studies have concluded that cleaning up these brownfields, where expansion or redevelopment is technically and financially complicated by contamination and other investment barriers, could total more than $700 *billion*.[18] Along with the choice to use recycled raw materials, locating an industrial project in an urban brownfield is one of the two most important environmental decisions any industrial developer can make. Industrial-location decisions affect the nature and economic viability of raw-material–supply decisions, and in combination these two attributes determine a factory's biodiversity impacts, transportation impacts, water- and air-pollution impacts—including GHG impacts—and water-use options. Location decisions also determine the extent to which a project can help alleviate poverty, enhance a community's social-services infrastructure, and preserve traditional, indigenous cultures and communities.

Stimulating cost-competitive and profitable investments that result in the cleanup of contaminated areas and reduce the pressure to convert green spaces is precisely the type of hands-on work industrial ecologists should focus on. Although I didn't know of a suitable site for the paper mill when I launched the development of the BCPC, I knew that locating at a greenfield was out of the question. In an urban setting a recycled-paper mill—because of the ample supply of wastepaper raw material and the proximity of a market for the mill's product—can provide additional economic and ecological benefits by reducing the costly, polluting vehicle miles that have to be traveled to obtain raw materials and get a product to its market (known in the trade as "off-take").

I took this brownfield-reclamation approach because it not only agreed with ecological criteria, but also because a representative of a local South Bronx community group told me that, while housing had been steadily rehabilitated in the area during the previous decade—the late 1980s and early 1990s—many abandoned industrial sites remained, and the community was as economically depressed as ever. Above all, it lacked environmentally clean, livable-wage jobs; overall unemployment was in the double digits, and teenage unemployment was reputed to be above 50 percent. The absence of jobs was destroying the fabric of families and creating other social problems in the area. It became quickly apparent to me that the viability and long-term continuation of businesses, and the preservation of the jobs that go along with them, is too often overlooked in discussions of sustainability, taking a backseat to more traditional habitat- and resource-based ecological considerations. In addition, I knew from my daily review of the government's *Federal Register* index, that programs existed to financially support brownfield reclamation; local governments, states, and the federal government all have an interest in this.

As discussed in chapters 4 and 5 of this book, although there are environmental benefits to be gained from locating at a brownfield, doing so is fraught with many technical and political obstacles, as well as economic penalties—and most of these have little to do with cleaning up the site's contamination. Consequently, throughout the BCPC's development phase I was constantly on the lookout for any and every subsidy available to offset the economic, technical, and political barriers associated with locating at a brownfield.[19] I was also seeking subsidies to offset the market impacts of the perverse, environmentally damaging subsidies that for more than a century have supported virgin-resource exploitation and green-space conversion.

Because of the infrastructure requirements of a paper mill, and because I sought to locate the project only where it was invited, it ultimately took fourteen months and almost a million dollars to identify the proper site for the BCPC. However, by choosing to locate at a brownfield—an abandoned rail yard—with a community group as a partner, the project-development team was able to anticipate the following environmental benefits and cost advantages:

- reduced utility-infrastructure-development impacts;
- reduced transportation impacts;
- reduced energy demand;
- reduced waste-management impacts; and
- the creation of more wealth and social services in an economically disadvantaged area.

Deciding that the mill would be located at a brownfield was only the first step in finding a location for the mill. Industrial-development infrastructure and operational issues related to sustainability also had to be factored in. Paper mills require specific infrastructure services—including a high-volume water supply, electricity and steam supplies, effluent-processing and -discharge systems, and roads—in order to function technically and economically, and these services had to be available or developed at the site. Plus, sustainable communities require livable-wage jobs and poverty-alleviation initiatives. Therefore, worker training was likely to be an essential and large-scale feature of the development effort.

Community Wealth

As I have mentioned, most industrial developers choose a site based on technical considerations and afterward inform the potential host community about it. I took the opposite approach: Although respecting the technical needs of the mill's operations was obviously a sine qua non for locating it, I was looking for community interests, rather than NRDC or our paper-company partner, to guide site selection.

The traditional approach to industrial-site development is not an inclusive one as far as community interests are concerned. An imposed-from-outside approach, though, inevitably instigates community alienation toward a project and, thus, organized opposition. Perversely, industrial developers often view their siting efforts as more likely to be successful when they manage to exclude environmental and community groups from the process. For industrial ecologists seeking to promote sustainable communities, this exclusive approach is exactly the wrong one for ethical as well as financial, political, social, and technical reasons. Projects that welcome community interests, and are respectful of and attentive to remedying past burdens imposed in certain regions, are appropriate from the perspectives of ecological progress, democratic processes, and community development. Benefiting from community input, these projects are also more likely to succeed during the permitting and development phase. This reduces the costs of litigation and helps bring in a more acceptable technical design at an earlier—less expensive—stage. According to Phil Sears, a New York City–based environmental planner with three decades of experience developing infrastructure and industrial projects, "[p]olitical opposition is the largest cause of failure of projects, no matter how smart or necessary a project is. Among other things, it takes a forceful political mentor to shepherd a project forward, and support from the local community gives the mentor a reason to support a project."[20] There are no road maps and few precedents on what, precisely, incorporating authentic, adequately representative community participation into a project actually means. Certainly, what I did with the BCPC—arranging for a community group to entirely own the corporation we established to develop the project, without successfully developing a more broad-based collaboration with other community groups—was an ideologically pure (i.e., inexperienced) but politically and operationally naive approach that turned out to be a huge strategic error; it contributed heavily to the BCPC's failure to get financed. Fortunately, as discussed in chapter 7, there are many forms of authentic community participation short of what I did. Correctly attending to this issue is central to industrial ecology and the ultimate success of any industrial development.

Although brownfields are routinely avoided out of a concern with the site-preparation effort involved, cleaning up a non-Superfund brownfield is, in fact, a doable activity, however complicated it may seem at first. With the enactment of the Small Business Liability Relief and Brownfields Revitalization Act,[21] which was signed into law by President George W. Bush in 2002, one important redevelopment hurdle has been lowered: Brownfield-developer liabilities have been reduced, and early-stage redevelopment funding has been increased.

Brownfield cleanups invariably involve multiphase efforts to characterize and map the type of soil conditions, pollutants, and gases present on the site, and they invariably also involve a multiphase approach to cleaning up the site. The BCPC was to be located on an abandoned, overgrown rail yard abutting the Harlem River and the Bronx Kill, which separates the Bronx from Manhattan, in the southernmost section of the South Bronx, in New York City. The site had served as a rail yard for more than a hundred years and is located in New York City's poorest census tract. It is zoned for heavy industry and offers excellent access to water, rail, and highway facilities. Adjacent to the site are two major highways— the Major Deegan Expressway and the Bruckner Expressway—and the Triborough Bridge, which connects New York City to Long Island. There is also an existing docking area on the Harlem River at the southwestern section of the site. The location is within a New York State Economic Development Zone as well as a Federal Empowerment Zone, underscoring the government's interest in attracting new manufacturing jobs to this historically difficult-to-invest-in area.

After being invited into the community by a local community-development corporation (CDC) named the Banana Kelly Community Improvement Association—Kelly Street in the Bronx, where the organization started its work, is shaped like a banana; hence, the name—my colleagues and I, together with the CDC and our private-sector collaborators, consulted extensively with diverse interests before proceeding with any project-development work. We reviewed the idea for the project with local community groups, local elected officials, the New York City Economic Development Corporation, the New York State Department of Economic Development, the New York City Department of Sanitation, private real-estate firms, citywide environmental organizations, and national environmental organizations that have their headquarters in New York City; besides NRDC, these included the National Audubon Society, Environmental Defense, and the New York Public Interest Research Group. We chose the site in collaboration with our community-group and paper-company partners to take advantage of the site's location advantages and, especially, local community groups' interest in hosting an environmentally positive, jobs-generating industrial investment: Community interests and local elected officials sent me, our collaborating paper company, and others working on the project more than two dozen letters in favor of locating the mill at the Harlem River Rail Yard site. Choosing the brownfield site and navigating through the cleanup and permitting processes were made easier—though they were still complicated—because of the participation of community interests and because poverty alleviation was also among the project's principal objectives, on par with the more traditional approaches to sustainability that emphasize ecological criteria. Alleviating poverty is fundamental to sustainability, as I discussed in the introduction to this book, but it has for so long been ignored by the traditional approach to environmental advocacy. Poverty was certainly threatening the health and well being of the desperately poor in New York City's South Bronx.

THE CHALLENGE OF INFRASTRUCTURE ISSUES

In any industrial development, infrastructure services—available water, effluent treatment, roads, energy, and other utilities—are critical. Although the infrastructure at a brownfield, which has already hosted some form of commercial activity, is likely to be more developed than at a greenfield, the essential task of tailoring the site to the needs of a specific project is still complicated. After determining the site's geographic location—ideally, a brownfield in a community that authentically supports the project because it comports with the neighborhood's development plans—the next steps are developing a suitable water, sewage, power (electricity and steam), and transportation infrastructure. As with virtually every other issue related to industrial development, every option for providing these services engenders different environmental consequences. For each of these industrial-development issues, the guiding principle I returned to each and every time during the BCPC development effort was what I have earlier stated should be the mantra of industrial ecology: "What can I do to heal ecological impacts related to this sector?"

Water

It is a sad fact that the vast majority of scarce potable water used in the world—indeed, virtually all of it—is used only once, contaminated to a greater or lesser degree, and then discharged, sometimes to a septic or sewage-treatment plant, often directly into a waterway. This has to change: According to a United Nations report released in March 2002, "more than 2.7 billion people will face severe water shortages by the year 2025 . . . [and] two out of every three persons on Earth will live in water stressed conditions . . . if the world continues consuming water at the same rate. . . . [A]nother 2.5 billion people live in areas where it will be difficult to find sufficient freshwater to meet their needs . . . [including] Europe, where one in seven of the population still do not have access to clean water and sanitation." Among other severe impacts, this situation "is the biggest threat to food production."[22]

Although potable water is safest for drinking and cooking, most *industrial* processes can be—and should be—run without relying on fresh drinking-water supplies. Industrial ecologists should design their factories to rely not on potable water but instead on cleaned-up sewage effluent and to produce what is known as gray water, which would otherwise be discharged as a contaminant into waterways. I refer to this as green water, given its environmental value.

Locating at a brownfield by definition means the site has previously hosted a commercial or industrial facility. This makes it likely that a sewage-treatment infrastructure exists nearby. Another potential benefit of this: If a sewage plant exists within a two- or three-mile radius, it would be possible to use cleaned and treated effluent instead of potable water as a process-water supply for the factory.

Almost without exception, all industrial operations require water, and virtually all industrial operations produce wastewater. Wastewater must either be discharged into the environment or, preferably, reclaimed for use. In general, water is used for three purposes at industrial facilities: (1) domestic water, (2) process water, and (3) cooling water. Consequently, industrial facilities ipso facto generate three types of wastewater: (1) domestic wastewater, (2) process wastewater, and (3) cooling wastewater. Domestic water is used by workers for drinking or showering. Process water is used by machinery during production or washes the product. Some process water is occasionally retained in the product (for example, paper coming off a papermaking machine is made up of about 10 percent water and about 90 percent cellulose fibers). Sometimes process water leaks or spills. Cooling water is used to cool machinery and energy-production systems. Obviously, all industrial siting decisions must take into account the need to clean up and dispose of large volumes of wastewater.

As with almost all other forms of consumption, the use of freshwater in the United States, at 1,873 cubic meters (m^3) annually per capita, is more intensive than in any other country in the world. By contrast, the annual per-capita demand for potable water in Germany and Japan is less than half the amount consumed in the United States, 580 m^3 and 730 m^3, respectively.[23] A large part of the reason for this is the low cost, in the United States, of wasting water and discharging wastewater after it is used. Industry and agriculture consume well over 90 percent of all water used in the United States, but unlike the situation in most other industrial societies, it is much more common for industries in the United States to discharge wastewater into municipal water-treatment plants.[24] Allowing private firms to use publicly owned treatment works (POTWs), what we commonly refer to as sewage-treatment plants, is a huge water-use taxpayer subsidy that substantially lowers the cost of water to industry, making it less expensive to waste this precious resource.

Hundreds of billions of gallons of sewage effluent are discharged each day into waterways throughout the world, and much of it, given the chronic absence of sewage treatment plants in most of the developing world—possibly most of it—is discharged without any prior treatment, undermining the biological viability of receptor waterways. In the United

States, an EPA report published in 2000 concluded that by 2020 the country will face a $23 billion shortfall *each year* for sewage-treatment–plant infrastructure needs. Ken Kirk, who currently (in 2002) heads the Association of Metropolitan Sewage Authorities, predicts that "systems will break down, pipes will crack, there will be overflows of sewage."[25] Shifting some of our industrial and commercial water use toward the capture of reclaimed water would not only reduce the demand for freshwater but would benefit sewage systems with added financial support for maintenance.

Although water-acquisition costs are invariably higher at urban brownfields than at rural greenfields (see Chapter 4), locating at an urban brownfield offers unique water-conservation and -remediation opportunities. In New York City, POTWs discharge between 1.24 billion gallons (in dry weather) and 1.33 billion gallons of effluent *each day*.[26] This astounding amount of water consumed in New York City is—as in virtually all other cities throughout the world—used once and then, after flowing down the drain, never cleaned up and recovered; instead, it is discharged, after treatment, into surrounding waterways. The daily amount of effluent discharged by sewage plants in New York City actually exceeds the amount of freshwater delivered to New York City residents by about 2 million gallons per day.[27] Despite its potential value, wastewater is not reclaimed for use. In New York City in particular this is a spectacular waste, since "ninety percent of the water . . . [New Yorkers] . . . use does *not* go to human needs."[28] In fact, the New York City Health and Buildings departments have rules that forbid reuse of gray water in any building that has potable water, because they are afraid of a cross connection and contamination of the drinking water. (This is but one of many examples of local regulations and zoning ordinances that conspire to stymie more sustainable industrial practices.) In New York City the only widespread application of water reuse taking place is for car washes, where water is used for a few cycles before it is discarded. Although this does help reduce demand on freshwater, it doesn't involve cleaning up the water, just using it multiple times.[29]

The characteristics of the pollutants contained in sewage effluent vary depending on the source of the effluent and the type of sewage treatment used. In general, the types of pollutants found in wastewater discharges to sewage plants include organic materials—including pathological and infectious liquids—inorganic materials, caustic and acidic materials, grease and oils, and some toxic materials. However, cities without intense industrial activity, like New York City, have relatively clean effluent, because there are few industrial toxins discharged into the sewage system. Sewage-treatment plants perform various treatments on the wastewater to reduce the environmental degradation that would result from discharging it directly into waterways. There are primary-, secondary-, and, much less frequently used, tertiary-treatment systems. In addition, industrial waste-water streams are, or should be, pretreated prior to discharge to a sewage-treatment plant. Although zero *discharge* of wastewater is not a practical goal, because there will always be some liquid wastes that must be treated and returned to waterways, experienced chemical engineers long ago con-cluded that "*zero pollution* [of waterways] is a practical goal that can be attained by every industry."[30]

Pretreatment of wastewater discharges to sewage plants can be as sim-ple a process as equalizing the flow rate to the sewage plant. By leveling hydrologic loading, a process known as equalization, industrial operators can avoid overloading a treatment facility. Neutralization of acidic or basic wastewater, removal of grease and oils in grease traps, and prevent-ing the discharge of toxic substances into wastewater are also types of pre-treatment programs.

Primary treatment targets the removal of suspended solids, usually with physical-separation devices such as screens, grit chambers, and grav-ity-sedimentation tanks. Sometimes suspended particles are removed by a process known as chemical precipitation, in which various chemicals (alu-minum sulfate, ferric chloride, ferrous sulfate, or lime) are used to coag-ulate tiny particles into larger particles; these are then physically removed.

Secondary treatment removes organic matter through the use of microbes. The microbes convert soluble organics into gases that are invari-ably vented—such as CO_2 or CH_4, both of which should be recovered because they are greenhouse gases—and into removable suspended organic solids, which are then removed by a physical-separation technique such as gravity sedimentation. Among other processes, tertiary treatment involves denitrification of the effluent prior to discharge. This is rarely done, despite the increasing prevalence of hypoxia, a low-oxygen condition exac-erbated by nitrogen loading, which causes adverse ecological conditions.

As the world's population moves toward 7 billion, and as climate change is expected to instigate more frequent and severe droughts, water shortages are increasing throughout the globe, including in the United States, and the regulation and metering of water use is expanding. In addition, more and more sewage effluent is being discharged as water-pollution–control measures expand and sewage-treatment plants proliferate. Consequently, there is both the increasing need for and increasing opportunity for industrial ecologists to focus their water-acquisition designs on effluent reclamation and, in so doing, help avoid exhausting, wasting, or polluting freshwater supplies.

Cleaned, reclaimed wastewater should be used for industrial and commercial processes, to augment potable supplies, and for agricultural irrigation. Although some regions of the world have been using reclaimed wastewater for a number of years, most notably regions in Africa and the Middle East (Israel relies on reclaimed wastewater for 70 percent of its agricultural irrigation), doing so is much less common in the industrialized world, including the United States (in California reclaimed-wastewater use is more common than anywhere else in the country, but it is still relatively rare). In all of the world's largest cities—and the number of large cities is increasing; by 2010 there will be 27 cities around the world with greater populations than New York City[31]—virtually no effluent is recovered and cleaned up for industrial or commercial uses. This is an enormous waste of water resources. Urban industrial facilities can and should make a huge difference in reducing that waste.

The BCPC's Water Supply*

Industrial ecology requires that sewage-treatment–plant effluent be considered a useful supply of water, not a waste product.[32] With this in mind I instructed the engineers designing the BCPC to rely on sewage-effluent remediation—not potable water—as the source of water for the opera-

---

*This is a conceptual leap for most industrialists, but it also creates daunting technical challenges. It's critical to understand these challenges up front, and thus I present them in more technical detail than some readers might wish. More casual readers may wish therefore to skip this section.

TABLE 3.4

The Characteristics of Influent Wastewater Stream to the
Wards Island Water Pollution Control Plant

Parameter	Value
Discharge flow rate	210 million gallons/day
PH	7.01
Biochemical oxygen demand (BOD)	100 mg/l
Chlorides	<50 mg/l
Total suspended solids (TSS)	87 mg/l
Nitrogen	8.5 mg/l

Source: Data supplied by Ron Wallace, plant manager, Wards Island Water Pollution Control Plant, New York City Department of Environmental Protection.

tional needs of this 330,000-metric-ton-per-year newsprint-recycling mill. The water was to be drawn from the 210 million gallons of wastewater generated daily, and discharged into New York City's East River and adjacent Long Island Sound, by Manhattan's Wards Island Water Pollution Control Plant (WPCP), about one mile from our site.

The typical characteristics of the influent stream to the Wards Island WPCP are shown in Table 3.4, and the complete cycle for the BCPC's process water is shown in Figure 3.1.

After undergoing primary treatment to remove grit and other inorganic solids, approximately 210 million gallons per day (mgd) of sewage enters the Wards Island WPCP for secondary treatment. This facility is a typical wastewater secondary-treatment plant, responsible for the removal of large amounts of organic matter using biological methods. The effluent from the plant is discharged into the East River and averages less than 210 mgd. The characteristics of this effluent are shown in Table 3.5.

Of the approximately 210 mgd of treated effluent destined for discharge into the East River, approximately 4 mgd was to be diverted to the BCPC for further treatment in an advanced remedial-process system designed specifically to make the water more suitable for the BCPC's operational and production purposes. These additional effluent-processing steps were to be located on-site at the Wards Island WCPC on a parcel less than one-half acre in size.

The first step in this advanced remediation system was an additional

FIGURE 3.1

The BCPC's Water-Acquisition and Cleanup System

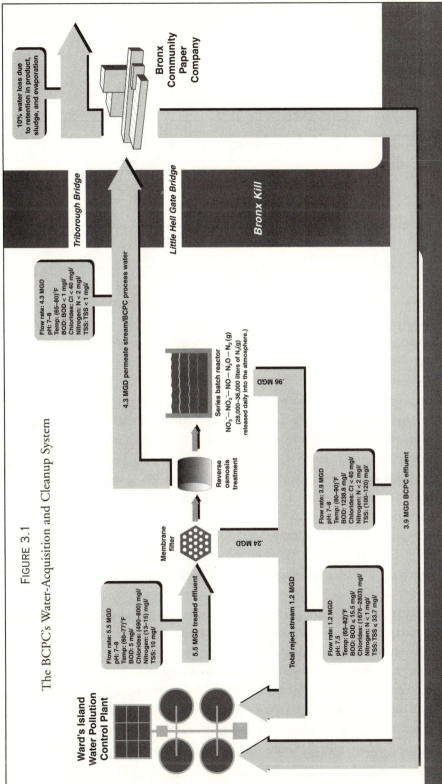

TABLE 3.5

The Characteristics of Effluent from the Wards Island
Water Pollution Control Plant Discharged into the East River

Parameter	Value
Discharge flow rate	210 million gallons/day
PH	7–8
Temperature	60°–77°F
Biochemical oxygen demand (BOD)	5 mg/l
Chlorides	490–800 mg/l
Nitrogen-based compounds	13–15 mg/l
Total suspended solids (TSS)	10 mg/l

Source: Data supplied by Ron Wallace, plant manager, Wards Island Water Pollution Control Plant, New York City Department of Environmental Protection.

reduction of the water's suspended and settled solids, represented by the total suspended solids (TSS) and the organic matter (in the form of the biochemical oxygen demand, or BOD). This was to be achieved by a microfiltration system designed to remove approximately 95 percent of the suspended solids from the Wards Island effluent stream going to the BCPC's supplemental remediation system. The collected material was to be mixed and shipped with New York City sewage-plant sludge, which is now marketed as a soil fertilizer. From this screening process, a treated effluent stream having a TSS and BOD concentration of less than 1 milligram per liter (mg/l) each was to be sent for further treatment. A liquid reject stream was also to be produced by the water-remediation system, and this was to have TSS and BOD concentrations of approximately 200 mg/l and 100–160 mg/l, respectively. This small 1 mgd reject stream was also to be reintroduced into the larger 210 mgd effluent stream at the Wards Island site.

After microfiltration, the remediation system's treated effluent was to be subjected to additional cleaning in a reverse-osmosis system designed to remove large amounts of soluble ions and dissolved solids. Of particular concern was the need to reduce the incoming stream's chlorides and nitrogen-based compounds (mostly in the form of ammonium and nitrates). Reverse osmosis breaks down and removes approximately 80 percent of the incoming chlorides and nitrogen-based compounds, and generates two streams.

One was to be a treated-effluent stream having a greatly reduced chloride concentration (less than 40 mg/l, reduced from 490–800 mg/l) and nitrogen-based–compound concentration (less than 2 mg/l, reduced from 13–15 mg/l). The second stream was to be another reject stream composed of the captured chlorides and nitrogen-based compounds, with a concentration in the range of 2,500–4,000 mg/l and 45–75 mg/l, respectively.

The reject stream from the reverse-osmosis system, because of its high nitrogen content, was to be sent to a series batch reactor for the sole purpose of denitrification. This additional step was intended to reduce nitrogen loading into the Long Island Sound, which, primarily due to excessive discharges of nitrogen, suffers from hypoxia in the sound's bottom-water habitat. The final result was the production of inert nitrogen gas that was to be either captured for commercial use (which is preferred because nitrogen is a greenhouse gas) or released into the atmosphere. Not surprisingly, market analyses designed to identify beneficial-use options for the nitrogen gas indicated that without some form of government or commercial subsidy supporting our attempt to capture and sell it, this would be uneconomical. Predictably, it is cheaper to do the ecologically wrong thing and vent this greenhouse gas to the atmosphere. This compromise in our industrial-ecology design underscores the importance and potential compromising effect of cost competitiveness on sustainable development.

As a result of the additional remedial processes just described, there were to be two reject streams produced after all the steps would have been completed: One from the microfiltration system and the other from the series batch reactor. By taking a control volume around the entire microfiltration–reverse-osmosis system and performing a mass balance, the chemical characteristics of this aggregate reject stream could be determined. This total reject stream could be recycled to the head inflow stream of the Wards Island facility in order to undergo treatment again.

The cleaned-effluent stream designed to emerge from the reverse-osmosis system was to serve as the process water for the paper mill. This "green water" would not be potable, but it would be sufficiently purified to reliably meet 80 percent of the needs of the mill for clean, nonodorous water. Approximately 300,000 gallons daily of this green water would be retained in the form of finished newsprint, which is 6 percent moisture,

TABLE 3.6

The Chemical Composition of Influent and Permeate Streams
to and from the Reverse-Osmosis System at a
Chlorides Concentration of 520 mg/l

Chemical compound	Feed (mg/l)	Permeate (mg/l)	Percent removal efficiency
NH_4^+	5.0	.50	92.0%
K^+	10.0	.40	96.8%
Na^+	325.8	10.60	97.4%
Mg^{2+}	34.0	.70	98.3%
Ca^{2+}	26.0	.50	98.5%
Sr^{2+}	0.8	0.00	100.0%
HCO_3^-	145.0	5.70	96.8%
NO_3^-	15.0	1.80	90.4%
Cl^-	530.0	15.30	97.7%
SO_4^{2-}	60.0	1.00	98.7%
SiO_2	12.0	.80	94.6%

Source: USFilter BCPC water-supply fact sheet, 1997.

TABLE 3.7

The Chemical Composition of Influent and Permeate Streams
to and from the BCPC Reverse-Osmosis System at a
Chlorides Concentration of 800 mg/l

Chemical compound	Feed (mg/l)	Permeate (mg/l)	Percent removal efficiency
NH_4^+	5.0	.50	92.0%
K^+	10.0	.50	96.0%
Na^+	500.8	17.70	97.2%
Mg^{2+}	34.0	.70	98.4%
Ca^{2+}	26.0	.50	98.5%
Sr^{2+}	0.8	0.00	100.0%
HCO_3^-	145.0	6.30	96.5%
NO_3^-	15.0	2.00	89.3%
Cl^-	800.0	26.10	97.4%
SO_4^{2-}	60.0	1.10	98.5%
SiO_2	12.0	.90	94.0%

Source: USFilter BCPC water-supply fact sheet, 1997.

or lost in the sludge and to evaporation. Tables 3.6 and 3.7 give a complete breakdown of the permeate stream's chemical composition under two chloride-concentration conditions.

For the BCPC, given the nature of the production processes of the mill, using expensive, ecologically valuable, fresh, potable water would have been highly superfluous, given the high quality of drinking water. When I conceived of the BCPC's water-remediation system, I sought to stimulate the development of a model that would show the potential for using cleaned effluent as process water for industrial and commercial activities, while at the same time limiting demands on freshwater sources. If even a fraction of the hundreds of billions of gallons of effluent discharged each day in cities throughout the world were captured for commercial purposes, it would provide enormous economic and environmental benefits. By designing the water-acquisition system to be larger than that needed by the BCPC, I sought to provide the benefits of acquiring cheaper, cleaned effluent to other commercial or industrial users in the community. Doing this was also a good financial strategy, since it allowed the BCPC to pay for only a fraction of the water-cleanup system's capital and operating costs and, at the same time, qualify for additional economic-development subsidies from the city and the state. Thus, the BCPC's water-remediation system was designed to allow the paper mill to integrate itself harmoniously with its surrounding water systems—both natural and man-made—and still remain economically sound. These are precisely the goals that lie at the heart of a successful industrial-ecological system.

Electricity and Steam

Although pollution impacts from electricity and steam power plants have been substantially reduced over the past thirty years due to the implementation of the original Clean Air Act of 1970 and the 1990 amendments to it, it is still the case that power plants that produce electricity remain the single largest stationary source of air pollution. In 1990 electricity power plants emitted 81 percent of all sulfur dioxide (SO_2), 36 percent of all CO_2, 37 percent of all NO_x, and 21 percent of all airborne mercury emitted in the United States.[33] Most of these pollutants are emitted by generating facilities that rely on fossil fuels—in particular, coal-fired plants.

In order to successfully redevelop an urban brownfield, from an environmental perspective, it is critical to avoid adding air-pollution burdens to this kind of area, which is typically more densely populated and tends to already suffer from higher pollution impacts than a rural greenfield area. In the case of the BCPC project, we planned to use a natural-gas boiler and a cogeneration facility to supply our electricity and steam. Moreover, energy in the steam was to be recaptured to the highest degree possible before venting the small fraction of steam that remained unrecoverable. Because we planned to use a high-efficiency natural-gas boiler (the fuel cells, photovoltaics, and passive-energy systems we also considered for certain energy tasks could not by themselves adequately meet the large mechanical demands of the mill), the only energy-related pollutants we expected our stationary boiler to produce were less than 12 tons annually of NO_x—a respiratory irritant, greenhouse gas, and contributor to photochemical smog—as well as an uncalculated amount of CO_2—a greenhouse gas that, as of this writing, remains unregulated.

We calculated with a high degree of reliability that the incremental increase in NO_x and particles pollution from our stationary source—the natural-gas boiler—would be more than offset by a corresponding reduction in regional pollution due to fewer impacts from mobile sources. This is because we designed the transportation routes for obtaining the mill's wastepaper supply and marketing its product so as to reduce the distances currently traveled by local recycling-collection vehicles and paper-delivery trucks. This transportation-impacts mass-balance assessment is a critical approach to industrial-ecology design that makes it possible to reduce pollution loading in the region and, in so doing, consider locating a mill in an urban area where air-quality problems may already exist. (Actually, the BCPC's site and its surrounding community, on a wide-open and breezy peninsula in the South Bronx that benefited from frequent and unencumbered air flows, were in fact in compliance with federal and state clean-air standards except for ozone, which is a regional pollutant affecting even semirural and rural regions outside the city.) Moreover, in the same way we oversized our water system to make it more economical and, therefore, of broader potential benefit to other businesses in the community, we also considered oversizing the power boiler. In so doing, we hoped to be able to attract an independent power producer to finance and operate the power boiler, which would again provide both an economic and an environmental advantage. Economically, having a third party finance and operate the boiler would result in a reduction of the mill's capital costs, making it easier to finance. And environmentally, by overscaling the boiler to a size beyond what the mill needed, and by making that boiler a cogeneration device that simultaneously produced steam, we could introduce a new high-efficiency gas-powered turbine into the deregulated electricity market in New York City and help shift demand away from the higher-polluting oil- or coal-fired plants that now supply steam and electricity to the region.

Transportation Energy Use

Besides the stationary energy supplies needed to construct and operate a mill, industrial projects engender transportation-related energy impacts when (1) workers commute to the plant, (2) raw materials, water, and chemicals are delivered, (3) finished products are transported, and (4) solid and liquid wastes are disposed. A brownfield location provides a greater range of options than does a greenfield in reducing these inherent energy impacts.

Unfortunately, every energy-efficient form of commuting—carpooling, public transportation, bicycling, and walking—has declined in use from 1985 to 1999.[34] Energy impacts associated with workers arriving and leaving the plant can be reduced in urban areas by promoting mass transportation and other alternatives to autos. Mass transport is usually not as readily available to workers at greenfield mills as it is at urban brownfields, nor are the longer, highwaylike routes to rural mills as conducive to bicycling. In planning the transportation strategy for the BCPC, I hoped to provide workers with financial incentives for walking, taking mass transit, or riding bicycles to work. Mills located at remote forested locations always require workers to drive to work, so incentives to take mass transit can't even be considered. If a rural-mill worker's car services one worker per vehicle, as cars—and trucks—overwhelmingly do at forest-based mills (and everywhere else in America, where, as of 1999, 78 percent of workers drive to work alone—and 87 percent drive either alone or with someone else),[35] this represents the least desirable, most polluting, and personally costly form of transportation option available.

The delivery of raw materials and chemicals to a factory, and the shipping out of finished products and wastes from the plant, also engender

TABLE 3.8

The Impacts from Transport Trucks Delivering Newsprint to
New York City: A Canadian Virgin-Paper Mill versus the BCPC[1]

Pollutant/Parameter	Virgin-paper mill	BCPC (metric tons/year)	Percent reduction
PM-10 (tons/year)	13.12	.765	94.16%
PM-2.5 (tons/year)	11.74	.685	94.16%
VOCs (tons/year)	15.91	.928	94.16%
Exhaust CO (tons/year)	77.27	4.510	94.18%
Exhaust NO_x (tons/year)	149.77	8.740	94.16%
CO_2 (tons/year)	15,323.22	894.600	94.16%
Diesel fuel consumed (gallons/day)	35,994.90	349.800	94.16%
Energy expended by transport trucks via fuel (million Btu/day)	3,720.00	216.600	94.17%

[1]The numbers are based on round-trip travel and the assumption of negligible idling time. Values for the percent-reduction benefit are calculated by taking the difference between the two mills, then dividing by the value for the virgin-paper mill.
Source: NRDC, Allee King Rosen & Fleming, and S. D. Warren.

energy impacts. If a paper mill is located closer to its raw-material supply and its offtake market—as a recycled mill would be in an urban area—huge energy-reduction benefits can be achieved. In the case of the BCPC, our location allowed for a whopping 94 percent reduction in vehicle miles that needed to be traveled to deliver the newsprint to New York City publishers, compared with delivering this product to the city from eastern Canadian mills. This meant a corresponding 94 percent reduction in fuel use and transport-related pollution (when trucks were to be used). (See Table 3.8.) In addition, because we chose the BCPC location to take advantage of waterway and rail-transport options, we expected to be able to reduce the energy use even when it involved shipping to and from far-away markets and suppliers.

As discussed earlier, locating at a brownfield means there will be some type of transportation infrastructure existing at the site. At the BCPC's site, three types of transportation infrastructure options—roads, rail, and barge—existed. Therefore, we avoided the development and energy-use impacts associated with building and maintaining new roads and sought to take advantage of rehabilitated but underutilized transportation infrastructures like barge and rail. Also, financiers liked the fact that if one form of transportation happened to be interrupted—if there were a truckers' strike, for example—other transportation options would have been available to get the product to market.

In one of the project's best industrial-symbiosis initiatives, the development (and what seemed like imminent construction) of the BCPC newsprint mill resulted in the *New York Post* moving its printing plant to the eastern border of the BCPC site, which itself rehabilitated a brownfield and resulted in the demolition of a diesel-bus depot that polluted the local community. For supplying that publisher, a conveyor belt was contemplated and, hence, virtually zero transportation impacts would have been generated. Also, there would have been a great reduction in the transportation impacts now caused by out-of-town—indeed, out of the country—suppliers. This would have provided very substantial energy savings and regional air-quality benefits, easily offsetting any new impacts from the natural-gas boiler we planned to build.

Finally, a mill can have a huge market influence over suppliers; being a supplier to even one world-class mill can mean procurement contracts totaling millions of dollars annually. Thus, it is possible—if the will of management were so inclined, as we expected in the case of the BCPC—to try and develop incentives for suppliers and transporters doing business with the mill to switch from vehicles that rely on diesel fuels, which generate dangerous and carcinogenic pollutants, to hybrid, high-efficiency, electric or natural-gas vehicles.

It is worth reiterating that none of these strategic considerations designed to reduce transportation-related energy use and the impacts resulting from it by locating at an urban site would have occurred had it not been for the presence of environmental advocates at the helm of the development initiative.

CONCLUSION

Clearly, the environmental benefits of developing a world-scale recycling project at a brownfield can make a substantial contribution toward advancing sustainable industrial production: Natural resources of all types can be conserved, habitat can be preserved, contaminated sites can be cleaned up, sewage water can be reclaimed, water and air pollution can be reduced, energy can be conserved, poverty can be alleviated, and the political and economic influence of environmentally beneficial production mills can increase.

However, the barriers to achieving these benefits are diverse and complex, which is why world-scale industrial projects relying on recycled materials aren't being developed, and they certainly aren't being developed at urban brownfields. In fact, as the next two chapters argue, it is clear that those locations and manufacturing plants offering the greatest environmental and social benefits—recycling mills at urban brownfields—are also those that suffer from the greatest technical, economic, and political obstacles.

NOTES

1. For more on this see Janine Benyus, *Biomimicry* (New York: Morrow 1997).

2. *OECD Environmental Indicators: Towards Sustainable Development* (Paris: OECD, 2001), Table 7.4A.

3. U.S. Environmental Protection Agency, *Characterization of Municipal Solid Waste in the United States: 1997 Update* (Washington, D.C.: U.S. EPA, 1998), p. 6.

4. The estimate of the paper recovered from private collectors is from Jaakko Pöyry, "Office Wastepaper Supply in the New York Metropolitan Area," prepared for the BCPC, New York, New York, 7 September 1994, p. 2. The New York City Department of Sanitation collection data are from Robert Lange, director of the New York City Department of Sanitation's Bureau of Waste Prevention, Reuse and Recycling, personal communication, 4 February 2002; the New York City waste-generation data are from Department of Sanitation, City of New York, "Comprehensive Solid Waste Management Plan Draft Modification," May 2000, Table 2.1–1 and Appendix 1.2–2.

5. For some useful assessments see Richard A. Denison and John Ruston, eds., *Recycling and Incineration: Evaluating the Choices* (Washington, D.C.: Island Press, 1990); R. A. Denison, "Environmental Lifecycle Comparisons of Recycling, Landfilling, and Incineration: A Review of Recent Studies," *Annual Review of Energy and the Environment* 21, (1996), pp. 191–237; and Frank Ackerman, *Why Do We Recycle? Markets, Values, and Public Policy* (Washington, D.C.: Island Press, 1997).

6. "Make That Recycled: A Buyer's Guide to Recycled Coated Freesheet Paper," *Alliance for Environmental Innovation and Business for Social Responsibility* (June 2000), p. 4. See http://www.environmentaldefense. org/documents/517_coatedfreesheet.pdf, downloaded 6/24/02.

7. *Effluent Limitations and Guidelines, Pretreatment Standards, and New Source Performance Standards: Pulp, Paper and Paperboard Category; National Emission Standards for Hazardous Air Pollutants for Source Category; Pulp and Paper Production,* proposed rule, 17 December 1993, 40 CFR Parts 63 and 430, *Federal Register* 58, no. 241, p. 66078.

8. Tapio Korpeinen, president, and John Wissmann, senior project manager, Jaakko Pöyry, personal communications, Tarrytown, New York, 19 July 1996.

9. "Bronx Community Paper Company in the Harlem River Yard: Final Environmental Impact Statement," prepared by Allee King Rosen & Fleming (AKRF), New York City, April 1996, pp.13 and passim.

10. Supro Mukherjea, senior vice president, Stone Consolidated, Montreal, personal communication, 19 July 1996.

11. "Bronx Community Paper Company in the Harlem River Yard," passim, and "Bronx Community Paper Company: Feasibility Study for the High-Grade Deinking Facility," prepared by Rust Engineering Company, Birmingham, Alabama, August 1994, throughout.

12. Edward O. Wilson, *Conserving Earth's Biodiversity*, CD-ROM (Washington, D.C.: Island Press, 2000).

13. *Pulp and Paper North American Factbook 1998,* (San Francisco: Miller Freeman, 1999), p. 183.

14. Ralph E. Colberg, *Emerging Trends in Southern Timber Supply and Demand Relationships* (Columbus, Georgia: Decisions Support, 1996), p. 7. Paper presented at the International Woodfiber Conference, Atlanta, 14–15 May 1996, pp. 3–5, 8, emphasis added.

15. Wilson, *Conserving Earth's Biodiversity.*

16. *Report to Congress on the Status and Trends of Wetlands in the Coterminous United States 1986 to 1997* (Washington, D.C.: U.S. Fish and Wildlife Service, 2000), p. 9.

17. *Federal Register* 65, no. 52, 16 March 2000, p. 14274.

18. Andrew C. Revkin, "New Pollution Tool: Toxic Avengers with Leaves," *New York Times,* 6 March 2001, p. F1, emphasis added.

19. In 2002 President George W. Bush signed the Small Business Liability Relief and Brownfields Revitalization Protection Act (now Public Law 107–18), which, among other things, provides small grants—up to $1 million—to help rehabilitate brownfields. Despite this, most of the logistical and financial barriers to brownfield rehabilitation remain.

20. Phil Sears, vice president, AKRF, personal communication, 10 January 2001, excerpted with permission.

21. Public Law 107–18.

22. Klaus Töpfer, executive director United Nations Environment Programme, keynote address *UNEP's 7th International High Level Seminar on Cleaner Production,* Prague, 29–30 April 2002; and, Reuters, "World's Water Fails to Slake Its Rising Thirst," *New York Times,* 24 March 2002, p. A 26, and BBC News, 22 March 2002, http://news.bbc.co.uk.

23. *Environmental Performance Reviews: United States* (Paris: OECD, 1996), pp. 63 and 65.

24. Ibid., p. 72.

25. For a summary of this report, see http://www.msnbc.com/news/522041 (posted 27 January 2001).

26. New York City Department of Environmental Protection, Bureau of Wastewater Treatment, "Monthly Average Dry Weather Flow, October 2000," Process Engineering Division, 27 December 2000.

27. Ibid.

28. Charles G. Sturcken, chief of staff, New York City Department of Environmental Protection, quoted in Andrew C. Revkin, "Beyond a Drought, Water Worries Grow," *New York Times,* 24 February 2002, p. A1, emphasis added.

29. Sears, personal communication, 17 January 2000.

30. Robert H Perry, Don W. Green, and James O. Maloney, eds., *Perry's Chemical Engineers' Handbook,* 6th ed. (New York: McGraw-Hill, 1978), pp. 26–48, emphasis added.

31. Peter Ravin, Ph.D. and president, American Association for the Advancement of Science (AAAS), keynote address to the AAAS Annual Meeting, Boston, 14 February 2002.

32. I am indebted to my former research assistant Thomas Chu for helping me design and assemble the diagrams, tables, and text for this explanation of the BCPC's water-acquisition and -cleanup system.

33. Alliance to Save Energy, et al., *Energy Innovations: A Prosperous Path to a Clean Environment* (Washington, D.C.: Alliance to Save Energy, 1997), p. 11.

34. John Wright, *New York Times Almanac* (New York: Penguin Reference, 2002), p. 363.

35. U.S. Department of Transportation, Bureau of Transportation Statistics, *National Transportation Statistics 2000* (Washington, D.C.: U.S. Government Printing Office, 2001), p. 50.

4. Confronting the Technical and Economic Facts

> Knowledge about the most significant
> potential obstacles to sustainability is needed.
>
> —Board on Sustainable Development,
> National Research Council

ACCORDING TO THE TEXTBOOK *Green Development*, "What's good for the environment is good for business. . . . [G]reen development offers many potential benefits: reduced operating costs of buildings and landscapes, improved sales or leasing rates, higher property values, increased absorption or occupancy rates, reduced liability risk, better health and higher productivity of workers, avoidance of regulatory delays during permitting processes, and even reduced capital costs."[1]

One has to wonder: If environmentally sustainable development is more profitable and cost competitive, why are industrial and commercial activities the world over dominated so overwhelmingly by environmentally destructive practices?

Despite rhetoric—and hopes—to the contrary, my eight-year experience developing the BCPC, and twenty years of international research, indicates that it is in fact more difficult, time-consuming, risky, and costly to develop environmentally superior industrial projects, especially at brownfields, than to develop polluting, resource-depleting projects at intact greenfields. In large part this is due to rarely discussed barriers to sustainability that are specific to urban areas—more complicated and lengthy site-characterization and preparation work; higher construction-labor costs; higher water, effluent, and utility costs; more intense political competition; and more lengthy and complicated permitting costs, with many opportunities for litigation. In addition, it is more difficult to get financing for environmentally innovative technologies, and using the most environmentally benign raw materials—recycled materials—imposes more financial risks and logistical hurdles than does using environmentally destructive virgin materials.

The frustrating, ecologically dire fact is that the best places to locate a manufacturing plant from the perspectives of environmental remediation and community development are the locations with the most complicated economic and political obstacles. The challenge for environmentalists, industrialists, green developers, and community activists is to figure out how to develop projects that can overcome these barriers in a cost-competitive fashion.

THE HIGH COST OF BROWNFIELDS

Industrial developers do not set out to purposefully hurt the environment. Nor do they set out to heal it. But there are powerful economic and logistical incentives encouraging them to avoid rehabilitating brownfields and to, instead, convert green spaces to industrial or commercial uses.

The cost competitiveness of an industrial project is a function of many factors, and the costs of working at a brownfield tend to make it a less competitive, and less timely, venture for industrial development. Assuming a market demand for the product exists, the choices about which raw materials to use and where a project should be located—and the variety of environmental impacts that flow from those decisions—are based on various costing assessments. Unfortunately, as Table 4.1 indicates, virtually all the costs associated with developing an industrial project at a rehabilitated brownfield and working in an urban location are disadvantaged in comparison with developing a greenfield. In addition to construction labor, operating labor, energy, water, land acquisition, zoning requirements, and permits, the costs that most substantially affect the ultimate

TABLE 4.1

The Economic Costs of Developing a Recycled-Paper Mill:
An Urban Brownfield Mill versus a Rural Greenfield Mill[1]

	Urban mill
Land acquisition	
Purchase price/rental	Disadvantaged
Permitting costs	Disadvantaged
Zoning impediments	Disadvantaged
Development risks	Disadvantaged
Water costs	
Inflow	Disadvantaged or competitive
Effluent	Disadvantaged
Energy costs	Disadvantaged
Raw-material costs	
Transportation	Advantaged
Per-ton cost	Equal or disadvantaged
Marketing/delivery costs	Advantaged or equal
Construction costs	
Labor	Disadvantaged
Site remediation	Disadvantaged
Equipment	Equal
Operating costs (exclusive of energy and water)	
Labor	Equal/Disadvantaged
Chemicals	Equal
Sludge disposal	Disadvantaged

[1]Before factoring in potential subsidies, financing, and tax structure. Not all disadvantages or benefits are of equal economic value.
Source: NRDC.

profitability of any industrial facility include site preparation, waste management and disposal, and raw-materials and product transportation.

To an industrial developer a greenfield site seems to offer unlimited and unencumbered possibilities. Site preparation there does not involve the lengthy analysis and cleanup of regulated and potentially dangerous contaminants that might need to be safely removed or encapsulated, causing delays and adding liability headaches. Delays are a problem for which industrial developers usually have the least tolerance: Once they identify the market opportunity and their firm gives the green light to develop a facility, they need to act on this promptly or else risk losing the market opportunity and company support behind the project. Moreover, at greenfields, a nearby water body or groundwater source seems to offer easy and cheap access to water supplies and effluent disposal. Although greenfields are too rapidly disappearing, they still exist in almost all regions of the world, and they rarely benefit from zoning protections, so developers can more easily choose their neighbors as well as the demographic characteristics of their future workers. Often locations are purposefully chosen where there are no neighbors.

This is not to suggest that greenfield development doesn't have any costly logistical disadvantages. It certainly does: Water and sewage infrastructure systems need to developed, roads often need to be built to the site, and power needs to be brought in or developed on-site. The pool of available workers is more restricted. Yet compared with rehabilitating a brownfield, and negotiating around industrial-development barriers endemic to urban areas, these issues are easier to deal with. Greenfield-related barriers mostly involve engineering and financial solutions, whereas brownfield rehabilitation involves overcoming not only engineering and financial solutions but also the remediation of some other firm's past mistakes and the resolution of more thorny social and political issues (which are discussed in chapter 5). The underlying economics and political psychology motivating the social and political issues that typically stymie brownfield rehabilitation are frankly more difficult to address and resolve—and are thus more threatening to the timing and ultimate viability of a development initiative—than most engineering problems faced at any greenfield.

CLEANUP*

Assuming a developer with community support can find a large-enough brownfield location that has the potential for hosting suitable water, effluent, transportation, energy, and other operational infrastructures that a

---

*Brownfield cleanups are technically complicated, but critical to the vision behind the BCPC. They are illustrated here at the necessary price of adding some technical detail, which more casual readers may wish to skip.

large industrial project needs, the first major cost is cleanup. (It took our BCPC team fourteen months to find a politically acceptable and technically workable site, despite very active support from New York City's economic-development agency, community groups, and eager private real-estate interests.) Although brownfields are almost reflexively avoided by industrial developers out of a concern with the site-preparation effort involved, in fact cleaning up a non-Superfund brownfield is feasible, no matter how complicated it may seem at first. However, though technically feasible, cleanups are nevertheless time-consuming and can sometimes be subject to legal challenge, which always worries a developer interested in taking advantage of a timely market opportunity. Brownfield cleanups invariably involve multiphase efforts to characterize and map the type of soil conditions, pollutants, and gases present on the site, and they also involve a multiphase approach to cleaning up the site and getting the needed liability sign-off from local and state regulators.

The BCPC was located on an abandoned, overgrown rail yard abutting the Harlem River and the Bronx Kill—which separates the Bronx from Manhattan—in the southernmost section of the South Bronx. The site had served as a rail yard for more than a hundred years, was abandoned in 1974, is zoned for heavy industry, and offers excellent access to water, rail, and highway facilities. Adjacent to the site are two major highways—the Major Deegan Expressway and the Bruckner Expressway— and the Triborough Bridge, which connects New York City to Long Island. There is also an existing docking area on the Harlem River at the southwestern section of the site. (See site plan on pages 2 and 3.)

A three-phase assessment of the site was carried out over a period of almost two years to characterize its environmental contaminants and design a remediation and mitigation program. Multistage analyses were performed to detect a wide range of pollutants, even at very low concentrations. Boring and soil sampling, mapping of gaseous emissions, assessing impacts on groundwater and surrounding water bodies and the impact of previously deposited volatile hydrocarbons on air quality were among the analyses performed. Historical information, including past regulatory records (such as local, state, and federal National Priorities List [NPL]; Comprehensive Environmental Response, Compensation, and Liability Information System [CERCLIS list]; and National Spill Reports

[NSR list] documents), aerial photographs (dating back to the early 1950s), boring logs, insurance maps (dating back to 1891), and utility lines pertaining to the site's use were reviewed and correlated with records about current environmental conditions and soil-gas surveys, to confirm the accuracy of current observations and direct the future remediation and mitigation activities.

The contamination assessments also included the obvious visual inspections. The site was overgrown with decades' worth of vegetation and revealed seven abandoned cars, abandoned metal drums, and coal slag throughout. In addition, there were makeshift shelters for homeless people and aging storage equipment, including old gasoline tanks. Historic insurance maps indicated that in the past the site hosted firms that traded in fireproofing products, which could have deposited asbestos; a gasoline station, which could have deposited oil, grease, and solvents; and an electric sign maker, which could have deposited polychlorinated biphenyls (PCBs).

More detailed analytical sampling identified the presence of surface soil contamination that included polyaromatic hydrocarbons (PAHs) and other semivolatile organic compounds, toxic metals, petroleum hydrocarbons—from coal residues—and pesticides. Although the contaminants were found at the surface, the site had a high water table, and initial concern focused on the possibility that these "surface" contaminants had leaked into groundwater. (Later groundwater-sampling and toxicity-characteristic–leaching procedures determined contaminants were not transported into groundwater.)

Identifying the contaminants through the process just described took more than a year. After that, cleanup took place. All storage tanks and old equipment were removed, as were surface piles, sheds, abandoned equipment, and contaminated soils that could be separated to a depth of three feet. The site was regraded with additional soils to a depth of at least three feet and encapsulated with asphalt. To preserve the effectiveness of these control measures, fill areas were protected from erosion and exposure to any remaining contaminants by a repaving plan approved by New York State as part of the environmental-remediation program for the site.[2]

The process of analyzing and cleaning up the entire ninety-six-acre site—BCPC was going to sit on thirty-six of the acres—cost less than $5 million and took just less than three years. The Galesi Group Inc. was the site developer, and it had a ninety-nine-year lease with the New York State Department of Transportation (DOT), the site's owner. In exchange for the Galesi Group's willingness to (1) try and attract investments to a site that required cleanup prior to industrial-development work, (2) guarantee a minimum annual rental payment to the state, and (3) invest in rehabilitating the site's rail infrastructure, the developer was rewarded with a state grant that paid for most of the site's entire cleanup, a ninety-nine-year lease at a competitive market rate, and indemnity backed by the state from any liabilities due to past contamination of the site.

The concessionary incentives given to the Galesi Group highlight major impediments to brownfield development, but not what might be the most important one: To what degree do existing contaminants need to be removed in order to be deemed safe enough for habitation? Most of the debate about how to expedite rehabilitation of brownfields centers on cleanup standards. The Comprehensive Environmental Response, Compensation, and Liabilities Act (CERCLA), which was passed by the federal government in 1980 and amended in 1986 to promote the cleanup of America's most contaminated sites—known as Superfund sites—sets forth only general requirements regarding the degree to which hazardous-waste sites must be cleaned. And there is even less certainty around the country concerning cleanup standards for most non-Superfund sites. The health-related and legal uncertainties about whether a site should be clean enough for children to play there or to allow factory workers to work there has made it extremely difficult to get brownfield sites redeveloped.

While it is true that site-by-site protocols can facilitate a cleanup and can make it more locally appropriate (e.g., this approach may offer the chance for more community input and encourages more detailed analyses of existing background levels of contaminants—those that exist in the area regardless of whether the project gets built), many environmentalists have historically feared site-by-site cleanup decisions out of an understandable concern that financially influenced local politicians and business-sympathetic local regulators will allow for cleanup shortcuts. However, it is worth noting that cleanup shortcuts can be very costly and counterproductive. A developer seeking to clean up a site to the best standards is more likely to benefit from local good will and the government support that can flow from that, including cleanup subsidies. By contrast, cleanup shortcuts seem to always become publicly known, and when they do, they throw a development initiative into turmoil. While many industrial-project developers who take shortcuts do succeed and environmentally inferior projects are often developed, these projects—at least in the United States—may be as likely to face delays due to government investigations and financing snags because of liability concerns. Moreover, local interests are more likely to fight against and successfully delay implementation of a compromised cleanup plan rather than a superb one.

It is also useful for environmentalists to recognize that while some market pressures certainly do push toward getting the cleanup job done cheaply and quickly, there are also market pressures pushing toward cleaning up the site as thoroughly and safely as possible. Among these rarely discussed nonregulatory pressures encouraging safer cleanups are (1) construction-company and, where they exist, union work rules that prevent laborers from working at a nonremediated contaminated site and (2) financing interests that want to be—indeed, must be—protected against any environmental liability that a poorly cleaned site will impose. Workers who fear for their health may, and should, refuse to do construction work on the site, and developers who knowingly send workers into contaminated sites face substantial liability risks. Moreover, the cleaner the site, the more easily a project will get its necessary financing and insurance guarantees. If a publicly traded firm is involved in the development, investors, the facility operator, and the public will need to know the site is clean, since Securities and Exchange Commission (SEC) regulations themselves require that environmental liabilities be revealed, described, and evaluated.[3]

Finally, it is important to remember that a project supported by the brownfield's host community is much more likely to satisfactorily resolve the debate about how clean the reclaimed brownfield needs to be than is a project subject to community opposition. This underscores the importance of incorporating community participation into brownfield-rehabilitation investments as early and as authentically as possible. The best way to do this is to plan to clean up to the most exacting standards possible. The costs are small compared with the overall development costs, and with the prospect of being sidetracked by community opposition.

So, as just discussed, cleaning up a contaminated site—even one, as in the case of the BCPC, that has been used as an industrial rail yard for more than a hundred years, and that is laced with toxic and volatile hydrocarbons and other pollutants—is complicated but certainly doable. But it takes time, much more time than converting a virgin greenfield. And this is a penalty most industrial developers won't tolerate, so it sends them packing off to develop a greenfield, where this penalty does not exist. By itself, this barrier can derail virtually any industry's consideration of locating at a brownfield. When combined with other barriers, including lengthy and politically uncertain permitting and zoning obstacles, it becomes quite obvious why so few brownfields are being redeveloped into ecologically valuable industrial projects, and why terrestrial habitat throughout the world remains so vulnerable.

PERMITTING AND ZONING

In most of the world, property rights are legally regulated. Consequently, in order to be constructed and to operate, industrial facilities virtually always require some form of government permission. This permission usually follows rudimentary technical reviews and perfunctory public hearings, and takes the form of written approvals, formal permits, or licenses that are granted on the basis of a variety of environmental, economic, and social criteria. Theoretically, the process for obtaining government permission to build and operate an industrial facility is designed to ensure and indeed enhance the environmental safety of the project, and to encourage public participation in decisions affecting the facility's design, construction, and operation as well. Unfortunately, in many, many instances—especially in the developing world, where business influence over government may be even greater than in the developed world, and in lower-income communities in the developed world—government and industry officials subvert the permitting process by undermining thorough technological evaluations. In fact, even where permitting regimes are properly implemented, the rigor of the approval process and the level of community input into it vary both by location and by technology. No permitting regime requires life-cycle assessments, and given the risky legal context in which permit reviews are carried out, certain attributes of even the most credible permitting processes can actually stymie technical innovation and interfere with authentic public participation.

The siting and development of any new industrial facility must, by law, proceed through an environmental review and permitting process. This is obviously appropriate, regardless of a facility's potential environmental value. The permitting process—and all of the social as well as technical barriers it imposes—reminds us that industrial ecology, and sustainability more generally, is not merely a question of good engineering. Industrial ecology provides benefits to our ecosystem only to the extent to which it gets implemented. The permitting process is one of the places where engineering formally meets political reality.

Although debate exists about what specifically constitutes the most effective, economical, and expeditious design of environmental regulations and permitting processes, there is no doubt about the value of environmental permitting. As the OECD has observed, "Over the last thirty years, [environmental] permit systems have proven to be very effective in achieving large reductions in pollutant emissions from stationary sources. Where major industrial accidents have occurred (e.g., Seveso, Bhopal, Schweizerhalle), the environmental permitting systems were either inadequate, non-existent- or poorly enforced. These incidents clearly demonstrate that strong, predictable and consistent enforcement of current regulations and permitting systems is a prerequisite to protect public health and the environment."[4]

Despite this, it is critical to remember that even in the most advanced industrial nations, permitting obligations are routinely ignored. A report issued in 2002 by the EPA's inspector general concluded that of the 19,025 major sources of industrial pollution in the United States, almost 40 percent had *not* obtained permits, even though all of these facilities were required to have them by no later than 1997. The most delinquent region was New England, "where on average only 37% of the permits had been issued. Among [all] states, [the worst situation] is New Jersey, where on average only 30% have been issued."[5] Permits are, in effect, a performance contract between industry and the public, based on each and every community's interest in—and right to—protecting its ecological health. Certainly the wholesale disregard for permitting by so many industries underscores the need for environmentalists to intensify their regulatory-oversight and -enforcement work.

Thus, it comes as no surprise that, when viewed against the backdrop of a dramatic worsening in global environmental problems such as climate change, conversion of green spaces, threats to biodiversity, deforestation, and depletion of freshwater resources, environmental permitting as currently practiced has substantial limits. Though it has been very effective in reducing gross pollution impacts and remains an essential regulatory tool, environmental permitting, even when it is practiced as it was intended to be, can hardly be said to regulate industry in line with long-term sustainable practices. Fossil-fuel dependent power plants, synthetic–organic-chemical plants in already environmentally overburdened communities, plastics refineries that produce lethal gases as a by-product, cyanide leaching of ores, and forest clear-cutting are all currently nonsustainable but theoretically permissible activities under today's permitting regimes.

Despite these limits, permitting is a necessary—and potentially progressive—reality that green developers must face. How strange it is then that industrial-ecology and green-development texts are invariably silent on the permitting processes required to convince regulators and the community at large that any well-designed project deserves real-world implementation. Alas, those working in the field of industrial ecology routinely ignore the process of environmental permitting. But this issue must be studied because, in fact, the environmental-permitting process in urban areas can actually make it more difficult for projects being reviewed to improve technology than is the case in rural, greenfield areas.

Why? State and local officials are responsible for implementing federal environmental laws. And they are implemented differently depending on whether a project is being considered for a greenfield or for a brownfield. The differences in implementation of these laws by local officials in rural versus urban areas is shaped by a number of factors, including these:

• Rural local governments have fewer regulatory and technical resources than do better-endowed large cities, so industrial projects in rural areas are in general less rigorously reviewed.

- Rural local governments are controlled by a smaller pool of political decision makers to whom businesses have greater access. These decision makers, like their urban counterparts, are swayed by local economic affiliations and, again like their urban counterparts, reveal political and regulatory sympathies for industries that make local political contributions. Because there are fewer officials to influence in rural areas, the politically influenced approval process is less complex.

- Rural local governments have fewer resources—and are hence less inclined—to defend themselves during the permitting process against potentially costly, drawn-out legal battles with industrial developers.

- Rural local governments tend to experience fewer opportunities for large-scale economic development.

- Rural areas, unlike urban areas, rarely have meaningful zoning restrictions.

Veteran environmental planner Phil Sears, who has been involved with environmental permitting in the United States for both government and industrial projects in rural and urban areas, describes the reason it is easier to get permits to convert rural greenfields than permits to rehabilitate urban brownfields:

> Based on my experience, in rural [greenfield] areas, many people are satisfied with their quality of life, but feel that economic opportunities are lacking. They worry especially about jobs and development for their children. They are more inclined to allow and even desire industrial development because of the economic opportunities it affords. In urban areas, the opposite situation prevails. People have a number of economic avenues they can pursue . . . [so] the urban population is far less inclined to accept the problems associated with industrial development. . . . This, of course, translates into a higher level of environmental review and the threat of litigation. The government bureaucrats [in urban areas] must ensure that every base is covered in the environmental review, and the government decision makers are less inclined to approve discretionary actions . . . even though I believe that brownfield redevelopment

and reuse of urban areas is the most sustainable approach to meet our industrial needs.[6]

Because rural areas tend to have fewer resources and a regulatory administration that is undeveloped compared with federal and big-city regulatory agencies, rural regulators, of necessity—if not by inclination—tend to rely more on industry engineers and industry data than do their counterparts in urban regulatory agencies. And community and environmental groups in rural areas—and in the developing world as well—also tend to have fewer resources than urban-based or industrialized-world community and environmental groups to produce technical counter-analyses for regulators to use. Moreover, fewer people are affected in rural locations, as populations are obviously less dense, and those that are affected often tend to favor attracting new industry, on economic development grounds. Because rural-based regulators have fewer resources to scrutinize a project and, at the same time, are under less countervailing pressure to stop it, they tend to hold a more tolerant attitude when it comes to permitting an industrial development or confronting site-specific technical adjustments to it, however last-minute they may be.

I know from firsthand experience that government administration and oversight in rural areas and especially in the developing world is a much more cozy political affair than is big-city government in the industrialized world. Local town-board members appoint building inspectors, and appoint as well the members of zoning and planning agencies. These "regulators" work collaboratively with developers of all stripes rather than as independent watchdogs, overseeing protection of the public health and the environment. This is especially the case when an industry comes to town offering the lure of jobs, political support, and tax dollars (no matter how illusory these turn out to be in practice). In the developing world, there is usually even less of a pretense that regulators are in any way independent of the positions expressed by the governing political establishment and its industrial sponsors.

Collectively, these influences have the cumulative effect of making it a less contentious and faster process to get permits and other local development approvals at greenfield sites than at urban sites. And they make it easier to adjust the technology design of a project without fearing litigation. Moreover, although it is preferable to locate a mill at an urban area to help remedy existing environmental problems, the fact that contamination risks exist means that the site's history justifies a more technically time-consuming and politically intense permitting and review process.

During the permitting phase the BCPC development team decided to approach the permitting process in the following way:

- We included affected communities in siting decisions, especially neighborhood groups, which can inform the project team about specific local ecological problems and which can deliver the support of local community boards and locally elected officials.

- We developed an understanding and a working relationship with all pertinent regulatory agencies, and were focused on designing a project to remedy environmental problems.

- We went beyond minimum regulatory compliance and instead pushed the regulatory and project-development teams to constantly look for opportunities to improve the environmental profile of the project.

- We vetted the development idea with statewide and other national environmental colleagues well in advance of choosing a site.

- We held public discussions on the project frequently in the host community and conducted special gatherings for members of the environmental community, seeking their evaluation.

- We disclosed as much information as possible and challenged legal advice urging secrecy.

- We thoroughly briefed media outlets well before anything was advanced or announced.

- We did everything "the long way"—no technical or political short-cuts—so any legal challenge the project would face would be less likely to have merit. In an urban area even the best and most inclusively designed projects are likely to face legal challenges.[7]

It is worth noting that the law governing environmental permits does not recognize efforts like these (although if our permits were ever challenged in court, these efforts would be recognized). Environmental regulations currently make almost no distinction between a community-supported project designed from the start to remediate environmental burdens and enhance the creation of wealth in an impoverished neighborhood, like the BCPC, and a project opposed by community groups that is likely to impose environmental burdens, like a hazardous-waste incinerator. Consequently, whether the industrial-development effort comports with the objectives of sustainable industrial ecology or not, the permitting process is now virtually the same.

In order to obtain state and local permits and approvals and mitigate the risks of litigation, an industrial developer must pretend to have more certainty about the production process under review at the specific location in question than is possible. Despite the obligations imposed by permitting, certainty about each and every technical aspect of an industrial project as it is being developed is almost impossible to achieve. And it is not even desirable. Site-specific design refinements attuned to changing local economic or ecological needs are inevitable and valuable, and this is particularly true of industrial projects whose purpose is to find innovative solutions, such as industrial-ecology projects. Thus, to date, industrial developers have been forced by environmental permitting to participate in a technological fiction. They have been forced to pretend to know precisely how to best fit an industrial project into its host community without either authentic input by the community—based on open dialogue and assessment of various options, which the process penalizes—or final engineering plans, which are drawn well after permitting is completed. (Why pay the high cost of finalizing engineering plans unless you first know you can obtain your permits, and without knowing about the restrictions they may require?)

Ironically, the permitting process imposes additional litigation risks on any developer who openly reveals this fact, and this is especially the case in urban areas, where the threat of litigation is higher because of a higher concentration of competing political constituencies, among other reasons. During the BCPC's permitting phase there were many reconsiderations of technical issues that I was advised by my lawyers not to discuss publicly, however much I wanted to maintain the most open dialogue with community and government interests. We reconsidered water-supply options: How much of the water we needed could come from reclaimed sewage effluent? How much had to be freshwater? We reconsidered the paper-bleaching technology—should we use hydrogen peroxide, ozone, or some other nonchlorine option? We reconsidered the location for the pipes that would carry the water to the mill and back to the nearby sewage-treatment plant. Should they get buried under a city park or should they be hung from a nearby bridge? Should we market the project's recycling residue or seek a zoning variance and burn it for energy recovery? To what extent could we redesign the site's barge facility to take advantage of water-transport options? How many wastepaper-supply trucks could we realistically hope to convert to natural-gas or hybrid fuels over what period of time, and how would that affect our air-pollution calculations? What should we do with the fugitive steam that couldn't get recaptured for energy recovery and couldn't be allowed to vent without a costly steam stack—as most paper mills do—because in the winter the vented steam, if not collected and properly channeled, would condense and freeze on nearby roadways? Despite the ecological and economic value of having easy and open public discussions about many of these issues—and despite my feeling the ethical obligation to do this—once our environmental impact statement (EIS) was completed and made public we could not share these thoughts with community and government interests because the permitting process requires certainty in order for the EIS to be approved.

Suffice it to say that members of the BCPC team *did* have many technical and political discussions about some of these issues after our EIS was completed, but they had to be done, in order to be protected legally, without as broad community input as we had wanted. Certainly this underscores the value of having environmental advocates intimately involved in the technical design and development of industrial facilities. Nevertheless, while the permitting process is supposed to enhance a project's legitimacy with a host community, the fact that changes in design can't be publicly considered without opening new litigation risks often results in a negative public perception. Community groups often, and understandably, feel as if they are being misled—or that something is being hidden from them—when they learn of adjustments they should have known about earlier but, because of the fear of litigation, weren't informed about. Thus, contrary to its intention and contrary to the spirit behind sustainable development, the permitting process often works to stifle dialogue among the pertinent community stakeholders involved with or likely to be affected by a project. In so doing, the permitting process as currently crafted and implemented works toward stifling technical innovation. It should not be so.

The environmentally progressive attributes designed into the BCPC, combined with the involvement of NRDC, and community interests, made it much easier for the project to comply with the technical criteria associated with New York City's infamous regulatory-permitting process. Still, the project had to go through many more reviews than it would have had we chosen to locate it in a rural greenfield (as was so often brought to my attention by some of my financial advisers). In urban areas within the United States, where most brownfields in need of rehabilitation are located, many different types of approvals are required to develop and construct an industrial facility. Some of these obviously relate to environmental permitting, but many do not and instead relate to the project's impact (including on traffic and roads) during construction, its impact during operation on existing infrastructure such as sewage systems, as well as whether it meets OSHA regulations. Plus, a site located in a less populated area that meets all air-quality standards (most likely a rural area) is subject to less stringent air-pollution–control requirements than is a site in a nonattainment area (most likely an urban area). This also tends to encourage greenfield siting.

In general, it is more difficult to develop projects in more densely populated areas, where debate is greater regarding its ultimate value and impacts. This has a profound effect on the ability of a project to get its necessary environmental permits and approvals, and it additionally tends to work against locating industry in urban areas.

Zoning

Zoning regulations, which are more restrictive and complicated in urban than in rural areas, also make it more difficult to develop an industrial-ecology project in an urban area. In an ideal world, zoning regulations designed to protect the integrity of communities, habitat, water systems, and other natural resources would guide all development planning, and would be especially protective of biologically rich and ecologically sensitive regions. But ours is not an ideal world. Quite the contrary: Those biologically diverse areas deserving the most zoning protections are very often the ones that are least protected from residential-, commercial-, or industrial-development schemes. And those brownfield areas needing the most innovative zoning inducements to attract environmentally beneficial projects are often locked into outdated restrictions that make such investments more complicated, rather than easier to advance.

Like permitting regulations, zoning regulations in both urban and rural areas are essential. However, while most urban areas are comprehensively and restrictively zoned, similar guidelines and restrictions generally do not protect rural areas. Given the high-density, mixed-use environment characteristic of urban areas, zoning restrictions in urban communities evolved decades ago. Moreover, because so many currently operating—but ecologically antiquated—industrial processes produce health-threatening pollution and involve the use of potentially dangerous chemicals and technologies, zoning regulations have been essential to protect public safety. The inevitable proximity of other land-use activities, such as residential housing, makes zoning compliance for large-scale industrial projects much more complex in urban areas than in rural areas, where they will inevitably engender more ecological damage. In rural areas, the process of obtaining development rights is typically quite simple. A local planning board or zoning board—should any zoning regulations exist at all—usually performs a cursory review of the project, applies few criteria related to ecological sustainability, and, strongly motivated by what it perceives to be a potential tax boost and employment windfall, grants a development approval. All of this transpires in fairly rapid order.

In urban areas, the process for obtaining zoning approvals, even if the project is located in an as-of-right development zone—one that doesn't require a discretionary approval from a zoning board of appeals—remains significantly more elaborate and time-consuming. Even in an as-of-right development zone, diverse city and state agencies weigh in on issues ranging from aesthetic compatibility with surrounding structures, to water supply, impacts during construction, traffic, noise, odors, and height. Finding brownfield parcels of property large enough and close enough to a high-volume supply of water and sewage infrastructure within a single land-use zone to host a world-scale industrial plant is itself a not-so-easy endeavor. And then the task of locating water-supply and effluent-discharge pipes to and from the project and nearby sewage-treatment plants also has to go through zoning reviews. Even trying to put a day-care center on-site for the children of workers requires zoning modifications. Many legal and engineering analyses, and reviews by city-planning agencies and their zoning experts have to take place before industrial projects can be built in urban areas. Plus, public hearings and opportunities for legal challenges, however potentially valuable for the community, add further uncertainly and risks to the endeavor, subjecting it to more marketing delays and political pressure than similar—or, indeed, ecologically inferior—projects in rural areas.

In effect, and despite their logic and value, urban zoning restrictions intended to make sure industrial projects get built and operate as good neighbors wind up pushing them to locate in rural areas, keeping them out of a city's brownfields entirely. This is not to say that industrial zoning regulations are unnecessary; they are clearly essential. It is simply to take stock of an important barrier to urban industrial ecology, one that can't be ignored: Why, after all, would an industrial developer choose to locate in an area facing more rather than fewer zoning obstacles?

The BCPC's Permitting Process

To the best of my knowledge, NRDC is the only environmental-advocacy organization in the world ever to have been involved in the process of *obtaining* construction and operating permits for a large industrial project. Like many other advocacy organizations around the globe, we are expert in *opposing* the efforts of industrial developers to obtain permits, and we've done that successfully hundreds of times during the past thirty years. There is no doubt that the expertise my colleagues and I acquired in stopping permits from being issued was instrumental in guiding us through New York City's labyrinthine permitting process, so we could successfully obtain the bevy of environmental approvals and permits the BCPC needed to be built and for operation. Perhaps most important, however, was that our experience working through the permitting process principally as an ecologically motivated advocate for sustainability and community participation—not principally as a financially interested advocate for the industrial development—revealed to us many of the barriers to sustainability inherent in the environmental-permitting process.

To develop the BCPC—or any industrial project in New York City—the Environmental Impact Statement (EIS) approval process begins with filing an Environmental Assessment Statement (EAS) form with the state Department of Environmental Conservation (DEC). In the EAS a developer can choose to claim that a project will either have an impact on the environment worth fully exploring—this is called a positive declaration—or that the project will not have an environmental impact worth a full environmental review, a negative declaration, or, in local regulatory parlance, a *neg dec*. The usual—and ecologically counterproductive—rule of thumb with permitting is always to go for the negative declaration first to see if you can get away with it.

With the BCPC my colleagues and I took the opposite approach, because we were confident about the design and environmental benefits of the project, had a community-group sponsor, and recognized the value of the permitting process in establishing the project's ultimate legitimacy in the community. Without ever seriously considering a neg dec, the BCPC's project team instructed its permitting attorneys to make a positive declaration on the EAS, to ensure a full environmental review and instigate as much community input as possible. We instructed the permitting attorneys and engineers to make sure all documentation was available in Spanish as well as English, given the high percentage of Latinos in the host community, and to try and make all technical discussions as comprehensible as possible. All industrial-development projects are required by law to hold two public hearings. The BCPC team held many more and in total convened more than 200 meetings or hearings on the project, 122 of them in the host community. And despite this effort and attitude by the BCPC's project team, there were still individuals who claimed we weren't attempting to communicate openly with the host community.

Asserting a negative declaration would have cut short a public review of the proposed project and, in all likelihood, subjected it to enhanced litigation risks and opposition. In the long term it would have resulted in more project delays and less community support. It may seem counterintuitive, but, in my experience, the fastest path to obtaining environmental approvals—certainly the legally safest path—is also the one incorporating the most substantial public review and input. Yet although it is more likely to be successful, that path remains a tedious one.

After the EAS is submitted, a lead agency is designated to oversee the environmental-review process. In the case of the BCPC, the lead agency chosen was the New York State DOT, which was also the owner of the BCPC site. Although it may have made sense for the DOT to be the lead agency for the BCPC's environmental-permitting process because it had the greatest familiarity with the site, obviously, as the site landlord, the DOT had an interest in seeing the property rented. This may have affected its impartiality in favor of the BCPC during the review process. But since our objective was to exceed the reporting and analytical requirements of the state's EIS process, whether or not the DOT was a sympathetic lead agency—and I have no evidence to suggest that they reviewed our work with any favoritism—made no difference.

To identify the environmental, economic, and social issues that the EIS will review, a scoping process must take place. There is no legal requirement for the scoping process to be open to the public or to involve the community in any formal way, but a developer can ask the lead agency to allow this, and we did. We convened both public and private scoping sessions to determine what should be reviewed in the full EIS. Besides the opportunity to include more authentic input for the project's design, which a public scoping session offers, convening such a session also helps insure a project, should it ever confront a legal challenge. At the public scoping session, as with all hearings and meetings throughout the project, we hired or otherwise arranged for Spanish and sign-language translators to be present. It is obvious that developers will always learn more about the particular ecological and economic concerns of a community and how to enhance its sustainability by listening to its residents.

After the EIS scoping process was complete—this included a public hearing and many community meetings, often running late into the night—a Preliminary Draft EIS (PDEIS) was prepared for review, which had to be submitted to the lead agency. Getting to this point took about eight months, in addition to the fourteen months it took us to locate a suitable site, and cost about $500,000 in engineering and legal fees, not including the full-time labor of three NRDC staffers (including me, a member of the senior staff). Once the PDEIS was approved by the lead agency, it was issued for public review as a Draft EIS. The Draft EIS then benefits from—or, as a traditional developer would say, is "subject to"— a forty-five-day public-comment period, during which dozens of meetings in the host and adjacent communities were held, including another formal, state-supervised public hearing.

Following the public-comment period, a Draft Final EIS (DFEIS) was prepared, and this was also presented for review to the lead agency, as well as other potentially affected city and state agencies, and other interested parties. After waiting the mandated sixty days to receive input from all of these interests—and actively encouraging any potentially affected or interested party to share comments—a Final EIS was prepared and submitted to the lead agency. The FEIS included responses to each and every comment received during the public-comment period.

All city agencies, regardless of their mission, are sent a draft of any DFEIS and offered the opportunity to comment. Representatives of one city agency, the Parks and Recreation Department, told me they "didn't get around to" reviewing the DFEIS until two days before comments were due, so they arbitrarily decided to oppose the project as an "eyesore" that would adversely affect an adjacent park. Given all the careful work our team had put into the EIS effort and our efforts to generate broad public input, I was rather annoyed—to put it mildly—at this cavalier and arbitrarily antagonistic attitude by midlevel city bureaucrats toward such a worthy development effort. Had they taken the time to read the DFEIS document before offering their opposition, they would have learned that Maya Lin, the much-admired artist and designer of, among other notable works, the Vietnam Veterans Memorial in Washington, D.C., was the designer of our mill. In great contrast to the "eyesore" view hastily and thoughtlessly offered by two Parks Department staffers, a Distinguished Professor at the City University of New York, writing in 1999 in an exhibition catalog for the Bronx Museum of the Arts—where drawings of the project were on exhibit—called the BCPC mill "the most impressive public artwork created in the Bronx."[8] Without our mill, the park adjacent to our site had unobstructed views of the city's largest sewage treatment plant, a giant utility power plant, and a maximum security prison. By contrast, the BCPC mill, the Parks Department "eyesore," was listed by the *New York Times* chief architectural critic Herbert Muschamp as one of the top ten architectural highlights of 1998, and the New York Municipal Arts Society listed it in a catalog of the 100 greatest ideas ever proposed for New York City. Such are the frustrations of urban permitting politics. Under normal circumstances, opposition by the Parks Department, however unfounded or ill-formed as it was in this case, could have greatly damaged the prospects of any industrial project under consideration for permits by the city. However, the opposition of the Parks Department was soon retracted after we contacted its commissioner and arranged a meeting for the BCPC team to describe our project's design to the less-than-careful midlevel administrators who initially submitted the comments opposed to it. In short order, the Parks Department became a supporter of the project.

Detailed reviews by the lead agency, and a hearing and review by the City Planning Commission (CPC), the local community board, and the New York State Public Authority Control Board, came next. As expected, the CPC warmly received Maya Lin's design. (This enthusiasm was, for me, a confirmation of Victor Hugo's observation that "The beautiful is as useful as the useful. . . . More so, perhaps.")[9] Then the EIS was approved. In total, the process took eighteen months, cost almost $1 million to complete, and involved four law firms, two engineering firms, full-time work by me and two NRDC colleagues, five senior engineering staffers at two paper companies, and two staff members from our community-group partner.

Following the completion, acceptance, and approval of the FEIS for the BCPC, which was announced by the project's lead agency, the DOT, in April 1996, project permits were sought. The air-emissions permit for our power boiler contained a few industry-sympathetic provisions designed to make compliance more "cost-effective" and "flexible," but which I viewed as potential loopholes for any less-than-environmentally-oriented firm that might one day take over the project's operation. Thus, after first making sure to formally accept the air-permit approval to build an industrial-size power plant—which is a rare and hard-to-obtain license—I then sent it back to the approving agency requesting a modification that would make the permit *stronger* and more enforceable. For example, while the original permit requested quarterly reports on the mill's emissions and effluents, I instead requested a modification that would require continuous emissions and effluent monitoring to be connected to the regulatory agency and a local library, to better serve the surrounding community's right-to-know and so interested regulators and community residents could access this information easily. I asked that the project be required to set up a Web site on the Internet reporting these data. I requested that environmental data collected by the mill monitors include reports for NO_x, CO, opacity, testing protocols, operating limits, etc., and that these be continuously (daily, every eight hours, quarterly, etc., as appropriate) transmitted electronically to the state DEC, the city Department of Environmental Protection (DEP), the EPA, and the local library. I also requested that the BCPC provide these agencies with the necessary computer equipment and software to receive such data. Interestingly, continuous monitoring, which is a more rigorous enforcement and right-to-know strategy, actually costs less than the labor-intensive process of filing quarterly reports. Even though it is more expensive to file quarterly reports, and even though regulated industries complain about the ostensible cost of complying with regulatory reporting, most industries don't want to install continuous-emissions monitors because they report environmental transgressions more promptly and accurately and make it easier to enforce compliance with environmental permits.

Finally, I also requested that language in the permit that allowed for "less stringent monitoring" if approved by the EPA be dropped. Because future air-quality or local epidemiological studies may need data on past discharges by the mill, I requested that data on emissions and discharges be kept for at least fifteen years—instead of the seven years originally requested—to facilitate and enhance the accuracy of local health research.

The attorney for the state environmental agency, never having received a permit-modification request asking for *more stringent* compliance procedures, told me he intended to have my letter framed. Nonetheless, he made sure his letter granting my modification request indicated that the air-permit enhancements being requested were voluntary actions applicable to this project only. This is a clear example of the value of having environmentalists in control of industrial development: Instead of being limited to fighting with regulators or trying to pass legislation against providing more enforcement and right-to-know access, we can work to open up industry to greater accountability by developing superior operating procedures at industrial facilities and by designing and obtaining more progressive and transparent permits for them.

Understandably, but ironically, environmentally innovative technologies and processes—the type that are needed to advance sustainability—are subject to more reviews than are conventional technologies, both by regulators and financiers. Consequently, additional environmental reviews and permits were required to develop the effluent-cleanup system at Wards Island. These permits included a water Pretreatment Approval from the city (DEP), a state storm-water–discharge permit (DEC), water-intake and wastewater-discharge approvals from the city (DEP), coastal-zone certification from the city (CPC), easements and street-opening permits from the city to allow for pipe placement (DOT, the Parks Department, and the Triborough Bridge and Tunnel Authority), a "no adverse effect" letter from the New York State Office of Parks, Recreation, and Historic Preservation (because the effluent-cleanup project was near a park and under a bridge), and building permits and other nondiscretionary approvals from the city (Buildings Department). Moreover, depending on the placement of the water-transport pipes, additional permits or approvals might have been required. This is because the BCPC mill would have been separated from the Wards Island sewage-treatment plant by a narrow waterway called the Bronx Kill. If we had opted to build a trench as the way for the pipelines to cross the Kill, we would have needed a permit from the U.S. Army Corps of Engineers, pursuant to Section 10 of the Rivers and Harbors Act of 1899, which deals with "Structures and Obstructions in Navigable Waterways." To avoid this, we designed our plant to transport the water with pipes hung over the Kill, not beneath it.

Most of the permitting processes described here and faced by industrial projects locating at urban brownfields are avoided at greenfield sites. The penalties related to time, political maneuvering (at the community, city, state, and federal levels), and cost disadvantages are by themselves enough to discourage industrial developers from considering an urban site for rehabilitation, regardless of the environmental benefits that would be realized. Indeed, one of the reasons I first decided to help develop an urban paper mill was because while I was contemplating the idea for the project, I discovered that Sweden's MoDo Paper company was willing to locate in an urban location rich in wastepaper. But MoDo officials were concerned about the labyrinthine permitting process in urban locations and, consequently, were reluctant to join our effort to build a mill in New York City without our assistance on permitting. We were told that the company wouldn't consider locating in an urban area because they didn't think they could successfully obtain the approvals to do so, and they were right: Without NRDC's participation during the permitting and development stage, it is unlikely that the project would have received an approved EIS and any of its permits.

CONSTRUCTION-LABOR COSTS

Construction-labor costs—the cost of hiring workers to prepare a site, procure and assemble the equipment, and financially guarantee the performance of the factory they build—are among the most important variables affecting the competitiveness of an industrial project. At urban brownfields, the prices for these services are almost always higher, often substantially higher, than at rural, ecologically unspoiled greenfield locations. Not only do these essential services cost more at brownfields, but the ability to acquire them at all is also more complicated.

The AFL-CIO, the New York City Central Labor Council, and various union locals enthusiastically supported the BCPC project. Beyond the ecological, economic, and social benefits the Bronx mill was going to offer New York City, the BCPC obtained union endorsements primarily because the project was anticipated to produce twenty-six hundred unionized construction jobs for twenty-two to twenty-four months, and to permanently employ more than four hundred unionized workers.

I accepted this universal support from organized labor for the BCPC as a badge of honor. But high costs and other labor-related issues were among the most potent obstacles our development team faced in trying to develop the BCPC. Most obviously, construction-labor costs in New York City are among the highest, if not *the* highest, in the United States and, arguably, among the highest in the world. For example, hourly labor rates for pipe fitters, ironworkers (structural and reinforcing), and electricians in New York City in 2000 were $40.54, $63.58, and $61.25, respectively.[10] But the cost to an employer is considerably more than the hourly rate, which represents only a worker's base wage and fringe benefits. Employers must also pay federal, state, and local taxes, unemployment insurance (and sometimes pay as well for a worker's tools). When these additional costs are factored into the total hourly labor cost to an employer for the workers listed above, the labor-related costs increase into the $70- to $80-per-hour range. During busy construction periods, the more sought-after—high-productivity—New York City workers get even higher wage rates, at what is known as "overscale," which increases their base hourly rate. This is good for them but bad for the cost competitiveness of the project, because it raises construction expenses even further. As discussed in chapter 5, the dilemma of higher labor wages being a barrier to sustainable development might be resolved by unionized workers taking an equity stake in the project—becoming co-owners of these projects—in lieu of asking for higher wages, which can prevent the project from being cost competitive at all.

A comparison of urban hourly construction-labor rates with those of more rural areas offers an insight as to why paper companies and other industries prefer to build their mills at greenfield sites, however ecologically inferior those sites might be. For example, hourly labor rates in 2000 for the nonunionized pipe fitters, ironworkers (structural and reinforcing), and electricians in Jones County (Macon), Georgia, were $10.00, $8.39, and $10.26, respectively (before factoring in the taxes and insurance costs the employer must also pay)—a small fraction (in some cases, less than 15 percent) of the hourly costs industrial developers pay for construction laborers in New York City.[11] Examples of construction-labor rates from other rural or forested counties where paper mills and other greenfield industries get built, such as Cowlitz County, Washington, and Elk County, Pennsylvania, also show construction-labor rates one third to one half as expensive as those in New York City. And because these laborers are not unionized, their work rules are more flexible.

The construction-company manager working on the BCPC project estimated that "For every $0.70 that you would spend on a laborer to build a paper mill in rural Alabama, you have to spend $1.29 in New York City."[12] The vice president in charge of paper production for the S. D.

Warren paper company, who for a while served as the president of the BCPC project, estimated that "construction labor costs in New York City are 135 percent the national average, and we usually build mills where labor costs are well below the national average. And in New York City we have to deal with costly union rules to boot."[13]

Though in some cases construction-labor costs are higher because of a slightly higher cost of living, New York City costs are more or less typical of those in urban areas throughout the United States. In cities like Chicago, Los Angeles, and Miami, which obviously also host many brownfields—and substantial supplies of wastepaper—construction-labor rates are comparable with New York City's and also substantially higher than those in rural greenfield areas. Thus, construction-labor rates in urban areas nationally tend to make it less likely for redevelopment to occur at brownfields than at greenfields. This is also true worldwide, whether in the developed or developing world. (See Table 4.2.)

Because paper is a commodity that is traded globally, the BCPC had to be designed to compete with the low-construction and production costs not only in rural North America but with mills in Asia and South America as well. In those areas the cost of labor is even less than in rural areas in North America, and the government subsidies promoting the use of virgin timber are sometimes even greater there than those historically offered in North America. The much lower labor costs and higher subsidies—including very cheap virgin wood and few environmental controls—offered to paper companies in the developing world more than offset the slightly higher transportation costs associated with bringing Asian- or South American–produced paper to North American markets.

Besides higher labor rates, there are other high transaction costs associated with acquiring labor in urban areas like New York City. These, of course, penalize those interested in developing an industrial-ecology project at a local brownfield. Some of these relate to the fact that laborers in urban areas are often unionized. I personally was a member of a union and have marched on behalf of union causes in street demonstrations, but as I considered the labor agreements being negotiated for the BCPC, I found some union work rules absurd. For instance, on a large industrial project that requires the services of different union locals, it requires a special job-

TABLE 4.2

Base Construction-Labor Rates Before Taxes or Any Other Employee Compensation

URBAN

City	Electricians ($/hr)	Fringe benefits	Pipe fitters ($/hr)	Fringe benefits	Structural iron workers ($/hr)	Fringe benefits
Boston, Mass.	31.55	13.30	30.96	12.19	25.50	14.60
Chicago, Ill.	30.50	13.51	32.70	7.84	30.00	14.09
Los Angeles, Calif.	27.55	10.78	25.78	11.14	24.83	14.09
Miami, Fla.	22.14	5.49	22.60	5.90	16.85	3.65
New York City, N.Y.	35.00	26.25	31.70	31.88	32.70	7.84
AVERAGE	29.35	13.87	28.75	13.79	25.98	10.85

RURAL

City	Electricians ($/hr)	Fringe benefits	Pipe fitters ($/hr)	Fringe benefits	Structural iron workers ($/hr)	Fringe benefits
Longview, Wash.	26.55	7.08	23.40	14.42	25.22	1.65
Johnsonburg, Pa.	26.02	8.84	20.51	10.44	22.03	11.68
Macon, Ga.	10.26	0.00	10.00	0.00	8.39	0.00
Westbrook, Maine	14.25	1.50	8.81	0.00	11.35	2.74
AVERAGE	19.27	4.36	15.68	6.22	16.75	4.02

Source: Compiled by NRDC, 2001, from U.S. Department of Labor Davis-Bacon Wage Determination Database.

site agreement—involving costly and time-consuming negotiation—to get the various locals, who are ostensibly all working on the same job, to guarantee they will take off the same days as holidays and start and end the workday at the same time. Union rules also occasionally require that certain types of equipment—e.g., pipes less than eight inches in diameter—be built at specific union-controlled shops within New York City.[14] For industrial projects, which typically require an enormous amount of piping, this can be a huge cost penalty, because it greatly limits the competitive-bidding options relating to equipment procurement. Nor does the absence of competition for acquisition of these pipes encourage the most efficient use of materials and other resources. Some work rules require costly foreman or other forms of supervisory personnel to be on-site, though they add no productive value to the construction project.

In addition, despite the reflexive support they receive from the progressive community—including people like myself—construction unions aren't particularly friendly to local, community-based laborers, who often can't get jobs at sites within their neighborhood, much less get into the union. Nor do unions offer special incentives to make environmentally superior projects more cost competitive. When I asked the head of the New York City building-trades union, with whom my BCPC colleagues and I had to negotiate a labor agreement, whether his union would be willing to hire local community laborers, the quick answer I received was a firm and unequivocal "No." The construction firm hired to build the mill did manage to obtain an agreement that the union local would try and assign laborers to the job who resided in the same zip code as the project. But this was for those few laborers already in the union who lived in the BCPC's zip code, and it would do nothing to enhance long-term livable-wage job prospects more broadly in the community. As for getting local community laborers into the union permanently, I was told in no uncertain terms that that simply couldn't happen. Getting into a union often requires personal connections. In addition, a certain amount of on-the-job time has to be spent as an apprentice, usually about three years. To quench local protests about nonlocal unionized laborers coming into a community with high unemployment to work on a job, unions have been known—to squash the protests—to hire some locals as apprentices for a period of time that is just under the amount necessary to get into the union full-time. They then lay off these apprentices, making it impossible for them to get into the union. A number of influential unions are reputedly nepotistic and, some minorities have charged, ethnically biased as well. None of this comports with any harmonious vision of sustainability that I know of.

Another labor-related obstacle for paper-industry officials is that most of the industry is not unionized and, due to mergers and mills closing, the number of unionized paper-mill workers has been steadily declining during the past ten years.[15] According to federal labor laws, if a company has a unionized workforce at one site, it must allow workers at its other production sites to vote on unionization. That is not necessarily a plus for attracting paper-company operators to invest at brownfields in urban areas with unionized workforces. The bottom line, however, is that, union or not, labor costs and the complications of cost-effectively deploying a workforce in an urban area pose significant obstacles for which creative solutions are required.

MANAGING WATER

It is more complicated and costly to find high-volume water supplies in urban areas for large industrial projects than it is at rural greenfields. This is especially true for paper mills, which use huge amounts of water—more than any industry on Earth—in their production process. Developing a system to reclaim water in lieu of using freshwater, as industrial ecology developers should, complicates the water-acquisition process further, despite its ecological value. Again, contrary to optimistic suggestions about how to sustainably supply water to a factory, acquiring industrial-volume reclaimed–sewage-water supplies at brownfields shows how trying to do the right thing environmentally can make the industrial-development process more complicated and costly.

Using freshwater for papermaking and many other industrial processes in a city environment is not only wasteful; it can adversely affect water pressure in the surrounding community. In most urban situations concerns about adversely affecting water pressure will make an industrial ecology project subject to lengthy water-impact analyses. Whenever high volumes of water are involved, and water pressure is adversely affected, environmental approvals can be justifiably denied. Obtaining water from non–freshwater sources, such as reclaiming sewage water, helps avoid this.

Water-acquisition costs in urban areas, where the majority of the nation's brownfields are located, tend to be substantially higher than water costs in rural greenfield areas. (See Table 4.3.) Along with the cost of obtaining raw materials, construction-labor costs, and energy costs, the price of water is among the most important variables determining whether a paper mill or any industrial project can be cost competitive. Incredible as it may seem, most paper mills in rural areas do not pay *anything* to extract water from nearby rivers or lakes. Commenting on the BCPC's water-supply costs, the production manager for one of North America's largest paper companies, who was involved in the BCPC devel-

TABLE 4.3
The Costs for Potable Water in Urban and Rural Areas

URBAN

City	Utility or manufacturer	Water rate ($/100 ft³)[*]	Wastewater rate ($/100 ft³)[*]
Boston, Mass.	Boston Water and Sewer Commission[1]	2.01	3.76
Chicago, Ill.	City of Chicago Department of Water[2]	1.60	Included in the water rate
Los Angeles, Calif.	Los Angeles Department of Water and Power[3]	1.50	2.28
Miami, Fla.	Miami-Dade Water and Sewer Department[4]	1.88	2.35
New York City, N.Y.	New York City Water Board[5]	1.31	2.08

[*]Based on demand of 5 million gallons per day. One gallon equals 7.48 ft³.
[1]Anthony Benedetti, community services officer, personal communications, January 2001.
[2]Thomas Russnak, field assessor, personal communications, January 2001.
[3]Richard West, rate manager, personal communications, January 2001.
[4]Anthony Kalata, rate manager, personal communications, February 2001.
[5]New York City Water Board, Water & Waste Water Rate Schedule, February 2001, p.1.

RURAL

City	Utility or manufacturer	Water rate ($/100 ft³)[*]	Wastewater rate ($/100 ft³)[*]
Longview, Wash.	City of Longview Public Works Department[6]	Price negotiated by project	Price negotiated by project
Johnsonburg, Pa.	Johnsonburg Municipal Authority[7]	2.69[**]	1.57[**]
Johnsonburg, Pa.	Willamette Industries[8]	0.18	Included in the water rate
Macon, Ga.	Macon Water Authority[9]	0.90	0.96
Westbrook, Maine	Portland Water District[10]	0.75[†]	3.99[†]
Westbrook, Maine	Westbrook Mill[10]	0.00	0.00
Skowhegan/Fairfield, Maine	Somerset Mill[10]	0.00	0.00

[*]Based on demand of 5 million gallons per day. One gallon equals 7.48 ft³.

[**]Although the Authority charges $2.69 and $1.57 per 100 ft³ respectively, these rates are not passed on to the paper mills. Willamette Industries operates an existing mill in Johnsonburg using approximately the same 5 million gal/day. However, it draws more than 99% of its water from a nearby river, free of charge, and consequently requires only 1 million gal/month from the utility.

This translates into a cost of approximately $3,582 a month rather than $540,003, if all 150 million gallons a month were supplied by the utility. The $0.18 per 1,000 ft³ reflects the actual price per 1,000 ft³ the mill pays for its 150 million gallons used per month.

[†]Westbrook Mills and Somerset draw water free of charge from nearby rivers and therefore do not pay the high costs of the Portland Water District.

[6]Bob Gregory, assistant city manager, personal communications, June 2001.
[7]Linda Tillack, office manager, personal communications, June 2001.
[8]Jennifer Smith, customer-service representative, personal communications, June 2001.
[9]Linda Fallona, director of customer service, personal communications, June 2001.
[10]Jim Black, vice president, S. D. Warren, personal communications, June 2001.

opment effort, stated, "The water costs at the Bronx site were a major disadvantage. There is no rural greenfield mill that I can think of where you pay for water by the gallon."[16]

For example, as shown in Table 4.3, rural paper mills in Skowhegan and Westbrook, Maine, pay nothing for their water supplies,[17] while a paper mill in the rural county of Johnsonburg, Pennsylvania, pays one eighth the water rate charged to all other businesses in the county. In Washington State, water costs for paper mills are negotiated project by project to help make each mill financially viable. New York City and other large urban areas have financed their water-supply and sewage infrastructure with financing bonds that must be repaid by water users and effluent dischargers. Given their fiduciary obligations to bondholders, these cities have less latitude than do rural towns to adjust their water-supply costs to the needs of each industrial project. And getting that adjustment done in a large urban area is politically time-consuming and complicated.

Undervaluing an asset leads to waste. It seems clear that if virgin-paper mills had to pay for the prodigious amounts of water they consume, they would use less of it. Because urban recycling mills are more likely to be located where water is more appropriately priced, providing free water to virgin mills is an enormous, and environmentally destructive, subsidy.

Rural paper mills do pay for the cleanup of the water they discharge back into the river or lake from which they take the water, as would any urban mill. But rural mills do not pay for their water supplies on a per-gallon or per-100 cubic feet (ft^3) basis, as is typical for factories in urban areas. Moreover, the characteristics of pollutants in effluent discharged by rural mills are less rigorously controlled than at urban sewage plants. Even if paper mills were charged for the volume of water they withdraw, as other industries sometimes are, rural greenfield areas, as Table 4.3 indicates, invariably offer cheaper freshwater costs than do urban areas. Thus, unless a strategy is designed to overcome it, the water-cost penalty for locating industrial projects, which routinely consume millions of gallons of water daily, at urban brownfields can be enormous.

The data in Table 4.3 also show that not only are water-supply rates lower in rural greenfield areas than they are in urban areas but, additionally, that special free-water arrangements are routinely made with timber-based mills. This is obviously done to attract additional economic development into rural counties, notwithstanding the adverse ecological consequences that will result from the conversion of greenfields, and the infrastructure and sprawl impacts that engenders.

Besides the higher water cost, there are other logistical hurdles associated with obtaining water at urban brownfield sites. Despite the value of avoiding freshwater sources for recycling operations, it is more complicated and costly to identify, acquire, and clean up alternatives sources from local sewage-treatment plants.

The BCPC's Water-Reclamation Plan

In the case of the Bronx paper-mill project, certain host brownfield sites had to be eliminated from consideration because they were not in convenient proximity to a sewage plant. After fourteen months of review—clearly, not all of which was related to water-supply considerations—a site was finally identified with a sewage-treatment plant located approximately one mile south. Although the idea of cleaning sewage water for use at the mill was an ideal objective, it quickly became apparent that this was not as simple as is the process of withdrawing freshwater from the nearby rivers or lakes typically relied on by rural, forest-based mills.

As discussed in the preceding chapter, the Wards Island Water Pollution Control Plant, the sewage-treatment plant the BCPC was going to rely on for 80 percent of its process-water needs, is owned by New York City. Consequently, to begin the process of acquiring water from this plant—an ecologically superior alternative to using potable water—we had to first sell the idea of cleaning up sewage effluent for use at the mill to senior city officials. While midlevel staff at the city's Department of Environmental Protection (DEP), who routinely work on water-conservation and sewage-treatment issues, immediately saw the innovative benefit of this decision, obtaining approval and political support for the effort required political calculations at higher city-government levels.

When we started on it, before Rudolph Giuliani was elected mayor of New York City, when an administration under Mayor David Dinkins was in office, the BCPC development team was dealing with an environmentally progressive DEP commissioner who had substantial independence as to how she could run her department. Being environmentally oriented and sensitive to the interests of her midlevel staff, this commissioner was enthusiastic about moving forward on the water plans for our project. Still, even with support from the top of the agency controlling New York City's water supply, a number of complicated and time-consuming logistical obstacles were before us.

First, we had to assess the characteristics of the effluent prior to the BCPC's cleaning it up. That was initially performed inaccurately. Our early effluent-quality assessments failed to take into account that the sewage plant from which we were planning on capturing water was routinely contaminated by water from the East River, because the tidal gates on the sewage plant were inoperative—they didn't close to prevent backwash into the plant—and it would cost the city hundreds of millions of dollars to get them to work properly. The city didn't plan on spending the money to correct this problem. This allowed brackish, high-chloride water from the East River to mix with the processed effluent. Then our Alabama-based engineering firm, whom we brought in on recommendation from our paper-company partner, learned, after many months of costly work, that the East River flows in two different directions, depending on the tides. When it flows south, it contains relatively low chloride levels, in the range of 250–400 parts per million (ppm). When it flows north, it contains briny seawater, and the river water mixing with the effluent greatly increases its chloride concentration, to levels as high as 500–800 ppm. Water with high chloride concentrations would corrode the pipes at the mill and contaminate the water used in the papermaking process. Unfortunately, the initial water samples we took from the effluent at the sewage plant were taken when the East River was flowing south, so initially we greatly underestimated the amount of chlorides in the effluent we were going to capture.

This was an expensive, time-consuming miscalculation. The fact that the chlorides in the effluent were intolerably high meant that we had to redesign the effluent-cleanup system to more aggressively remove chlorides. Ultimately we designed a reverse-osmosis and membrane-filtering system that would reduce chloride levels from more than 500 ppm to less than 40 ppm. Had a local engineering firm—more familiar with the directional flows of the East River—taken the river-water sample, perhaps we would have avoided our assessment mistake. However, there are not many engineering firms that can design a world-scale paper mill. The companies that build mills rely on these few firms, and virtually none of them are based in large urban areas; instead, they are based near rural areas, where the mills are. Despite my hope to use a local engineering firm to work on the mill design—we did use a local engineering firm for environmental permitting, zoning, and architectural work—we had no choice but to accept the choice of the engineering firm our paper-company collaborator wanted. Perhaps in Alabama all the rivers flow in one direction, so the fact that the East River flows two ways didn't occur to our consultants.

Our second obstacle was that eliminating unexpectedly high chloride levels was not all we had to deal with in terms of contaminants. We sought to remove other pollutants from coming into the mill's process water and to remove pollutants as well from the effluent the BCPC was going to return to the sewage plant. Besides designing a system to remove chlorides, we designed a system to remove additional suspended solids and, most important from the perspective of water ecology, to remove nitrogen. When it flows north, the effluent discharged into the East River from the Wards Island sewage plant winds up in the Long Island Sound, which, as already mentioned, suffers from nitrogen-induced hypoxia.

Although designing a nitrogen-reduction process improved the BCPC's environmental profile and, in so doing, ultimately helped our project obtain much needed development financing and subsidized loans (through the Clean Water Act's State Revolving Fund program), designing this system nevertheless added time, costs, and logistical complications to the mill's development process. Financiers were also concerned about what they viewed as our innovative water-acquisition strategy. Though they appreciated the ecological objectives we were trying to accomplish, it is so much easier to get financial backing for commercially proven rather than environmentally innovative—read: unproven—technologies. As the United Nations Environment Programme has observed, "Even though a company has established environmental objectives, this does not automatically result in a lower 'hurdle rate' for environmental projects."[18] My experience suggests that environmentally innovative technologies are often penalized by current financing practices. Proven, commercially operating technologies are more likely to obtain needed performance guarantees from construction firms and equipment vendors. Innovative technologies have less experience against which those guarantees can be confidently offered. If the effluent-cleanup system failed to perform as expected, the mill couldn't operate and produce product. If no product was being produced, the mill's financing obligations obviously couldn't be met. Consequently, despite all the trouble we went through to design the effluent-reclamation system, financiers informed us that we had to design and build capacity for a redundant, freshwater-supply system as well!

Because the cleaning and reuse of sewage water is not routinely done, and if done improperly it may pose contamination threats, the process of using cleaned effluent had to go through an EIS. Although the entire mill project was subject to a full EIS—unlike most rural greenfield mills, which avoid this lengthy regulatory process—adding specific details about precisely how the effluent-cleanup system was going to work as well as details about what the mill would do if this system failed, and obtaining an equipment vendor's assurances about the reliability of the system to satisfy the permitting agencies, added time and costs to the EIS process.

Additional logistical hurdles associated with using reclaimed wastewater abounded. As mentioned earlier, the Wards Island sewage plant was located about a mile from the mill site. Between the sewage plant and the mill were a city park, a railroad bridge, and a bridge for cars. The railroad bridge—the Little Hell Gate Bridge—is a beautiful structure that was built in the 1930s by a giant in bridge design, Moravian engineer Gustav Lindenthal (in New York City he also designed, or redesigned, the Williamsburg, Queensborough, and Manhattan bridges). The bridge is appropriately designated by the city as having "potential landmark status." One option for running pipes from the sewage plant to the mill would have required that they be run across or under city parkland, which would require a hard-to-obtain easement from the New York City Parks Department and was potentially subject to its own EIS. Alternatively, the pipes could have been hung off the Little Hell Gate Bridge, which would require approval from the railroad companies that use the bridge—Amtrak and Conrail—as well as a critical review from the city's Landmarks Preservation Commission. Digging a trench under the Bronx Kill would not only require permits from the U.S. Army Corps of engineers, as mentioned earlier, but would also require hard to obtain easements from the city's Parks and Recreation Department because a small city park sits between the BCPC site and the sewage plant supplying its water. To avoid the possibility of defacing a potential landmark, and to avoid interring pipes within a city park, we decided to run the pipes from a bridge located farther away from the sewage plant, the Triborough Bridge. This would not require a new EIS, though it would require approvals "only" from the TriBorough Bridge and Tunnel Authority. This is an intimidating agency to work with but is heavily influenced by the governor's office; thus, we hoped to get swifter logistical cooperation than most supplicants because of Governor George Pataki's support for our project. Had we chosen to rely on the environmentally inferior process of sourcing freshwater, none of these expensive and intricate efforts would have been needed.

After finally managing to accurately characterize the effluent coming out of the sewage plant, getting the DEP to support our plans to use recovered effluent at the mill, and designing and pricing the technologies used to clean up the effluent, we had to find a one-acre parcel adjacent to the sewage plant on which to locate the water-cleanup system. This required a complicated-to-obtain easement from the city, since the sewage plant is located on city property and negotiating for the transfer of city property to the private sector, regardless of how seemingly small the process, can take teams of lawyers more than a year. So to avoid this, the BCPC project team decided that the effluent-cleanup process would be owned by the city but paid for by the BCPC. Then we had to negotiate with the city also about who would operate the system—would it be the city officials who run the large treatment plant, mill employees, or city officials paid by the mill? These were all time-consuming and politically influenced decisions that, given the change in mayoral administrations and the lack of interest in the BCPC by Mayor Giuliani, then new at City Hall, went on for more than two years. Negotiations were made all the more complicated by the fact that the positions held on some of these issues by DEP permanent civil servants were at odds with the positions held by Mayor Giuliani's political appointees. Actually, the perspectives of the mayoral appointees shifted whenever new political appointments were made. Reconciling the perspectives of these two interested parties—the mayor's office and DEP staff—and obtaining a firm commitment from the mayor's office (under Mayor Giuliani the DEP commissioner could no longer decide these types of technical issues without political assessments first being made by City Hall staff) made the water-acquisition process one of the most complicated and time-consuming aspects of the mill's development, even though it offered one of the project's greatest ecological innovations.

Most of our paper company partners, however, weren't interested in ecological innovations:[19] They were interested in getting a papermaking machine on-line as swiftly and cheaply as possible, and the delays caused by the design and implementation of our water-cleanup process turned into a huge penalty for the project. Had we been willing to employ the less sustainable practice of drawing and discharging freshwater, our logistical hurdles and the financial burdens of resolving them might have been fewer.

While the social and political sides of development obstacles associated with locating industrial projects in politically complex urban areas will be discussed in more detail in the next chapter, having to deal with uncertain, costly, and time-consuming local politics to obtain a water supply for any development project is not a circumstance most rural greenfield projects have to consider. Indeed, their situation is usually just the opposite: Political office holders in rural areas compete to attract industrial projects to their area—however environmentally detrimental this might be—and this is why water and other development costs tend to be so much lower there than those in urban areas, which have a more diverse and contentious, and contaminated, economic infrastructure.

COPING WITH ENERGY EXPENSES

Although *transportation*-related energy costs at urban mills might be advantaged relative to rural mills—due to the shorter distances between wastepaper supplier and producer, between producer and market, and because of the broader opportunities for workers to rely on mass transit, bicycles, and walking—unless subsidies are provided, urban brownfields also suffer higher *operating* energy-cost penalties relative to rural locations. Although rural virgin mills consume more energy per ton of product produced than would an urban recycled paper mill, they will still pay substantially less for their energy. There are three reasons for this: (1) They burn the bark, chemical residues, and sludge by-products that are produced from virgin-timber processing, while many urban areas prohibit

TABLE 4.4

Industrial Electricity Costs at Urban and Rural Locations

URBAN

City	Utility	Summer rate ($/megawatt)*	Winter rate ($/megawatt)*
Boston, Mass.	NSTAR[1]	43.23 (June–Sept.)	25.93 (Oct.–May)
Chicago, Ill.	Commonwealth Edison Co.[2]	41.83 (May–Sept.)	38.99 (Oct.–April)
Los Angeles, Calif.	Los Angeles Department of Water and Power[3]	51.08 (June–Oct.)	49.61 (Nov.–May)
Miami, Fla.	Florida Power and Light Co.[4]	40.92	40.92
New York City, N.Y.	Consolidated Edison Co. of NY[5]	101.47 (June–Sept.)	72.14 (Oct.–May)

*Based on 35 MW continuous demand.

[1]Chris Mullaney, customer-service engineer, personal communications, July 2001.
[2]Cheryl Scannell, account manager, personal communications, July 2001.
[3]Larry Chacon, utility marketing representative, personal communications, July 2001.
[4]John Lehr, product manager, personal communications, July 2000.
[5]The Consolidated Edison Company of New York, published rates for large commercial and industrial users, Rate 9-II.

RURAL

City	Utility	Summer rate ($/megawatt)*	Winter rate ($/megawatt)*
Longview, Wash.	Cowlitz County Public Utility District[6]	28.49 (May–Aug.)	37.39 (Sept.–April)
Johnsonburg, Pa.	Allegheny Power[7]	35.041	35.041
Macon, Ga.	Georgia Power[8]	25.43	25.43
Westbrook, Maine	Central Maine Power Co.[9]	06.32 (Dec.–Mar.)	26.10 (April–Nov.)

[6]Gary Huhta, senior power resource engineer, personal communications, July 2001.
[7]Mike Geitner, major account manager, personal communications, July 2001.
[8]Paul Price, business customer consultant, personal communications, July 2001.
[9]Peter Bartlett, key account manager, personal communications, July 2001.

sludge and other forms of waste-based combustion; (2) energy-supply taxes and transmission-distribution costs are typically higher in urban areas than they are in rural areas; and (3) paper-mill utility boilers have until recently been exempted from Clean Air Act regulations, and this has allowed them to both pollute and to avoid the costs associated with proper environmental controls that are required in urban areas. As Table

4.4 indicates, comparing industrial-energy costs at paper mills in urban areas with industrial-energy costs in rural areas reveals that, on average, energy costs at greenfield sites have been about 30 percent lower.

In the case of the BCPC project, buying electricity off the grid was prohibitively expensive: Local industrial electricity rates in New York City were the second highest in the nation (second to Hawaiian Electric). Because we located the project in a state economic-development zone, however, the project was freed from having to pay any taxes on the electricity bought off the grid. This amounted to a 47.5 percent saving. Nevertheless, this was still less competitive than the price for energy that competing virgin mills paid. Because electricity deregulation had recently been enacted in New York State, we were able to find a power-plant developer who was willing to finance a power boiler dedicated to the project if a little excess generating capacity was designed into it to sell in the local market. Of course, we still had to get an air-emissions permit for that boiler (which, as described earlier, we did).

Most factories, paper mills included—whether they are virgin- or recycled-paper mills—also require steam to operate. Consequently, not only does an industrial-ecology developer have to find competitively priced electricity for the mill, but a new steam boiler may need to be financed and built as well, adding costly infrastructure expenditures to the mill's development. The project was located too far from any steam-generating plant—no industries remained in the economically desolate area we were trying to revive—so we had to plan to build one and go through the necessary environmental-permitting process. It was to be a high-efficiency, natural-gas–fueled steam-and-electricity cogeneration plant. Also, an elevated roadway—the Triborough Bridge—bisected the mill site, and local transportation officials were understandably concerned that in the winter the BCPC's unrecoverable steam, which from a rural mill would typically vent freely, would condense and then freeze and cause dangerous roadway conditions. Therefore, the BCPC also had to design a steam stack at a $10 million added expense, to channel the flow of the steam that couldn't be economically recaptured for energy recirculation away from the bridge roadway.

As mentioned in chapter 3, to help overcome the higher energy cost typically faced at urban brownfields, we sought to overscale the power boiler to attract an independent power producer to finance and operate it, which would provide both an economic and an environmental advantage. Economically, having a third party finance and operate the boiler would result in a reduction of the mill's capital costs, making it easier to finance. And environmentally, by overscaling the boiler to a size beyond what the mill needed, we could make that boiler a cogeneration device that simultaneously produced steam and introduced a new high-efficiency gas-powered turbine into the deregulated electricity market in New York City. In so doing we were seeking to use the BCPC to help shift demand away from the higher-polluting and less-efficient oil- or coal-fired plants that now supply steam and electricity to the region.

THE DIFFICULTIES OF USING RECYCLED RAW MATERIALS

Factories are designed to receive specific types of raw materials and get a specific product yield from them. The financial viability of manufacturing plants depends on their ability to generate the designed-for product yield. While it is true—although underappreciated—that there is substantial variability in the quality of virgin resources delivered to manufacturing plants, including virgin timber delivered to paper mills, relying on recovered materials collected from post-consumer sources plagues industrial projects with more quality variability and logistical uncertainty than does a reliance on virgin sources.

Post-consumer recycled materials are the used items that residents and commercial establishments separate for recycling that would otherwise end up in a landfill or incinerator. The amount of post-consumer materials collected by a recycling program and their quality depends on a number of factors, including participation rates by households and commercial establishments, public education about and compliance with rules as to what should and what should not be separated, collection schedules, and the effectiveness of post-collection processing facilities to remove contaminants. While obtaining virgin raw materials involves a fairly straightforward business deal focused around price, quality guarantees, and delivery schedules, obtaining a steady, adequate supply of recycled raw materials isn't as straightforward.

As recently as 1991 the United States, out of the eighteen most indus-trialized nations, ranked fifteenth in paper recovery.[20] Part of the reason for this is that the collection of recycled raw materials is so often dependent on politically determined budgeting decisions and government operations. Thus, the business of acquiring a steady supply of recycled materials is inherently more complex and risky than the more direct business-to-busi-ness situation typical of providing a steady supply of virgin raw materials.

For example, for budgetary or even ideological reasons, cities can cut back on collection frequency and the programs—like public education—that support participation by residents. This situation plagued the BCPC, and it continues to plague New York City as of this writing.[21] On June 12, 1996, I called the official I was negotiating with at the New York City Department of Sanitation (DOS) to advance the BCPC's contract to acquire wastepaper from the city's recycling program, and I was informed that then-mayor Giuliani's 1996 budget essentially decimated the city's wastepaper-collection program, a move that would have been in violation of both the city's Local Law 19, and a court order for the city to *expand* its recycling program to comply with the law. I was told that the mayor was proposing to

- change weekly collection of recyclables to once every two weeks;
- eliminate expansion of the paper-collection program, and;
- eliminate public education on recycling.

This sent an icy chill through everyone involved with the project: Not only did it threaten the BCPC's raw-material expectations, but it also communicated a lack of concern about the project by the mayor and the DOS. Despite the plentiful supply of wastepaper in New York City, that radical change in the city's recycling program, if implemented, would have wiped out any possibility of convincing paper companies or investors that the raw material for the BCPC would be available and insu-lated from political games. DOS officials told me they couldn't negotiate with the BCPC project on the paper supply if they didn't know if they would have a program in place to effectively collect it. This was taking place even though the BCPC had always intended to pay the city for the paper, even though the city usually paid others to get rid of it, and despite the fact that millions of dollars had been spent to develop the BCPC on the assumption that the city's recycling program would be in place—indeed expanded as the law required—to supply the mill.

The BCPC was designed from its inception to remedy environmental problems—and help alleviate poverty—in New York City and provide a long-term waste-management service to the city's sanitation department. Nevertheless, with the exception of only a handful of city officials, the city's political and administrative establishment—and the potentially affected businesses that relied on the city's wastepaper—treated our development team as if we were any other vendor trying to make money off the city.

Ironically, however illogical it might seem, because of legal constraints that come into force when the public sector controls raw materials, the BCPC faced a real risk of having to pay more for locally collected and processed old newspapers (ONP) than would out-of-town mills relying on the same New York City wastepaper. This is because in order for a city to sign a noncompetitive, sole-source contract for a service (in this case, the provision of unsorted wastepaper), the contract has to be a revenue contract—that is, it has to provide the city with revenue. Given the large scale of the mill investment and the enormous amount of bonds that would be outstanding to finance it, investors would never allow its raw-materials supply to be subject to interruptible request-for-proposal (RFP) bidding competition. Thus, the BCPC needed a sole-source contract with the city for its wastepaper. However, as anyone familiar with the pricing structure for wastepaper recovered from a municipal-waste stream knows, cities often have to pay to have wastepaper carted away; they don't tend to get paid for it (in recycling jargon this is known as paying a negative price).

Processors who intermittently bid for the wastepaper through RFP competition do not have to have a revenue contract—because theirs would not be a sole-source contract—and therefore they can be paid to take the paper away. But unlike these processors, the mill could never legally get paid to accept the wastepaper—because, as just mentioned, sole-source contracts always have to provide revenue to the city. Unlike a sole-source contract, RFP bidding is the only way the mill could get paid to accept the city's wastepaper during market downturns. But financiers were requiring the mill to have a sole-source contract to ensure that its raw-materials flow would never be interrupted by a losing RFP bid. Consequently, the mill would always have to pay at least one dollar per ton to the city for its paper. But if it paid the city even only one dollar, it would still have to pay a paper sorting cost of thirty-five dollars to forty dollars, which is what it costs to sort out the appropriate grade of paper the BCPC needed from all the other paper discarded in the city. Thus, competing mills out of the city could actually wind up paying a lower price to New York City ONP processors—who were getting paid to take away New York City's wastepaper—than the Bronx mill, which would always be paying for this paper.

Granted, with adequate political support from the mayor's office there were ways to modify this adverse market situation, but that would have required cooperation from a supportive mayor, which for political and ideological reasons—discussed in chapter 5—wasn't forthcoming from Rudolph Giuliani. Even if the mayor were favorably inclined toward supporting the BCPC (his opposition was no surprise; the project was supported by Hillary Clinton, his then-opponent for the U.S. Senate seat he coveted, and it was located in a part of town run a by a borough president, Fred Ferrer, who was among his political rivals), the fact that so many political considerations had to be factored in during the normally straightforward process of acquiring raw materials underscores some of the logistical disadvantages faced by developers of recycling facilities.

However great an idea the BCPC seemed to be to most people—in the United States and abroad it was the subject of many favorable articles, book excerpts, and radio and TV shows—the fact was that there was already a waste- and recycling-collection infrastructure doing business in the city and with which the mill would compete for raw materials. Good intentions do not elevate us from the ruthlessness of the market. Even though the city's current wastepaper-collection program is based on export to out-of-state mills or mills abroad is environmentally and economically substandard, from a strictly business perspective an in-town local mill wouldn't necessarily benefit all the haulers who are presently collecting, processing, and marketing these materials. Nor would it benefit the wastepaper brokers who would be cut out of the city's wastepaper-export market, because the paper collected by the city would no longer be exported. (Though it would reduce the pollution those longer-distance export vehicles cause.) Waste haulers, especially giant waste firms like Waste Management and Allied Waste Industries, and large wastepaper-brokerage firms, have huge political influence in large cities like New York, where they do hundreds of millions, perhaps billions, of dollars' worth of business each year. These companies were regularly lobbying the mayor, his informal advisers, and his staff against supporting the BCPC financially or politically. And they were persuasive, especially since a former Giuliani deputy mayor, reputedly the mayor's best friend, and the state's former attorney general, one of the mayor's political allies, went to work for these firms after leaving their government jobs. None of these political obstacles plague the acquisition of virgin raw materials at mills in rural greenfields.

The bottom line is that while using recycled materials offers great environmental advantages, and locating a mill in an urban area can reduce truck traffic pollution, trying to advance these policies as a business strategy engenders logistical and financial complications, if not outright penalties, for industrial-ecology developers. And these penalties can actually increase if the mill is most ideally located (from an ecological perspective) near its raw-material supply. Although environmental benefits only partially affect a company's profitability—for example, by making permitting compliance easier and providing lower costs for raw materials and product transportation—the financial penalties can sink a project's competitiveness entirely. Unless sustainability-oriented policies are somehow put in place to resolve these issues in a timely and profitable fashion, there will be penalties for many firms wishing to locate at urban brownfields and use recycled materials. I think the best way for things to change is for environmentalists to assume greater control over businesses and industrial development in general and, in that way, more substantially influence both the economic and political spheres that are now controlled by anti-environmental business interests.

Perhaps, had the BCPC delivered political contributions to the mayor and other elected officials in the city, as other potential vendors with the city routinely do, this situation might have been somewhat different.

This problem in acquiring the raw-materials supply for the mill occurred just as the project was moving to finalize engineering and cost estimates. But to establish these estimates, which we had to do to continue making accurate presentations to potential participants and investors in the project, we needed to be assured that we would have a paper supply from the city and a pricing formula that financiers would accept. If the wastepaper supply wasn't going to be available from the city, many of our financial projections would be undermined, as would many of our assumptions about the environmental value of the mill. Even though the mayor didn't destroy the city's recycling program—an NRDC lawsuit successfully stopped him from doing so—the unending uncertainty about whether the city would commit the paper to the mill, because it would have to divert the paper from large waste haulers who were profitably exporting it and who financially supported the mayor, contributed to the BCPC's failure to hold onto its financing.

CONCLUSION

The obstacles to sustainable industrial development at brownfields in urban areas would plague any industry, not just recycled-paper mills. Obviously, some industries face more logistical obstacles converting their virgin processes to recycled raw materials above and beyond the problems associated with efficiently acquiring them. But along with the obstacles associated with acquiring a steady volume of recycled raw materials at a competitive price, all industries seeking to locate at an urban brownfield will struggle with longer and more controversial permitting time and cleanup logistics, more lengthy site preparation, higher water costs, high construction-labor costs, and greater political hurdles. These issues help explain why so few industrial-ecology investments have been developed anywhere, and why they are especially likely to be stymied at ecologically ideal brownfield sites in the foreseeable future.

Unfortunately, financial and technical barriers to sustainability are only part of the bevy of barriers sustainable industrial projects face in urban environments. As the next chapter reveals, equally disadvantageous and burdensome social- and political-market hurdles also stymie our efforts to develop ecologically healing industries.

NOTES

1. Rocky Mountain Institute, *Green Development* (New York: John Wiley & Sons, 1998), p. 6.
2. More in-depth discussions about this information can be obtained from the following documents: "Harlem River Yard Hazardous Waste Site

Assessment Phase IA Report," prepared by TAMS Consultants, New York City, February 1991; "Harlem River Yard Environmental Site Assessment Phase IB Report," prepared by TAMS Consultants, New York City, February 1992; "Harlem River Yard Environmental Site Assessment Phase II Site Investigation Report," prepared by TAMS Consultants, New York City, 1993.

3. SEC rules and generally accepted accounting principles (GAAP) impose specific requirements on companies for environmental disclosure. According to Item 101 of Regulation S-K, "appropriate disclosure shall be made as to the material effects that compliance with Federal, State, or local provisions which have been enacted or adopted regulating the discharge of materials into the environment may have on the capital expenditures, earnings, and competitive position of the registrant and its subsidiaries. The registrant shall disclose any material capital expenditures for environmental control facilities for the remainder of the current fiscal year and its succeeding fiscal year and for such future periods as the registrant may deem material. . . ." [17 C.F.R. 229.101 (c) (xii)]. Similarly, Item 103 of Regulation S-K requires reporting of "any material pending legal proceedings, other than ordinary routine litigation incidental to the business, to which the registrant or any of its subsidiaries is a party of which any of their property is subject" (17 CFR 229.103). Environmentally related proceedings must be disclosed if they are material, they involve a claim for more than 10 percent of current assets, or they involve the government and potential monetary sanctions greater than $100,000; from Robert Repetto and Duncan Austin, *Coming Clean: Corporate Disclosure of Financially Significant Environmental Risks* (Washington, D.C.: World Resources International, 2000), p. 8.

4. *Environmental Requirements for Industrial Permitting, Vol. 1—Approaches and Instruments* (OECD: Paris, 1999), p. 11.

5. John J. Fialka, "EPA Report Says Pollution Control Effort Is Hurt by Bureaucracy, Lack of Funds," *Wall Street Journal,* 12 March 2002, p. A28.

6. Phil Sears, vice president, Allee King Rosen & Fleming, personal communication, 15 August 2001, excerpted with permission.

7. More than twenty-five years ago, during a graduate-school seminar on politics, one of my professors, Bernard Brown, said that in the course of his long life he had come to believe that he "could stand on the corner of Fifth Avenue and 42nd Street and offer everyone who passes a free lunch, and someone will express opposition." Certainly, developing a large industrial-ecology facility in New York City, despite its environmental and social value, is not immune from this lesson.

8. Distinguished Professor Marshall Berman, "Views from the Burning Bridge," *Urban Mythologies: The Bronx Represented Since the 1960s,* catalog for an exhibit at the Bronx Museum of the Arts, 8 April–15 September 1999, p. 82.

9. Victor Hugo, *Les Misérables,* first published 1862, translation copyright: The Folio Society, 1976 (London: Penguin Classics), p. 38.

10. Julia Stone, compliance specialist, U.S. Department of Labor, personal communication, November 8, 2000. General wage determinations issued under the Davis-Bacon and related acts, ME000001, PA000002, FL000001, NY000003, ME000001, IL000009, CA000033, GA000059, and WA000008.

11. See note 10.

12. Tony Winson, vice president, Morse Diesel International, personal communication, 27 June 1997.

13. Jim Black, vice president/paper production, S. D. Warren, personal communication, 2 October 1995, excerpted with permission.

14. Gary Simpson, president, NAB Construction Corp., personal communication, New York City, 25 September 1995.

15. Lynn Baker, associate director of communications, Paper, Allied-Industrial, Chemical, and Energy Workers International Union (formerly the United Paper Workers International Union), personal communication, 12 February 2001. Since 1983 general union membership in the United States has declined by one third.

16. Jim Black, personal communication, 20 February 2001, excerpted with permission.

17. Ibid.

18. UNEP, *Promoting Cleaner Production Investments in Developing Countries: Issues and Possible Strategies* (Paris: UNEP, April 2000), p. 6.

19. As discussed in chapter 7, there was a decided difference in perspectives on environmental and technological matters between Swedish paper-company executives and their counterparts in the United States. Based on my twenty years of experience working with regulatory and corporate officials in Europe and the United States, the latter show much less interest in, knowledge of, and sympathy toward more technically innovative and socially progressive approaches to both papermaking and the social impacts of business.

20. James E. McCarthy, *Report for Congress: Recycling and Reducing Packaging Waste: How the United States Compares to Other Countries* (Washington, D.C.: Congressional Research Service, 8 November 1991), p. 3.

21. Kirk Johnson, "Recycling; Glass, Metal and Plastic May Become Plain Trash," *New York Times,* 14 February 2002, p. B5.

Designing the BCPC

INTRODUCTION
Working with Maya Lin

CONCEPT DESIGN

COLLAGES

INTRODUCTION

Working with Maya Lin

On a warm spring day in April 1993 I returned to my office at the Natural Resources Defense Council in New York City from a business lunch and was buttonholed by our office manager, Cathy Verhoff: "Allen," she said, "you need to call Maya Lin. She just called and wants to talk with someone who knows about the environmental impacts related to different construction materials." "Maya Lin?" I asked. "Yes, Maya Lin. She called the switchboard out of the blue."

Almost instantly I decided that the artist and architect Maya Lin, designer of the National Vietnam Veterans Memorial in Washington, D.C., the Civil Rights Memorial in Montgomery, Alabama, and other inspiring monuments, would be the perfect person to design the BCPC mill. There is a quiet yet essential cause-oriented passion about her work, and I knew that putting the BCPC design in her hands would make the project an even more important initiative.

I called Maya, and we chatted. "I would love to talk with you about the environmental attributes of construction and artistic materials," I said, "and I have something else to talk with you about—an environmental- and social-remediation project NRDC is coordinating. Can I come see you ... now?" When she said yes, I was out the door.

At the time, despite her fame and the luxuries she could afford, Maya was living in a walk-up tenement in Chinatown and working out of a nearby storefront in what was then a very nonchic part of the city. Inside I saw giant plywood tables topped by intricate three-dimensional cardboard models, drawings, shaped glass, large shiny black stones, sculptures, two assistants, phones on the floor, and a smiling Maya Lin in jeans, a ratty sweatshirt, and cowboy boots.

I gave Maya some of the book-length reports I had written on garbage management in Japan and Europe, an NRDC annual report, and a catalog on green building materials. When I explained NRDC's ecological and social objectives for the BCPC and told her we had partnered with a South Bronx community group, it took all of fifteen seconds for her to look at me warmly, nod her head, and say, "I want to do this." We chatted for another hour or so about her current works, her vision for a monument to extinct species that she wanted to locate simultaneously in different parts of the world, her fascination with ecology, with water, how hard she found it to reproduce the shape of a stone, and her commitment to environmental teaching.

I quickly recognized that Maya is a kindred ecological activist, a social visionary, and, of course, an artistic genius. I have no idea how I got back to the office. I'm fairly certain I floated back. I couldn't stop smiling. I kept thinking I was one of the luckiest people on Earth, that Maya and I would bring a very special gift to the people of the South Bronx.

We didn't have a site yet. Maya wanted to help evaluate sites and meet with project engineers. She wanted to spend time in the community. She wanted to visit some recycled paper mills. She wanted my help in making sure we chose the most environmentally sound materials.

Maya walked each potential location, some of them very contaminated, all of them in remote corners of the poorest parts of the South Bronx. She measured them and drew schematic designs for each.

Initially, her favorite site was an old giant warehouse—the largest indoor space in New York City—owned by a bankrupt company, because she liked the idea of recycling a building to build a plant that would recycle paper. Everything is connected in Maya's world. She would draw her latest concept for me on small white sheets of tracing paper, which I squirreled away like the local grocer who let Pablo Picasso pay him with pencil drawings on grocery bags.

The Swedish paper-company executives adored her. They invited her to visit them in Stockholm, which we did together. However, when American engineers and American paper-company officials became involved, project coordination for me was often nightmarish. The idea of an artist designing a world-scale production mill was something they couldn't stomach, and I was bewildered by the rudeness Maya faced. Watching the attitude of these parochial and, unfortunately, representative businessmen toward Maya led me to contemplate the idea of "cultural obstacles" to sustainability, which I discuss elsewhere in this book.

By the time the BCPC team had chosen a site—more than a year after my initial meeting with Maya—her participation in the project was as important to me as any other of the environmental and social objectives we had built into the design.

In spite of Maya's international reputation, I had to fight regularly with American paper-company engineers and some of the financiers on the team about her role. She had committed to working with the engineers to keep the project cost competitive; however, it seemed to me, money was not the issue. There was something about her gender, perhaps her ethnicity, certainly her intellectually brilliant and progressive nature that just intimidated these older paper-industry males in white shirts—always they wore white shirts.

I finally let it be known I would brook no more objections to her participation. I knew we were designing a landmark, and that like the gas station designed by Frank Lloyd Wright and the theater sets designed by Picasso, the function of the project would, in the public's eye, ultimately be less important than the luminous vision of Maya's design.

Her design helped the BCPC project sail through its required review before the New York City Planning Commission, and her full model for the mill was featured in "Designing Industrial Ecology," a Christmas-time 1997 Municipal Arts Society (MAS) exhibit in Rockefeller Center. Herbert Muschamp, the *New York Times* chief architectural critic, gave the design an extremely favorable review on the front page of the Arts section, comparing "Maya's BCPC project" favorably to Frank Gehry's design for the Getty Museum in Los Angeles. Muschamp named it one of the ten architectural highlights of 1998. In 1999 Maya's BCPC design was included in an exhibit by the Bronx Museum of Art Writing in the museum catalog, Distinguished Professor Marshall Berman of the City University of New York described it as "the most impressive public artwork created in the Bronx."

Together Maya and I not only traveled to visit paper mills and assess materials in Maine and in Sweden, we spent countless hours with engineers, equipment vendors, and government officials. We met with potential operators. We talked about the educational potential of the mill. Working for eight years alongside Maya Lin has been the single most enjoyable and inspirational experience of my professional career.

Before she designed the mill, Maya wrote down what she wanted this model industrial-ecology project to accomplish—for the community, for the city, for the workers, for visitors, for the environment. Maya always first writes out what she intends her work to accomplish emotionally, conceptually, visually, and then seeks to build something that achieves that. Her "BCPC Concept Design, Program Analysis and Schematic Design," presented to the BCPC's board on February 1, 1994, synthesizes an extraordinary artistic vision with an urban-recycling factory's function, producing a unique social purpose. In crafting it, Maya taught me more about what the BCPC mill could be than any other person. It is published here for the first time, with, of course, Maya's generous permission.

Following Maya's essay you will see some of the remarkable, fanciful collages that she produced for the hugely successful "Designing Industrial Ecology" exhibit, viewed by thousands. To me, these collages provide a sort of industrial surrealism, with powerful social and environmental commentary visually woven throughout. They are among my most favorite Maya Lin creations and reveal a fanciful side of this transcendental artist never seen outside the MAS exhibit.

ALLEN HERSHKOWITZ
Waccabuc, New York
July 24, 2002

CONCEPT DESIGN FOR THE BCPC
Maya Lin, February 1, 1994

The goal is to create a humanistic center whose purpose is not just to recycle waste paper, but to create a positive environment for the people that work there, the community it is placed in, and the people who will tour the facilities. I envision a group of buildings that will be integrated closely with each other and with their site. Attention shall be paid to the spaces between and surrounding the buildings, with the design of a green space/park that unifies the entire recycling facility and welcomes people to this place: creating an environment where the buildings and landscape are interconnected either physically or visually, in which the buildings do not define distinct boundaries between themselves and the environment, but open interfaces to them. Conceptually and physically, the center will express a redefinition of man's relationship to the environment.

The need to create spaces that are harmonious with their sites is critical in making people realize and rethink how sensitive we are to our surroundings. A critical element will be the design of the landscape surrounding the center. Fortunately, the recycling facility has a key element that will be crucial in developing this green space. In the recycling process, water is a major component. Whether it is used in a liquid state in the de-inking process or whether it is used as steam for energy to run the plant, the amount of water needed to produce paper is enormous, and it leads me to emphasize water in the design. The creation of a wastewater natural wetlands marsh that will clean the water used by the plant will not only incorporate another strong recycling process, but it will also afford us the opportunity to create a unique and beautiful landscape that will surround and become a part of the recycling center. The acknowledgement and incorporation of water in the design should, at times, simply expose the workings of the center—its presence is a natural one, illustrating its use throughout the facility. The use of water will give the project a strong sense of what this place can be about—recycling, the life cycle, the natural cycle of replenishing resources.

The buildings should be responsive to and derived from their site. They should express the processes that take place within them—allowing people to tour the facilities and acquire an understanding of the recycling process. Attention shall also be paid to the spaces between the buildings. These 'negative spaces,' normally unplanned and unthought of are potentially of great importance in the design. The placement of the storage facilities, the sorting center, the de-inking facility and, later, the paper-making facility can shape and form courtyards between the buildings, outdoor rooms that frame views towards the buildings as well as out to the site. An entrance can be signified through this design and pedestrian areas can be defined and separated out from vehicular traffic. Understanding the various paths through the building—from how the paper gets sent from one building to the next, to how people work or tour the facility—is of great importance in shaping this plant.

Rethinking transportation needs and traffic flows will be critical so that we do not accept the car/truck as a given and allow it to overpower the character of the place as a trucking thoroughfare surrounded by a parking lot. All too often the physical size of the transport infrastructure overwhelms all else. Instead the roadways should be closely studied so that they are efficient but not overwhelming to the plan. Careful separation of truck routing and pedestrian traffic flow should not only create more human scaled spaces, but should prove to be more efficient for the facility.

The goal is not to reinvent how each building functions but to possibly rethink the planned assumed shape and traffic flows of the recycling facility, working very closely with the papermaking process and meeting its needs and requirements. But, as opposed to jumping to architectural conclusions with standardized solutions for the simplest shed construction or parking and roadway locations, we should question if there is not a better approach that would be as efficient but more site sensitive and humane.

The buildings in their material usages, their method of construction and their functioning (energy usage and waste output) should be state of the art in terms of environmental sustainability. The fact that the center is a factory more than an office building will give us certain opportunities to experiment with less high energy/hvac requirements. Wherever possible, I would like to rethink when we need to heat or cool a building to its maximum—I think the opportunity to save energy and still create a comfortable work environment is crucially important in the design of this project. Daylighting can also be utilized since all of these structures are, for the most part, single story buildings. Skylights can be incorporated that will not only reduce the amount of lighting required, but can also make the interiors wonderful spaces to work in.

The Bronx recycling center should be about interconnectedness, creating a place in which people can come and learn not only about paper recycling, but about how we can successfully integrate a building within its site, create a natural water treatment marsh that surrounds and becomes a part of it, redefine the idea of a factory as being not removed from the community but a part of it, and rework the relationship between pedestrian and vehicular traffic. In so doing, we can create a place that begins to redefine the relationship between man and the environment.

The Site

The siting at the waterfront, along with the amount of water needed to produce paper, leads me to emphasize water in the design. The opportunity to utilize the use of water in the design should not be overlooked. In both its fluid state as an element people pass by and as a waste treatment marsh or in the form of fog/steam for the energy to run the plant, I think the use of water will give the project a strong sense of what this place can be about—recycling, the life cycle—the natural cycle of replenishing resources.

Again, the goal of the buildings both in their material usages, their method of construction and their functioning-energy usage and waste output should be state of the art in terms of environmental sustainability. I think the opportunity to save energy and still create a comfortable work environment is crucially important in the design of this project.

Program Elements

The Buildings

We must study the buildings both individually and as a group, and develop each building so that it is an efficient component of the larger whole. My interest is not in reinventing the wheel—or determining to any degree how to reinvent the inner workings of a paper plant—but to be familiar enough to possibly intervene aesthetically in their general shaping. My focus will be on optimizing traffic flows, increasing natural daylighting, decreasing sound levels, creating spaces that are warmer, easier to work in—understanding that we are basically working with a factory, not an office type, and studying the factory type to optimize its potential. Taking advantage, for instance, of the conditions at hand, the temperature in such a structure is normally subject to exterior conditions due to the large open areas that need to be left open for deliveries and pickups of the materials—this could work to our advantage to create temperature zones that are more energy efficient by configuring the building to take into account the different functions within each building and separating out parts within each structure.

Paths through the Facility

- the path people take
- the path vehicles take
- the path the paper takes
- the path the water takes

These paths need to be charted and carefully interconnected to create, in the end, a place in which people can come and learn not only about paper recycling, but about how we can successfully integrate a building within its site, how we can address the relationship between pedestrian and vehicular, and where we can redefine a working factory to become a place.

Traffic Flow

Probably one of the most important aspects of this design will be to allow for maximum efficiency of the paper plant yet not to let the roadways, parking facilities, and shipping routes completely overwhelm and dictate the atmosphere surrounding this plant. We will create two simultaneous traffic flows—one for vehicular and one for pedestrian—understanding that within each group subsets exist:

1) everyday shipping and receiving of trucks
2) visitors coming to the plant
3) workers, day-to-day
4) visitors to the site

The goal is to address the issue of the car/truck, yet not let it become the driving force that dictates the planning and character of the space. Once you allow the vehicular paths to dictate the architectural configurations you have sacrificed the pedestrian to the vehicular.

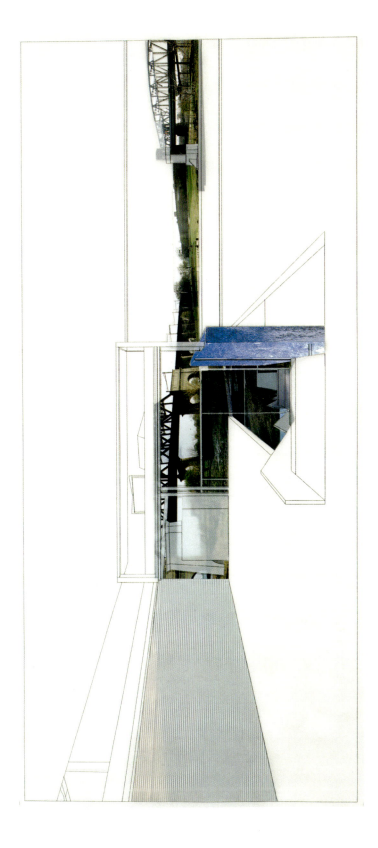

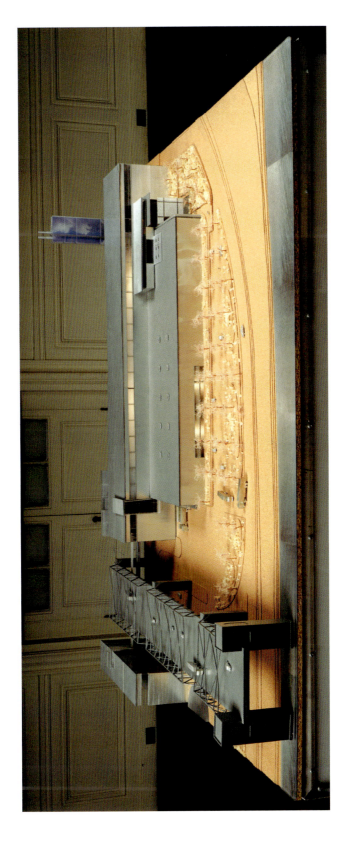

5. Clearing the Social Market

> Hunger can make a man do evil
> just as much as money can.
>
> —Graham Greene

IN ORDER FOR an industrial-development project to obtain a site, permits, and financing; get built; and successfully operate, it must satisfy two market forces: (1) Financial-market forces and (2) social-market forces. In chapter 4, I discussed some of the numerous financial-market forces—the technical, financial, and economic issues—that confront industrial developers at urban brownfields. Less frequently discussed by industrial ecologists are the social-market hurdles that any sustainable industrial-development project must clear as well. These social, political, and cultural forces are powerful development barriers at urban brownfields and, again, they tend to be less potent at rural greenfields.

These are some of the social-market obstacles that can interfere with any sustainable urban industrial-ecology development:

- Existing businesses benefiting from the status quo use their political and market influence to sabotage the development of a new, potentially competing project.

- Community groups fighting over turf can bring their conflict to bear on the project's development activities.

- Accommodating the political needs of local community boards may enhance democratic opportunities for public oversight but, from the perspective of an industrial developer and financiers, adds time and complications.

- Frequently changing political winds make it more complex to develop an industrial project in more politically competitive urban areas.

- In urban areas some construction companies try to litigate their way into large multimillion-dollar projects.

- Union rules and biases, construction-company problems with unions, and antagonism toward unions by unorganized laborers add delays, costs, and public-relations problems to projects being developed in the union environments more typically found in urban areas.

- Different worldviews and differences in anticipated rewards based on the disparate skills and resources brought to a project's collaboration may cause stress within the development coalition.

- The traditional players in the industrial-development world are not enthusiastic about participation by environmentalists or community interests.

UNDERSTANDING THE SOCIAL FORCES SHAPING MARKET POSSIBILITIES

It is a truism that politics is not rational. And while industrial decision making, attuned to the bottom line, may be more rational at the economic level of the firm, such decision making is very often irrational at the larger ecological and societal levels. Nor are industrial decisions immune from irrational factors like personal sentiment and ego gratification. Thus, the quick-return, ecologically inconsiderate, self-interested, irrational influence of individual and group psychological factors on political and economic decision making must be anticipated and factored into a development project's strategic planning. Social issues—status-seeking consumption; political ideology; and ethnic, racial, and class-based animosity—affect all commercial activities, including industrial development.

The cause and nature of some of these social obstacles to industrial development—some are imposed by community groups, some by elected officials, some by faceless bureaucrats, some by unions, some by self-interested development hustlers who pass themselves off as community-spirited activists—have intimidated many progressive observers into not publicly discussing these very real barriers to sustainable development. Some of these social obstacles are prompted by political interests historically and ideologically embraced by reformers. In fact, one prominent green developer with whom I have worked urged me not to discuss barriers to sustainability caused by unions in this book. When I wrote him to ask that he list the union regulations that impose obstacles on sustainable industrial developments, he responded, "It's a long story, but being anti-union in the press is not wise." I know he knows of such obstacles—he's a seasoned developer, and we've confronted some of these obstacles together and discussed them privately during many of our lengthy chats together—but he refused to discuss them for attribution. If sustainability advocates feel they can't openly discuss any particular barrier to sustainable development out of a fear that we might be viewed as being out of sync with a prevailing ideology, we certainly have less of a chance of figuring out how to overcome that barrier. Our obligation to future generations requires that we openly discuss all barriers to sustainability.

Investors in industrial projects, like all investors, have a keen interest in seeing their project become operational and revenue generating as rapidly as possible. The financial hurdles that characterize urban-brownfield rehabilitation, described in the previous chapter, make realizing this investor objective more complicated. Compounding the effect of adverse financial and technical barriers with added social-market barriers makes it apparent why industrial-ecology investments at urban brownfields are so rare.

Although it is true that social forces generally complicate the process of navigating the market forces affecting an industrial development, they can also help advance the development of an industrial plant. The way to achieve this is by creating the proper type of project collaborations that are needed to boost industrial developments. For example, to get a project started, the NGO participants in the collaboration—community groups and environmentalists—can generate political and philanthropic support for the project. This support can help obtain funding for the higher-risk, hard-to-finance, early-development stage of the project. Usually this type of government and philanthropic funding is available to NGOs only, not to for-profit corporations. In turn, this funding and political support can then be used to pay for work to be performed by the for-profit sector, like site evaluations, initial engineering and design work, preliminary legal work, financial assessments, and obtaining environmental permits.

Nevertheless, on balance, the bevy of social and political obstacles that often emerge in urban areas make maneuvering through the higher-cost environment endemic to urban-brownfield sites more politically complex and, hence, more financially risky than greenfield development. Unless these obstacles are properly anticipated, carefully attended to, and strategically managed, opposition to the project can emerge that might derail it, however irrational these obstacles might seem from the perspective of industrial ecology.

THE CHALLENGE FROM EXISTING BUSINESSES

Although the intentions of NGO developers—environmentalists and community groups—are likely to be to advance socially and environmentally valuable industrial-ecology models, many other interests in the community are likely to view such projects in a less public-spirited light. Good intentions do not elevate us above the ruthlessness of business as usual. Existing business and political interests will view an industrial-ecology–development effort either supportively, competitively, as an opportunity to personally acquire financial or political rewards, or even as an opportunity to express personal or ideological resentments.

Obviously, any new business coming to town is likely to benefit some commercial interests and threaten others. For example, all urban areas, in the developed and developing world alike, host some type of an infrastructure—government, private sector, or scavengers—that one way or another collects and processes recyclable wastepaper, other recyclable materials, and wastes. In New York City, for example, where wastepaper management is a very big and competitive business—wastepaper being among the city's top three exports—that existing commercial infrastructure involves tens of millions of dollars of investments owned by multibillion-dollar recycling and waste-related businesses. If New York City would have shipped its collected wastepaper directly to the Bronx recycled-paper mill, the commercial processors now managing wastepaper might have been cut out of the lucrative local wastepaper-processing business. The firms processing New York City's wastepaper understandably lobbied the mayor's office aggressively not to support the BCPC's development. Former city and state government officials working for these firms lobbied their contacts and former colleagues in government against our project. Other important government officials, some already predisposed to disliking environmentalists, some hoping for a post-government job with waste-hauling firms, gave them more than a little assistance and encouragement. So did certain interests in New York City's financial community, whose banking and securities firms serve the powerful interests of the virgin-based forest-products industry.

Nor was it just the local waste haulers and the paper-processing industry that tried to stop our mill. Other sectors of the paper industry— including paper brokers and out-of-state, typically Canadian, mill operators whose newsprint market included New York City—also tried to prevent the BCPC from succeeding, out of a concern about what the mill would do to their existing market relationships. One New York City–based wastepaper broker convinced a potential paper-company operator and investor, to whom he was selling wastepaper collected in New York City, not to continue working with us. Tellingly, that same wastepaper broker then contacted me, offering to bring in another paper-company investor to operate the mill, if *he* could participate in the project as the wastepaper broker and marketer of the product. Such are the ruthlessly competitive—and often ethically suspect—ways of business. Similarly, a CEO of a large Canadian paper company that shipped virgin newsprint into New York City, precisely the market with which our mill was designed to compete, called me at home one evening and told me "Allen, I don't want to see your mill happen, but if it does happen, I want to run it." Indeed, most of the interest in our BCPC mill by paper companies seemed to me to be defensive: They obviously weren't in it to

advance industrial ecology or to broaden the availability of environmentally superior products in the market but rather to protect their market
position. So, although it is true that environmentalists must mix more
substantially with business leaders to advance sustainable-ecology objectives, NGO participants in an industrial-ecology collaboration should
always be attentive to the fact that less-than-collegial—and less-than-
ecologically-rational—competitive behavior characterizes most business
relationships.

THE DIFFICULTIES OF WORKING WITH COMMUNITY GROUPS

It is an understated fact that community groups, like their counterparts in
the for-profit world, fight vigorously over turf. Ignoring this reality, pretending that all public-interest institutions and the people working for
them don't suffer from their own ego-driven, competitive, and self-
interested needs, can only lead to frustration and failure. Obviously, that
doesn't mean there aren't strong, civic-minded groups. But it is naïve to presume that officials at all community groups, by virtue of their oft-stated
public-interest objectives and not-for-profit status, always have the public
interest foremost at heart and that they will always work collaboratively to
advance the best interests of their community, above all else. Alas, this is not
a new insight: As Victor Hugo wrote 140 years ago, "The ostensible purpose of the ABC Society was the education of children, but its real purpose
was the elevation of men."[1]

In many cities there are intense rivalries among community groups
that can and do displace their professional objective of community development. I've seen it up close in, among other areas, New York City,
Chicago, and Central America. Sadly, I have seen representatives of community groups hurl unsubstantiated technical and personal attacks on the
personnel and priorities of other community groups. While developing
the BCPC I had the disheartening experience of seeing competing community interests fabricate dire public-health and political-corruption
charges and circulate this misinformation throughout the community
and to the media. I've run across community activists who have requested
and accepted money—sometimes under the guise of a consulting con-

tract—from developers of environmentally and socially destructive projects, and in exchange have offered their support. In an economically disadvantaged community, where so many real risks deserve attention, and economic development is so essential, these local activists can play a pivotal role by raising anxieties about fabricated, illusory impacts or, more helpfully, by addressing fears about real ones.

Although I prefer to spare the reader the unpleasant details—and spare myself the demeaning experience of having to recount them—I have seen people who label themselves community activists physically intimidate and verbally abuse, in the most ugly, aggressive language, people with whom they disagreed or from whom they personally wanted some project-related benefit. I myself experienced physical intimidation, ethnic slurs, requests for payment, and abusive language from both women and men professing to be community-oriented grassroots environmental reformers. We in the BCPC project were accused of being racists or shills for corporations. These epithets were thrown by individuals—admittedly, by only three or four people, but they were situated well enough in the activist community to be noticed—who all let me know, privately or in otherwise very clear terms, that for a certain amount of money paid to them, or a lucrative "consulting" contract, they would turn around and rally community support for my project. One person who claimed to head a local group, and whose request for seventy thousand dollars from me—to "take care of the problems" her group was planning to cause our project—was rejected, wound up turning from a project supporter to claiming at a public hearing that building the BCPC would "violate the Universal Declaration of Human Rights and the United Nations Convention on the Elimination of Genocide [sic]."[2] Eric Halphen, the celebrated French prosecutor, once opined "Racism is worse than corruption."[3] During the time I was involved with the BCPC project, I experienced both, and none of it came from within the for-profit sector.

Sadly, baksheesh—extortion—is all too often a fact of life and a barrier to sustainability in the world of urban development. It can add up to lots of trouble, unpleasant moments, and delays for developers who are unprepared to deal with it. Although I never considered paying off any so-called activists for their support, a number of the business participants in the project thought that giving money to the people making these requests—since they were grossly distorting the facts about the project and were trying to raise public, political, and possibly legal opposition to it—would be a prudent, least-cost thing to do. After all, they reasoned, the project was a half-billion–dollar investment, so why not spend a few hundred thousand to get rid of a few opponents? I suspect that logic is just what the "opponents"—who weren't really project opponents as much as they were project hustlers—were counting on. At the end of the day neither the BCPC team nor any firm affiliated with it paid anything to these interests—our project's guideline, recited mantralike whenever we faced an ethical fork in the road, was "What would pass the *New York Times* front-page test?"—and we still managed to get the project's needed permits and government funding. But the disruption in planning and implementation that these threats imposed made it harder to advance the mill. We blithely never expected opposition of any kind to arise against a project invited into the community by local interests and designed by socially progressive environmentalists. Still, the opposition we did face was minor compared to what it would have been had we not been work-ing in collaboration with a community group.

It is sad but true that very often local politicians do not feel politically or personally strong enough to challenge these deceitful people in public. These are disturbing facts, but they are facts nonetheless. And they stymie ecologically progressive industrial development. None of this comports with the open dialogue and rational exchange of views that sustainable development is thought to require, or the harmonious vision of sustain-able communities that environmentalists seek to inspire. Nor does it fun-damentally alter the fact that collaborating with community interests remains essential for sustainable development to succeed.

THE INTERESTS OF LOCAL POLITICAL LEADERSHIP

Political leadership at the local level is typically quite far from being driven by a concern for advancing ecological sustainability. Besides being indebted to business interests and other political contributors, local politi-cians are invariably affiliated with and supportive of—because they are supported by—particular community groups, and they are less supportive of competing groups. Politicians can try (with the BCPC at least two did this) to alter the composition of the industrial-development team and redirect the distribution of benefits toward their own supporters. When these overtures were rebuffed, one legislator withdrew from actively helping the project while another became an active opponent. This underscores the value of having numerous and diverse community groups participate in any industrial-ecology collaboration rather than just one or two, which are likely to become the envied targets of the intensely competitive behavior that sometimes characterizes relations among these groups.

I recall my surprise when a legislative assistant of a local state senator called me out of the blue one afternoon and said that if we were willing to replace the BCPC's community-group partner—the Banana Kelly Community Improvement Association—with a community group of her legislator's choice, she could make sure that the group threatening to give us trouble, for reasons having to do with turf and anticipated financial rewards, would back off. Although millions in revenue and local investments were going to result from our project and hundreds of permanent jobs were going to be generated, and despite the ecological and public-health benefits that the community anticipated from the BCPC, the project-development team was being pressured by so-called community interests in a less-than-community-spirited kind of way. And very unfortunately, the leadership at the community group we did partner up with turned out to be no less competitive with other community interests, refusing to share the project's upside potential outside the sphere of their own affiliated neighborhood interests.

The same type of political calculation applies to working with local community boards. Where they exist, community boards have been designed to strengthen local-input on development proposals and other community matters. Elected political officials appoint members of local community boards—which are typically nonexistent in the rural areas where greenfield mills are located—and these members also tend to be aligned with the interests of particular individuals, local businesses, and community groups. Choosing the "wrong" partner among any of these interests can cause a problem for a development effort with the local community board, as I learned firsthand. Little did I know that the community-development corporation we partnered with for the BCPC was not the first choice of the community board within whose jurisdiction we were working. The board sometimes deployed adolescent tactics to show that choosing the wrong community group could make life unproductive for our project. Sometimes BCPC colleagues or I were called by the district manager of the community board to come to a meeting, only to show up and be told the meeting was canceled. Sometimes we were called to come to a meeting by the district manager of the board, only to find when we arrived that no one from the community board showed up because no one had been told of the need for a meeting. Sometimes we were asked why we didn't show up for a meeting we had never been informed about.

This situation did not inspire confidence in the for-profit interests whom we were trying to convince (incorrectly) that the South Bronx was no less favorable a development climate than any greenfield area. Since local community boards are influential during the environmental-permitting process and with local politicians who might be asked to offer their opinion on a development grant from a city or state agency, running afoul of the local community board can cause problems. While most community boards are legally upstanding and politically healthy vehicles for democratic processes, the local community board the BCPC project faced in the South Bronx had a notorious reputation for ego-driven conflicts, biased political allegiances, and favoritism. That, I believe, is one of the reasons investment interests avoid the area. In general, whether or not one runs afoul of the local community board, just having to deal with the board, however useful it might be from the perspective of gaining community input, is another hurdle not faced by developers of greenfield projects in rural areas.

The BCPC's Struggles with Politicians

I would not be the first to observe that some political leaders are almost pathologically motivated by the need to have their ego massaged. And as one moves up the political ladder, this only becomes more true. It is critical to recognize this and pay obeisance to it—otherwise some of the political and administrative hurdles a large industrial development project will face, especially in an urban area, can become much more burdensome to resolve. Every industrial-development project needs someone on the team who can stomach the sycophantic flattery demanded by certain elected officials and influential bureaucrats. Indeed, an entire industry exists to service this type of work. Alas, as a technically oriented rationalist, I evinced a profound distaste and an innate ineptitude for this required skill and, I was told, the BCPC project suffered because of it. Given that the political base of many politicians is aligned with specific community-group interests, some local political leaders may see affiliating with the "wrong" community-group partner as a fatal affront. Someone must be there to soothe these ruffled egos. Ego-driven personalities always emphasize what someone has done wrong and the importance of their own position. They ask, "What can you do for me?"

I was told in no uncertain terms that as far as Bronx Borough President Fernando Ferrer was concerned, I had no right to choose the community-group partner for participation in the BCPC, even though we accepted an invitation from that group to collaborate on our industrial-development venture and did not go out and "choose" the community stakeholder. The now-former-borough president—who fancies himself a progressive reformer—made it clear to me that when it came to development projects and community groups that might benefit from development projects, he was the decision maker, he chose the group, and if he didn't, he wouldn't support it, regardless of its merits. Without his own handpicked community-development allies in the game, he did not actively support our efforts to obtain permits. More important, through his appointees to the federal New York City Empowerment Zone Board for the Bronx, he effectively made it impossible for our project to acquire any of the $300 million in economic-incentive funding available from the New York City Federal Empowerment Zone, even though our project was the largest, indeed the only, manufacturing plant slated to be located in that impoverished, job-needy zone. Clearly, it was more difficult to make investors and potential paper-company operators comfortable with the idea of working in the Bronx, a location paper mills have never settled into, with the borough president's office cool to the project. This was made even more complicated by the fact that some senior officials at our community-group partner, Banana Kelly, turned out to be themselves vigorously driven by self-interest and the need to control turf. As the project became very real, they wouldn't agree to share any of the potential rewards it might offer with the broader coalition of community interests we wanted to work with, however much it would simplify our project-development work, and however much it would more broadly and effectively benefit the community.

In rural communities, as opposed to urban areas, there are often less diverse social and political complexities requiring accommodation with a development project. There tends to be less political competition for the economic spoils in rural areas, and rural areas "benefit" from—from an industrial developer's point of view—the political consistency characteristic of fewer electoral turnovers. This lower-risk situation adds the benefit of predictability to industrial-development projects and is less characteristic of more politically competitive urban areas.

Being more politically competitive, urban areas present industrial developers with the specter of more frequent changes of elected officials and administrative appointees. When I first launched the development of the BCPC in 1992, New York State's governor was Mario Cuomo, with whose office, agencies, and commissioners we began to develop a working relationship. Less than two years later, George Pataki defeated Governor Cuomo, so we had to get to know and develop working relationships with his new team. Locally, Rudolph Giuliani, whose team we then had to get to know, defeated New York City's mayor, David Dinkins, with whom we had been also working for almost two years. As a result of these political changes, the BCPC project had to accommodate and negotiate with three different Sanitation Department commissioners, four different presidents of the city's Economic Development Corporation, two different commissioners for both the city and state departments of environmental protection, and two different state economic-development commissioners. Added to this political mosaic was the fact that when *local* political competitors felt they were being outmaneuvered for the project's anticipated spoils, *federal*-level politicians, including members of Congress, were dragged into the struggle over potential spoils, as were members of the local City Council, the State Assembly, the State Senate, and the local community board.

All of these political realignments and obligations engendered unending strategic revaluations and plagued the project with time-consuming reexplanations related to technical and market issues and politically driven reevaluations of negotiations on technical and financial matters that we had considered complete. Under Mayor Giuliani, the project had to hire lobbyists—and only certain ones were persona grata with him—to get access to his staff, because the mayor's interests were overwhelmingly motivated by the interests of his close personal friends and political supporters and, alas, his political ego. Ultimately the mayor behaved as though our project were aligned with the political machine in the Bronx that opposed him—though of course it wasn't. As just discussed, the BCPC was not being actively supported by Bronx Borough President Fernando Ferrer. But the mayor's perception that because the BCPC was located in the Bronx it would offer political benefits to the Bronx borough president was enough to discourage his support. As it turns out, there was much about the nature of the BCPC team—and the competition we presented to the waste-hauling firms that financially supported the mayor and some of his advisers—that displeased some of Mayor Giuliani's aides but appealed to others. And there was much about the nature of the BCPC team that warmed the heart of some of Governor Pataki's advisers but antagonized others. All this made for more uncertainty about whether the project would get what it needed from the state or the city—wastepaper, cleaned sewage water, tax-exempt financing, cooperation from various agencies during construction, grants, and subsidies—which is an intimidating uncertainty that projects in rural areas don't struggle with as much.

LITIGATION INTIMIDATION FROM CONSTRUCTION COMPANIES

Sometimes construction companies in urban areas may try to litigate their way into a large multimillion-dollar project. I know this from direct experience. This more refined and rarely discussed form of extortion originates from competing construction or other business firms who want "a piece of the action." The type of industrial-ecology projects we need to develop to alleviate global ecological problems need to be large, both to provide a meaningful market-scale alternative to destructive ecological practices and to maximize a factory's resource productivity in the context of global competition. It is not every day that a large—let's say, half-billion-dollar—construction project comes to town (even in a place like New York City, which is used to big ventures), and the competition to get the contract to design and build the project, supply equipment to it, and do the legal work related to issuing its bonds and financing is always intense. Industrial ecologists and advocates for sustainability rarely factor these influential struggles into their considerations of the barriers they face. (Never in my life was I offered more lunches in posh restaurants, more tickets to the World Series, the U.S. Open, the Knicks, and the Rangers than when I coordinated who would be eligible to sell services to the BCPC project. When I accepted, I very much enjoyed giving the tickets to NRDC's unsuspecting mail-room staff. I just loved the look on their faces after I handed them free and up-close corporate box seats to the World Series at Yankee Stadium. And never was I asked to contribute to so many political campaigns, which I never did.)

Sometimes a construction firm that doesn't win the contract straightaway from the development group will launch a lawsuit against the developer and the construction firm that did win the bidding, or against others involved with the development group—or against both, as happened during the BCPC project—claiming that some role in the project was previously promised and that they were left out of the deal was a violation of some previous agreement. (Based on my review of a list of court cases related to a construction company known for this kind of intimidation, it occurs more frequently than one might suspect.) The disgruntled construction firm litigates to get a cut of the business. Although the firm will usually litigate for a huge amount, perhaps the right to build the entire project, it may settle for a "small" portion of the contract. However, even a 10 percent contract slice on a $600 million industrial project amounts to a whopping $60 million construction contract, which is well worth the $100,000 or so in legal costs a construction firm might have to invest to get the development group or the winning construction company to settle out of court to allow things to move along. Or, if no out-of-court settlement is reached, a judge could decide to allocate a "small" 10 percent slice of the project to the losing firm. In any case, this type of commercial lawsuit is not unheard of in cities, and it plagues industrial development—and perhaps other large-scale development—in urban areas. This risk makes an industrial firm more reluctant to build a new, more ecologically efficient mill and instead encourages mergers that result in acquiring existing, inefficient mills. Moreover, it can also put a chill on the willingness—and ability—of NGOs to participate in industrial-ecology collaborations, since most NGOs have relatively small budgets compared with the amount that such a large lawsuit against them, as a project participant, might seek to recover.

THE IMPEDIMENTS THAT COLOR DEALING WITH UNIONS

Besides the high price of union wages in urban areas—as compared with labor rates in rural areas, which I discussed in chapter 4—union rules and biases, and construction-company and community problems with unions, can also add delays, costs, and public-relations problems to projects being developed in the union environments more typically found in urban areas. In the same way that reformers are inclined to assume that virtually all community groups can be relied upon to do no evil when it comes to local economic development, political progressives—myself included—often harbor a bias that makes us reflexively support unions. Many of us believe the enormous, socially and ecologically unconcerned concentrated power that characterizes industrial-capital interests must be countered by organized labor to reduce the exploitative relationships industrial-capital interests will invariably pursue. The approach taken by unions to respond to corporate power, though, has too often been limited to raising wages and increasing work-rule protections. While these benefits are extremely valuable in protecting union members from exploitative industrial forces, unions have structured these safeguards in such a way that they have become huge impediments to more sustainable industrial progress.

Currently, high construction-wage rates and work rules in urban areas, as previously mentioned, make it difficult to competitively build industrial-ecology projects where they are most needed. Thus, construction workers lose out on the potential work, the community loses the opportunity to expand its jobs, and the environment suffers, because environmentally destructive factories are able to remain in operation without more efficient, environmentally superior competition. However, if union employees were given a financial, equity stake in the project's outcome—as so many senior corporate officials routinely get as incentives to fuel their company's growth—some of the work rules that understandably protect workers but nevertheless plague construction projects in urban areas might fall away. Perhaps unionized construction workers would choose to receive ownership benefits, such as annuity dividends or stock options, in exchange for keeping their wage rates and work rules more competitive with those of rural mills. In fact, many of the interests that receive the greatest return from an industrial development—financiers, developers, and operators—routinely defer their return until the project is up and running. They then get enormous returns that dwarf the wages offered to workers who build the project. Why shouldn't workers who build the project be offered the same lucrative option? Instead of being an obstacle to sustainable development, unionized workers might partner with—indeed, they should develop partnerships with—environmentalists and community interests to develop and *own* industrial-ecology projects and profit handsomely from them.

I argued that the BCPC explore such a worker-owned approach but, as I wasn't the project's owner (early in the BCPC's development I mistakenly ceded complete ownership to our community-group partner, Banana Kelly), my voice in behalf of this innovative cost-containment approach had little influence with investors, *with our community-group partner, and with unions.* It was dismissed as unworkable by the unions, too generous by the community group that wanted to protect its spoils, and too "radical" by the financiers, though I saw nothing radical about it: To me it seemed like a sensible cost-containment strategy.

Most industrial developers have little appreciation of the need for unions or their essential, historic value and, in fact, seek to avoid unions wherever they can. The higher construction and materials-acquisition costs unions impose makes developers' aversion to them seem justified. And unions' traditional insensitivity to ecological needs has alienated many of their potential supporters in the progressive environmental movement. Ultimately, if urban industrial-ecology developments are to succeed at the large scale needed to save the planet, unions must be brought into the movement to develop sustainable industrial investments and, like their counterparts in the environmental and community-development world, they must take on a greater degree of ownership. But that will happen only if union leaders are inclined to negotiate in favor of this type of role and if workers themselves are willing to restructure *some* of their financial returns to benefit industrial-ecology developments at urban brownfields—rather than penalize these projects, as they do now. Although it is possible that union pension funds might get invested into projects that use union labor, as a way of encouraging such projects to proceed, this beneficial approach to industrial development has rarely been used in any meaningful way that has given workers more control; thus, union management may not be receptive to it. I vividly recall the cold meeting my BCPC financial colleagues and I had with the union staff overseeing the AFL-CIO pension funds, where we discussed using union investments to offset higher labor rates and increase equity for the workers in the project. It became clear almost immediately that I wasn't meeting with progressive union organizers—much less ecologically sensitive progressives—but, instead, with very conservative bankers seeking the lowest-risk, highest-possible return in the shortest time frame. The ecological and progressive nature of the project had zero bearing on these stewards of union funds consideration to invest in it.

Important attempts have been made in recent years to try and bridge the gap between union labor and environmental objectives, but the sad fact is that, more often than not, unions still cannot be counted on for their commitment to environmental policies—just look at the short-sighted union support for oil drilling in the Arctic National Wildlife Refuge or union opposition to even modest enhancements in automobile fuel-efficiency standards. Making matters worse, because of the barriers to sustainability that unions impose, their seemingly inflexible attitude about these barriers, and their opposition to progressive environmental policies, many environmentally oriented business interests—and some community groups—have become quite hostile to unions. (I discovered, much to my chagrin, that our community-group collaborator was perhaps the most anti-union of all the BCPC participants. This was because, in trying to develop or rehabilitate affordable housing units, Banana Kelly had had a history of battles over high-cost construction-union wages and work rules.)

DEALING WITH THE CULTURE OF BUSINESS

Different worldviews and the disparate skills, resources, and expectations brought to a project's collaboration will cause stress within the coalition brought together to develop a world-scale industrial-ecology project. This complication must be anticipated and overcome, because those who try to develop an industrial project without collaborating with diverse interests are less likely to incorporate ecological considerations and community-development objectives. From the perspective of self-interested corporate developers accustomed to being autonomously in charge of their own destiny, developing an industrial facility without getting involved with environmentalists and community activists is a more attractive, familiar, and less complicated approach. There is a reason for this: Maintaining successful collaborations requires enormous personal energy, diplomatic skills, knowledge about—or a willingness to learn about—diverse issues outside one's field of expertise, and a more inclusive worldview. Few people share these extraordinary traits, whether they work in either the for-profit or the NGO world.

Obviously, individuals who commit their professional careers to environmental reform and community development have different worldviews than do those who have committed their careers to accumulating wealth in the for-profit corporate sector. While most of those in the NGO world authentically tend to emphasize humanistic, environmental, and social considerations—though some are less public spirited and more ego driven than being in the not-for-profit field might suggest—participants from the for-profit sector will tend to emphasize exploitation of market opportunities, fast-track profitability, and cost-cutting options. For an industrial ecology project to succeed—indeed, for sustainable communities to be established and prosper and for the ecological health of the planet to be saved—the resources and worldviews of both sectors are needed. But once corporate industrial-development personnel are brought into the picture and financing the project becomes the paramount concern, many of the project's original objectives, the very objectives that may have helped it obtain its initial development funding from government grants or philanthropic sources, may become secondary to the objective of getting the deal financed. Individuals—especially those from the NGO sector—who may have contributed critical assistance early on in the life of the project, assistance without which the project may never have gotten its early political support, development funding, or environmental permits, become much less necessary (hence, less influential) as the deal advances.

Industrial-development projects, including ecologically beneficial ones, are first and foremost business deals. Consequently, relationships among the participants are characterized very much by a "What have you done for me lately?" atmosphere, and it is not at all uncommon to see the people who are very important to getting the deal finished trying to compromise the interests and cut out the rewards of those who were essential for getting the project launched. There is even a term in the financial world for this routine behavior: *cram-down*. For not-for-profit participants less driven by financial gain, who are more likely to be loyal and equitably reward those who provide essential early assistance, the "What have you done for me lately?" approach is likely to seem abhorrent. But to businesspeople in the for-profit world it is a routine way of life.

Of course, it is critical to remember that no sector has a monopoly on virtue: In the case of the BCPC, officials working for our community-group partner behaved, in my view, in a most disloyal manner toward the other participants in the project. What's more, I believe that, as much as any other single factor, the self-interested, shortsighted behavior of our community-group partner's senior executives, which was reported prominently in the local newspapers, ultimately caused the demise of the BCPC project.

Obviously, each collaborator in an industrial-ecology project brings different experiences, skills, and strengths to the table. While this is one of the obvious virtues of collaboration, it is also one of the reasons collaborations are stressful and difficult to maintain. I have often referred to the existence of experience gaps and information gaps that made managing the BCPC's project collaboration unduly complicated. There are also less frequently discussed and underappreciated cultural barriers[4] to sustainable development; thus, the standard way of evaluating and doing things in business makes harmonious, empathetic collaboration—perhaps more essential an attribute than any other for sustainability to succeed—almost impossible to achieve. Consequently, I often saw my role in the project as a cultural broker, trying to get the diverse interests in the

BCPC collaboration to understand one another's needs and smoothly work together. It is hard to explain to industrial developers in the for-profit sector why ecological and community-development concerns must be respected. And it is hard to get NGO participants to accept that a 15 percent or 20 percent return on investment isn't good enough, because higher returns are available to investors in other countries or other industries.

For instance, however obvious it may seem that beautiful buildings are more warmly welcomed in communities than ugly industrial boxes, it actually required enormous and frequent efforts to explain to the BCPC's for-profit participants why I insisted on having Maya Lin, one of the world's greatest public-space artists, design the mill. These corporate officials opposed Lin's participation even after she assured them her design would not increase the project's cost. Most corporate officials have spent their entire careers learning how to ignore the aesthetic potential or the social implications of their work, sometimes even ignoring basic human needs. Instead, they have psychologically trained themselves—consciously or otherwise—to separate out the anti-social, sometimes horrific consequences of their industrial business life from what they know is right and wrong in their personal life.[5] Countless times during my work on the BCPC project, as I tried to engage the humanistic side of the business-people on my team, I was reminded of social observations by Victor Hugo. Most of the time I was drawn to recall his characterization of the businessman Thenardier in *Les Misérables:* "Thenardier had silently withdrawn without saying good night, not wanting to treat with excessive friendliness a person whom he intended to fleece handsomely in the morning."[6] Environmentalists and community-group interests tend to work in behalf of human needs and so in general have less tolerance for this psychological and emotional bifurcation of business life and personal life, refusing to ignore the environmental, social, and ethical downside of what we do, no matter which domain of our life our actions fall into.

While corporate officials tend to have little patience for incorporating environmental and social goals into their agenda, they similarly have little inclination or need to train environmentalists or community activists in the realistic—what some would call ruthless—ways of industrial finance, construction and engineering, marketing, and global competition. Thus, while collaborations are essential to successfully develop a world-class industrial-ecology project, they are complicated to assemble and maintain.

OLD-GUARD RESISTANCE TO
ENVIRONMENTALISTS IN BUSINESS

Many traditional players in the development world are not enthusiastic about participation by environmentalists. Public rhetoric notwithstanding, the government, corporate, and financial officials typically involved in industrial-development projects have a long-standing, well-entrenched bias against environmentalists getting involved in development deals. Admittedly, environmentalists have rarely tried to assist industrial development, so this resistance is to be expected. Most industrial activities and economic incentives have worked against sustainable practices for centuries, so it should come as no surprise that environmentalists have historically opposed corporate investments and operations. Nor should it come as a surprise that regulatory approaches and the worldview held by government and corporate officials implementing and complying with regulations also do not comport with sustainable practices.

Some environmentalists may have logically decided, as I have, that for strategic reasons the time has come to help facilitate certain types of industrial development, but that doesn't mean we will get a warm welcome from entrenched development interests. Nor does it mean that the broader community of environmental NGOs will breezily embrace this more collaborative approach. Because environmental organizations have a history of opposing industrial-development projects, they are likely to have clashed in the past with some of the very same government officials or institutions with whom they will have to deal to advance an industrial-ecology project. These government officials will not easily forget those past battles. Nor should we: The fact that there were—and remain—such battles suggests that the regulator we may now be willing to work with has in the past facilitated ecologically destructive, nonsustainable practices and may still be willing to do so.

In the case of the BCPC, we were coordinating the project's development at the same time that NRDC was litigating against New York City's

lackadaisical implementation of its recycling law. NRDC was also petition-
ing the U.S. EPA to stop paper companies from using environmentally
harmful chlorine-based bleaching technologies. And NRDC was legally at
odds with New York City's approach toward the protection of its watershed.
Although all these legal interventions were initiated and handled by different NRDC staffers from those of us working on the BCPC, a number of
city and state officials in important positions relating to the BCPC were not
very understanding or tolerant of our multifaceted approach to sustainability. Therefore, at least some of the officials in the Department of Sanitation
who were subject to NRDC lawsuits because they weren't meeting the
requirements of our local recycling law were less than thrilled to be working with any NRDC staff on arranging the paper supply for our mill. And
some, but not all, Department of Environmental Protection officials who
oversaw the city's water system, and who were subject to NRDC action in
behalf of watershed protection, were less than delighted to be working with
NRDC staffers on arranging for water supplies to the BCPC mill.

Even at the *New York Times,* which based on my experience is about as
smart, well mannered, and upstanding a business operation as one could
ever hope to deal with, it took a few meetings before senior corporate officials became comfortable collaborating with NRDC staffers. This is
because we were also part of an activist network that had successfully
stopped clear-cutting of old-growth timber in British Columbia by a
paper company that had happened to be a supplier to the *New York
Times's* western edition; our coalition had publicized that the *Times* was
using that supplier, trying to embarrass the newspaper so it wouldn't buy
newsprint made from those clear-cuts.[7]

Although I see no incompatibility between promoting ecologically
positive, sustainable industrial practices through development collaborations and, at the same time, aggressively litigating to stop ecologically
negative government and industrial behavior—after all, the goal is sustainable ecological health, and there are many strategies needed to attain
that—many in government and industry are less tolerant of a "no permanent friends, no permanent enemies" approach toward environmental
reform. Their wariness is understandable: Working to regulate or litigate
against their firms, and attacking the environmental record of their businesses in the press, is much of what we in the environmental movement

have done during the past thirty years. Most of that criticism against them was valuable and needed, but it would be too much to expect this not to affect our relations. The BCPC team—in particular NRDC staffers—was often subject to hostile government officials who resented that we could maintain such an uncompromising moral high ground, asking for collaboration on our terms while rejecting their (inferior) development objectives in other areas.

Not all regulators and government officials the BCPC team dealt with held this anti-NRDC, anti-environmentalist worldview, but enough of them did to make our project's development progress more complicated, despite the obvious value our project would bring to the city and the state. To me, these officials were potent examples of people who let their egos drive their work at the expense of the public interest: They sought nothing more than personal emotional payback in trying to stymie what we wanted, because in other ecological and economic areas we were in the way of their getting what *they* wanted. And they were an unfortunate complement to the ego-driven, sometimes less-than-upstanding local officials the project had to deal with as well.

Moreover, some government officials, like certain sectors of the population at large, dislike environmental organizations and professional activists in general, regardless of whether they have ever interacted with us. Though their ranks are fewer and fewer with each passing year, there are those who resent environmental groups looking like valuable political forces or economic developers under any circumstances. They hold a business-*uber-alles* approach to life. In my experience it is a sad fact that most people in government and the corporate world do not place a high priority on sustainable industrial behavior, and so they more easily allow personal sentiments, biases, historical antagonisms, and narrowly defined, short-term business objectives to interfere with proposals to collaborate with environmentalists on developing industrial-ecology projects.

CONCLUSION

As just cataloged, a wide range of imposing—yet sometimes nearly invisible—barriers plague the development of sustainable industrial projects at those locations where they would provide the most ecological and social value: Urban brownfields. It's a mistake to think these barriers are only, or even primarily, those related to cleaning up sites or coping with liability issues. In fact, as should by now be clear, those are relatively small, though quite real, parts of the overall cost of any large-scale industrial-redevelopment project. Too often overlooked is the fact that brownfield redevelopment in urban areas takes place in a local social context and much broader global market context. These are rife with challenges that simply don't apply at greenfield sites and with which we have only begun to contend, as environmentalists and as a society. The lesson from this chapter, however, should be clear: We ignore these challenges at our own peril—or, rather, that of our projects, which will almost certainly face an early demise if this resistance is not met adroitly. Finding ways to meet these challenges is the subject of the next chapter and the remainder of this book.

NOTES

1. Victor Hugo, *Les Misérables*, first published 1862, translation copyright: The Folio Society, 1976 (London: Penguin Classics), p. 555.

2. The actual name of the treaty is The Convention on the Prevention and Punishment of the Crime of Genocide. Besides the patently unethical behavior involved, and the absurdity of the charge, that particular allegation was most offensive to me: The Convention on the Prevention and Punishment of the Crime of Genocide was instigated in response to the Nazi concentration-camp atrocities during World War II, and each of my parents and many other relatives of mine spent time in two of the worst of those camps. I refrain from providing the date, place, and nature of hearing where this remark was made to assure that this person cannot be identified.

3. Geoff Winestock, "Unable to Send Candidate To Jail, Halphen Gives Candidate Reluctant Nod." *The Wall Street Journal Europe*, 30 April 2002, p. 1.

4. As far as I can tell, this term, as it is applied to sustainability, was first used by Professor John Ehrenfeld at the Green Goods Conference in Stockholm, 1992. Ehrenfeld, formerly of MIT, is president of the International Society for Industrial Ecology.

5. A petty example, but an example nonetheless, of how pathologically antisocial business environments can be was reported in the *Wall Street Journal* this year when the National Collegiate Athletic Association (NCAA)

basketball tournament—known as March Madness, due to the popular interest it generates—took place. According to the *Journal's* front-page story, "Seedings for the NCAA men's basketball tournament were announced Sunday, but employees of Anchor Glass Container Corp. won't learn about it from computers during work hours. The glass manufacturer uses software . . . to block access from company PCs. 'I measure my success by complaints,' says Dennis Grow, Anchor's technical services manager." Carlos Tejada, "A Special Report About Life On the Job and Trends Taking Shape There," *Wall Street Journal,* 12 March 2002, p. 1.

6. Hugo, *Les Misérables,* p. 371.
7. The *Times* did stop buying newsprint manufactured by the offending company, MacMillan Blodel, but claimed it did so for business reasons, rather than as a response to pressure from environmentalists.

6. Getting Practical: Implementing Industrial Ecology

Care for the environment and the concomitant
need to build a sustainable society is not a fad
but an irreversible necessity.

—Marcel Jeucken

EVERY SITUATION IS DIFFERENT. Some industrial-ecological developers may face obstacles more difficult than what I faced in the Bronx; some may face far simpler ones. I believe, however, that my experience in the Bronx has taught me many useful guidelines for pursuing industrial-ecology projects, regardless of the situation. They constitute a coherent approach to overcoming the barriers—whether social, technical, economic, or political—and can help enable developers to navigate the minefields in the path to building a new kind of industry.

GUIDELINES FOR THE NEW INDUSTRIAL DEVELOPER

The most obvious guideline of sustainable industrial development is, first of all, do no harm. In ecological terms that means, among other things, do not develop projects that will have the net effect of adding greenhouse gases into the atmosphere or that will emit hazardous pollutants, and avoid converting green spaces into industrial and other types of commercial spaces. Clear-cutting a forest, converting it to a plantation, or digging a virgin-ore mine to acquire raw materials converts green spaces, which are supporting biologically diverse habitat, to industrial spaces. Similar ecological burdens are imposed when industrial projects are located at other types of intact green spaces—prairies, meadows, deserts—instead of at brownfields. As long as alternatives, such as relying on recycled secondary raw materials—agricultural wastes, municipal wastes, industrial wastes, commercial wastes, etc.—and locating at formerly used industrial sites, are an option, industrial-ecology projects should avoid turning to virgin resources or green-space locations.

However, I contend that to advance sustainability today, industrial-ecology projects must go further: They must attempt to remedy a known environmental problem, because virtually all industries are currently causing important environmental problems. Not only is this an appropriate goal, it is also a sound basis from which to approach local politicians, whose support is needed to realistically implement any industrial-development project.

I learned firsthand that to get support from both grassroots environmental groups and community-development corporations, and in so doing benefit from the powerful political support they can muster, the developer of an environmentally valuable project must authentically attempt to expand the economic benefits locally, in a politically just fashion. Industrial-ecology projects should not merely create additional wealth for a few individuals, one community group, or a few large corporations. Because livable wages and wealth enhancement are attributes of sustainable communities, industrial-ecology projects must authentically try to spread the wealth-creation potential of the project beyond the typical and narrow beneficiaries of industrial development.

But specifically how can a facility be designed and operated to remedy diverse ecological and social problems? These issues require the embrace of extensive and complex fields of expertise. Based on the day-to-day decisions I had to make about the design and development of the Bronx paper mill, a project intended from its inception to promote sustainability—technologically and socially—I gained both conceptual and pragmatic insights about the industrial-ecology development process. The following are four general guidelines.

Don't Expect to Find Sustainability Engineering Standards

Developing a world-scale industrial-ecology project is complicated by the fact that there are no universally accepted or professionally standardized indicators of sustainability or biodiversity. Nor, to date, is there scientific agreement on how to define, measure, or monitor sustainability or biodiversity. And with very few exceptions—most notably, in the United States, the Green Building Council's Leadership in Energy and Environmental Design (LEED) standards (which are, alas, oriented primarily toward commercial and residential space)—there are no sustainability-driven ecological engineering design and operating standards. (Plus, despite the potential value of the LEED standards, as of this writing less than twenty-five commercial buildings in the world have been certified as meeting it.) The applicable standards have yet to be developed. Most industrial designers and engineers are familiar with the International Organization for Standardization (ISO) management standards. ISO 14000 and 14001 are the specific standards for Environmental Management Systems. Firms that operate in accordance with these operating standards can boast that they operate their production facilities in a safe, efficient, and clean manner, and that they are continuously seeking to identify options to improve their standard operating procedures. To their credit, guidebooks designed to help industrial managers implement ISO standards do briefly touch upon—by mentioning as a concept to think about—the broader, outside-the-facility goals of promoting sustainability, though these guidebooks don't specifically mention any precise approach to do so. Preserving biodiversity, and remedying exploitative, poverty-perpetuating relationships related to the acquisition of raw materials, also needed to advance sustainability, are not mentioned. A basic limit of the ISO approach, viewed from the perspective of promoting sustainable development, is that it doesn't articulate specifically which environmental, social, or operational attributes promote sustainability.

The ISO admirably asks plant managers to "identify environmental aspects . . . that have significant impacts on the environment" but does not identify what is ecologically "significant" and how that "significant impact" might relate to supporting sustainable ecological systems at different scales. ISO guidelines encourage policies to be designed to "control [the] environmental impact of raw material sourcing . . . [and] the impact of new developments" but does not specifically mention avoiding virgin raw materials and greenfields. ISO asks managers to set "objectives and targets . . . [that are] quantifiable" but does not specify what these goals might be.[1] Essentially, the ISO standard properly calls for a commitment to comply with environmental regulations and, to its credit, for an adherence to both upstream and downstream pollution-prevention practices. In fairness, ISO standards certainly offer ecologically committed industrial managers the conceptual incentives and justification to design and implement policies related to the broader, systemic goal of sustainability. However, as I discovered when my colleagues and I set out to design the BCPC mill and its water and raw-material acquisition system, as well as its offtake marketing infrastructure, critical details about how to specifically advance sustainability are missing from ISO guidelines. Moreover, certain industrial processes that are inherently incompatible with sustainable business practices—particular types of synthetic-organic-chemical–manufacturing plants and virgin-timber–based paper mills—can achieve ISO certification. New York City's transit authority is ISO certified, but still operates a fleet of mostly diesel-powered buses, despite the carcinogens diesel fuel is known to generate. The point here is that while ISO certification valuably encourages "clean production" techniques, and asks plant managers to consider reducing upstream (when raw materials are acquired and at the factory) and downstream (during a product's use and when it is disposed of) impacts, it does not qualitatively assess or provide specific guidance about how to do so from the perspective of sustainability. Nor does this certification process consider other attributes related to a sustainable community, such as prioritizing brownfield redevelopment, treating the creation of local jobs as an asset to be nurtured rather than a cost to be cut, and providing workers with social-services supports, like child care and affordable, convenient transportation.

The lack of specificity as to what actually constitutes sustainable practices—ecologically and socially—is largely a result of the fact that few world-scale industrial projects other than the BCPC have incorporated ecological sustainability into a project's initial objectives as seriously as profit making. Essentially, the field of sustainable–industrial-ecology development lacks large-scale experience, and clearly environmentalists lack experience with it; this hampers our understanding of precisely what constitutes sustainable practices. When I set out to develop the BCPC, I purposefully wanted to develop a sustainable industrial enterprise, even though the term was almost as unrefined then as it is now and there were no real-world, large-scale industrial models from which to learn.

Clear the Market

By having to identify and help choose the development team; mill location; political approach; raw materials; energy and water supplies; engineering and construction strategies; chemicals; and approaches to financing, permitting, and other technical attributes that would ultimately define the BCPC, the project development team had to make decisions that would not only advance a concrete real-world definition of sustainability but that would also "clear the market," i.e., be cost competitive, profitable, and socially acceptable. Both market forces confronting industrial development—the financial market and the social market—must be cleared. This is an aspect of sustainability that is rarely discussed: Sustainable manufacturing plants must be financed, built, and operating to be of any ecological or social value. It is not enough to have an innovative technology. Sustainable projects must also be cost competitive: As I've said before, good intentions do not elevate us above the ruthlessness of the market. It was within this real-world, competitive–global-market context that those of us working on the BCPC project were forced to refine our understanding of and approach to both the concept and details that define sustainable industrial development.

Be Prepared to Make Strategic Compromises

Evolving economic and technical adjustments are unavoidable—and beneficial—characteristics of scientific pursuits and all market economies. Perhaps no failing was as decisive in undermining the productivity and efficiency of the post–World War II–era state-owned Eastern European industries as their inability to improvise and innovate in response to changing market, technical, and social conditions. The single strongest feature of successful market-based economies is the rapidity of information transfer they foster—indeed, that they require. Therefore, to competitively respond to the changes open markets perpetually instigate, a willingness to compromise and be flexible must also be part of the approach to sustainability. Unfortunately, the environmental permitting process, discussed in chapter 4, penalizes evolving technical adjustments with legal risks. Also, too often the value of technical adjustments and strategic compromises elicits a charge that progressive principles are being abandoned. Tactical compromise does not mean principles are being forsaken; in fact, it may mean exactly the opposite: Accepting a compromise may reveal so passionate a commitment to making progress that we agree to seize what is achievable at the time, with an eye toward using that step forward to build a better foundation from which to seize more in the future. To truly deliver tangible ecological benefits to the world, environmentalists must emphasize a practical side to idealism. As Emerson said, the "Ideal" is "better," not the illusory unattainable "best." "That Better," he said, "we call the Ideal. . . . The Ideal is the Real."[2] If it is not real, it cannot be ideal, because no one is benefiting. If it is not real, it is only an idea, without tangible improvements. While ideas are obviously essential to help us make sense of the world and define our place in it, ideas cannot, unless implemented, repair ecological damage, alleviate poverty, or feed the hungry.

The industrial market and consumer behavior have been nurtured on centuries of nonsustainable incentives and the nonsustainable industrial practices that have resulted from them. Can we realistically expect to develop a sustainable industrial-ecology project in this still-biased market context without making environmental, social, or technical compromises, or without relying on government or philanthropic assistance? Because barriers to sustainability are still pervasive, sometimes the best technology is truly not affordable or is logistically impossible to execute. Although we may not always be able to incorporate the absolute best design one might think of, a sustainable industrial development should at a minimum always be better—more efficient, less polluting, with fewer biodiversity and climate impacts—than current industrial practices. Plus, vigilant attention to public-health protection, resource conservation, species preservation, and host-community benefits must *all* be considered as objectives of the industrial ecologist.

Technologies are forever being improved, and physical reactions can never be 100 percent efficient. Economic circumstances and technical innovations are ever changing. Consequently, while adhering strictly to the precautionary principle and the scientific facts at hand, we must adopt an open approach in the fight for sustainability, because economic viability and cultural and scientific definitions of the "best" vary by place and over time. As we advance sustainability we need not fear confronting the complications we face due to market variability, economic limits, and technology changes. As long as our aim is right—"Look at the mark, not your arrow," Emerson said[3]—we should in fact welcome some degree of social and scientific uncertainty, as a license to originate innovative environmental and social approaches, as long as the health of the public and other species' habitats are protected.

Echoing the Dalai Lama's teaching that experience refines us,[4] sustainability theorist Tom Schuller wrote that "[v]alues as well as competencies are only truly learnt when they are applied."[5] This is critical to recognize if we are to advance more sustainable practices. According to the National Research Council's Board on Sustainable Development, "[u]ltimately, success in achieving a sustainability transition will be determined not by the possession of knowledge, but by using it."[6] It is essential to bear this in mind as we struggle to identify exactly what sustainable industrial ecology is and what it is not. The fact is that compromises—choosing the "better" option because the "best" option is too costly or is logistically impossible—is part of our evolution toward sustainable development, not a retreat from it. An example of the need to compromise because of economic uncertainty and, hence, evolving technical understanding of just what constitutes sustainable development is offered by Jonathan F. P. Rose, an accomplished "green developer" who, besides assisting me with the BCPC project, has worked throughout the United States on planning and developing environmentally responsive housing and commercial space.

> As a firm, we are committed to building environmentally responsible, or "green" buildings. . . . When specifying materials, we try to find materials manufactured within 400 miles to reduce transportation impacts. We also seek to use materials that come from recycled resources, or that are recyclable, and to use materials that do not off-gas volatile

organic components. However, this always results in trade-offs. For example, linoleum is a natural flooring material, but it must be imported from Italy. Should we use it or not?

We would love to use more sustainably harvested wood, but have not been able to find roof trusses, kitchen cabinets, doors, and other materials made out of certified wood [which is grown and harvested in a more sustainable way]; or if we do find them, they are often custom made on the west coast. These are out of the price range for our projects, particularly affordable housing projects."[7]

Apply the Precautionary Principle

Biologists recognize a phenomenon called emergence. In life, new characteristics and properties emerge at each higher unit of biological activity—known to biologists as integrons—which cannot be predicted merely from an understanding of lower-level components. For example, the behavior of organs cannot be predicted simply by studying their cells, and the behavior of individuals cannot be predicted just by understanding the structure and function of their organs. Populations behave differently than any study of individuals could predict.[8] Emergence helps explain why it is impossible for us to foresee the consequences of our impacts on ecological systems and biodiversity—on the life sciences—with the kind of certainty we've grown to expect from the much more predictable physical sciences. As science writer Carl Zimmer has noted, "Biologists [must] tolerate a level of mystery in their work that would drive your average engineer or computer programmer crazy."[9] The life-sciences concept of emergence urges caution in predicting the consequences of any activity, especially a large industrial activity, that has effects at several ecological levels and that might affect life-sustaining biological phenomena. Examples of industrial projects with uncertain, emergent biological implications abound: dams that flood entire upriver regions; the blanket introduction of genetically modified organisms into the food supply; concentrated developments in wetlands above complex subsurface aquifers; the development of salt refineries in biologically diverse and complex marine environments; and the manufacture of synthetic organic chemicals that cause mutations, cancers, and other major health risks if released into the environment, which invariably happens. The biological phenomenon of emergence—a logistically and intellectually limiting scientific fact—compels environmentalists to argue that industry, regulators, and individuals should adopt the "precautionary principle": In the absence of certainty, actions should be taken that prevent or reduce risks, until and unless those risks, and how to control them, become fully understood with the certainty of the physical sciences. Because of emergence we will always have to be cautious about impacting the environment and also always have to settle for the incrementally better, rather than the best—and ultimately unknowable—behavior.

UNDERSTANDING SYSTEMIC BARRIERS TO SUSTAINABILITY

Making sustainable industrial technologies economically competitive in the face of wide-ranging counterincentives is the conundrum each industrial-ecology–project developer has to solve. To a very substantial degree, the market is currently inhospitable toward sustainable industrial development. Centuries of incentives promoting nonsustainable production and consumption have created powerful market and cultural obstacles. Historically, standard operating procedures in industry, supported by government regulations, bureaucratic rules, and financial subsidies, and supported as well by consumer behavior, have not encouraged the competitiveness of large-scale, world-class industrial-ecology investments. The biases built into our global industrial system, and supported internationally by government and consumer preferences, promote exploitation rather than conservation of virgin resources, end-of-pipe pollution control rather than pollution prevention, high-volume waste generation, disregard for traditional and indigenous communities, and conversion of green spaces into industrial, commercial, and residential zones.

Based on my experiences developing the Bronx recycled-paper plant, it became clear to me how nonsustainable biases had evolved in the marketplace and serve as barriers to change.

- Environmental problems begin with the development of specific production technologies, since without production technologies there can obviously be no industrial production. Each manufacturing technology is designed to accept specific types of raw materials, use specific amounts of water, and spew specific amounts of pollutants. In effect, social and ecological choices are made in the guise of technology choices. For example, the pulping technology used for de-inking recycled paper cannot be used to process virgin timber. Government policies, by making virgin raw materials cheaper to use and more easily acquired than they would be without financial and research subsidies, have facilitated the investment in and development of industrial equipment designed to process virgin resources. At the production site, processing virgin resources almost always generates higher levels of pollution, and uses more energy and more water.

• Designing equipment to process virgin resources leads manufacturers to locate their industrial plants near virgin supplies—hence, paper mills are generally located near forests and not near cities, despite an abundant supply of urban wastepaper. Smelters are located near their source of virgin ores. This usually involves converting and infecting green spaces and other undeveloped areas.

• Because manufacturers promote products made from these virgin-based processes, consumers—industrial, commercial, and retail—expect and request product specifications associated with virgin-based quality.

• To control the impacts these industries impose when they process virgin resources and convert green spaces, government regulations and research programs presume the use of these same virgin resources. This itself further encourages a virgin-based approach to industrial production, by shaping environmental compliance and research subsidies toward virgin-based technologies.

• Engineering firms designing these technologies have become expert at designing virgin-based technologies. In effect, this promotes their use.

• Lawyers and other consultants administering compliance for these industries have become expert in understanding compliance and design issues related to virgin-based technologies, and this also promotes their acceptance and use.

- Industrial lobbyists seeking subsidies from the government craft those incentives based on assumptions related to virgin-based processes.

- With virgin-based technologies being the standard, it is more difficult to acquire technological-process guarantees, or regulatory-compliance guarantees, from equipment vendors for less commercialized, environmentally innovative technologies that are not virgin based.

- This, in turn, makes it more difficult to obtain financing for nonvirgin-based or environmentally innovative technologies from investors, since investors insist on production guarantees to reduce their downside risks. And with more obstacles to financing, there is little chance that nonvirgin-based or environmentally innovative technologies can successfully compete in the marketplace.

The goods and services available in the market—and the jobs and relationships that have evolved to deliver them—shape human consciousness, and the market has been built on ecologically nonsustainable, so-called "disposable" practices. In effect, most of us hold nonsustainable worldviews, because day in and day out we consume and produce products in a nonsustainable context. This is not a new insight: Alvin Toffler, among others, described these trends more than thirty years ago in still relevant chapters of *Future Shock* titled "The Death of Permanence" and "Things: The Throw-Away Society."[10] We know that the market—driven primarily by individual self-interest—places a high value on short-term gains that usually rely on the long-term desecration of resources rather than long-term stewardship. Our focus on price, performance, fashionableness, and being attended to—the fundamental attributes driving the marketplace—does not encourage people to think about the upstream or faraway human and ecological impacts that commodity-production processes engender. Clearly, this has led to the proliferation of environmentally problematic and, often, disposable products (and, more than a few social observers have argued, disposable relationships), rather than environmentally superior or durable products. Consequently, consciousness will also need to change, to accept and encourage more sustainable consumer behavior. But consciousness and culture will change toward more sustainable assumptions only when economic behavior changes, and that will happen, if it ever happens, because environmentalists—the catalysts for sustainability—have increased their influence in the industrial-production sector.

Change Must Happen in the Marketplace

So the dilemma is this: If the nonsustainable market so substantially shapes our consciousness and culture, these will change only if and when the market does. If the market shapes our politics, regulations, and bureaucracies, and the market has been built upon nonsustainable practices, then politics, regulations, and bureaucracies will also continue to support sustainable developments only when the market becomes more sustainable. It is a catch-22. Political influence by industrial interests essentially controls our political process, and industry now relies overwhelmingly on nonsustainable practices, supported by the government programs they disproportionately influence, regardless of their inherent ecological damage.

Clearly, sustainable behavior in all spheres of political and economic life will creep forward only when environmentalists claim more influence over the industrial sector. Environmentalists are history's catalysts for sustainability. As Emerson observed, "if men [sic] can be educated, the institutions will share their improvement."[11] But even when we increase our influence over industry, the barriers to reform will remain huge, because humanity's dominant worldview, supported by literally hundreds of government programs at the local, state, federal, and international levels, continue to prop-up and subsidize nonsustainable consumption practices and policies related to public lands; road building; below-cost timber sales in national forests; water use; irrigation; agriculture; and auto- and truck-based transportation, totaling hundreds of billions of dollars in subsidies *each year*. Nonsustainable lifestyles and the policies to support them have existed for centuries, and most people in the developed world—along with the industrial infrastructure that supports us—profit handsomely from this. Alas, when it comes to our society's ecological inconsideration of future generations, Thoreau's observation still rings true: "There is but little virtue in the action of masses of men."[12]

One fairly recent example is that the U.S. government's energy-research budget in the fifty years between 1948 and 1998 totaled about $112 billion dollars. Of that, 82 percent was directed toward some type of subsidy for nuclear or fossil fuels, even though these fuels generate enormous and often irreparable environmental impacts. No vision of sustainability includes a continued reliance on fossil fuels, much less subsidies for their use. Examples of other nonsustainable-subsidy programs include radioactive-waste–disposal research and services, "clean coal" technology research, and diesel-engine research.[13] Subsidies for these types of energy programs are particularly damaging to efforts to promote sustainable industrial behavior, because sustainable industrial processes need to be more energy efficient and less disruptive and polluting than a reliance on fossil fuels could ever achieve. Energy savings generate some of the greatest cost savings that make sustainable industrial processes potentially more competitive than nonsustainable industry. If government artificially makes energy less costly through subsidies—as it has for more than a century—the economic advantage of sustainable industrial practices relative to nonsustainable practices is reduced.

The key, then, is that environmentalists must figure out how to change the market—which overwhelmingly influences the consciousness of the masses—in spite of all the institutional momentum working against sustainable production. If industries relied on more sustainable practices, then government subsidies and research programs would more likely be designed to support more sustainable industrial approaches. In an economy based on nonsustainable practices, it's not surprising that in trying to stimulate sustainable industrial investments, ecologists hit market—cultural, practical, and psychological—obstacles. And with government programs historically created to support nonsustainable industrial practices, it is also not surprising that most politicians don't understand how to use government resources to promote sustainability.

How can environmentalists hope to change the built-in market advantages of business-as-usual? And how can we develop the leverage to do so?

BUILDING BRIDGES: THE POWER OF COLLABORATION

Having environmentalists develop or run the business has an important by-product: We no longer have to rely on government to mediate our relationship with industry. The development of a large-scale industrial project, especially an ecologically oriented industrial project, is a complex undertaking, requiring the expertise of many different participants. Fine-tuning a project to remedy ecological problems is impossible to do without direct dialogue and collaboration among many sectors. The key is to coordinate those participants needed to overcome the many and diverse obstacles in the way of developing, financing, building, and operating ecologically superior industrial designs and practices, and still remain cost competitive. This requires more than subcontracting our interests to government: It requires genuine partnership and a shared vision for a project.

This approach—the one I developed to advance the BCPC—involves direct dialogue with those in the industries targeted for reform. (See Figure 6.1.) Unlike government-dependent advocacy, which I described in chapter 1 and which often subverts environmental sciences or economics in the name of getting legislative compromises enacted, direct dialogue with corporate engineers, financiers, and CEOs tends to build scientific and economic understanding. When they are not involved in legislative or regulatory obfuscation, industrial officials tend to respect sound science and engineering. To a considerable extent they have to: Having properly operating, precisely engineered production facilities depends on it. Nonadversarial dialogue is essential to advancing knowledge and sustainability. And by working together to construct cost-competitive industrial-ecology factories, environmentalists, community groups, and unions

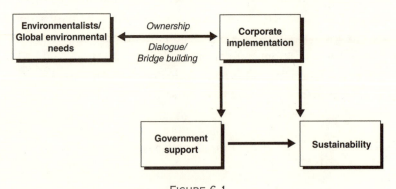

FIGURE 6.1.

A New Collaborative Advocacy Paradigm to Promote Sustainability can most effectively push aside the destructive influence of the worst corporations.

As opposed to the adversarial legislative and regulatory processes, a more collaborative approach helps build bridges among the participants, and bridge building between adversaries must indisputably be part of the environmentalist ethic in the twenty-first century. Angry people cannot create a peaceful world. Truth requires an open dialogue, whether these are scientific, social, or financial truths. Consequently, maintaining an adversarial relationship with decision makers in industrial firms makes it harder to achieve needed reform. Ecological reform must be based on an accurate assessment of our environmental and social situation and technical options. Collaboration among diverse interests makes it more likely that the science, engineering, and social coordination needed to advance the diverse issues that promote sustainability will be evaluated accurately and, indeed, creatively. As the biologist Ernst Mayr has observed: "Often it is feedback from outside one's narrow domain that is decisive for a conceptual advance."[14] In the market-based collaborative-advocacy paradigm I envision, conceptual advances will be more likely because diverse perspectives will be working together. With this new scenario, government compromises need not mediate the environmentalist's relationship with ecological objectives or with industry, but instead can be used to support an industrial-ecology collaboration as a strategic facilitator (e.g., by supplying tax incentives, research, worker-training grants, or other types of subsidies that may be needed to advance the industrial-ecology project).

In the future, one hopes, there may be no distinct field known as industrial ecology or sustainable design. All business plans and practices will then support and preserve the ecosystems that we need to survive on a biologically diverse and healthy planet. But until that time, environmentalists must reorient their work to directly stimulate environmentally superior industrial developments. After all, offering investors an opportunity to work together rather than imposing obstacles in their path to profit is more attractive to them. As Thoreau said in *Walden*, we "attract more flies with fruit than manure."[15] Most important, given the magnitude of the investments needed, the complexity of the technologies that must be designed, constructed, and operated, and the complex political context through which industrial investments must navigate in order to become real, we simply cannot achieve our sustainability objectives without collaborating.

CONCLUSION

Environmentalists promoting sustainable manufacturing plants need to learn a host of new skills not typically employed in our traditional advocacy work. Normally, we engage in filing legal briefs, arguing before a judge, or negotiating with legislators and regulators. Recently we're more frequently begging corporate officials to voluntarily minimize the ecological impact of their business, and we continue to beg consumers not to buy products manufactured in environmentally destructive ways. We pretend they have a meaningful choice, but mostly they don't. Buying land, taking it out of commerce forever, as Edward O. Wilson has written, is ultimately "The Solution."[16] But it's hard to imagine that the relative handful of land trusts doing this incredibly valuable work, influential as they are, will in the long term successfully outbid global transnational corporations for most of the important habitat on the planet. Indeed, much of it is already gone.

Developing industrial-ecology projects, however, requires a broader—indeed, an entirely different—range of expertise. To advance the BCPC industrial-ecology project, my colleagues and I had to engage in negotiations with financial backers in the for-profit, government, community, construction, engineering, and philanthropic worlds, as we sought to acquire development funding, proper engineering designs, and environmental permits. We had to learn how to supply development services, such as hiring industry experts to staff the development team. We also had to obtain political support from community groups for—rather than against—an industrial-development project; assess the competency of equipment vendors, engineering, and construction firms; coordinate press relations; and obtain various forms of financial support, tax incentives, or investments from various government agencies.

Only by being responsible for the strategic planning and the funding and doing the hard labor involved in bringing together the necessarily diverse participants needed to successfully develop a world-class industrial-ecology project can we expect that ecologically better factories will gradually begin to operate and help the market evolve into a more sustainable system. Under the best of circumstances this will take many decades. Much will be lost; many species will disappear and, indeed, many will die prematurely because of pollution during that time. Yet this realistic approach—eco-realism—a blueprint for a new environmentalism, is ultimately likely to become the most effective way to stop the ecological damage imposed by current industrial practices. Developing cost-competitive, replicable models that can remedy past ecological problems and outcompete the bad factories that currently dominate the market is within our grasp.

NOTES

1. Don Sayre, *Inside ISO 14000: The Competitive Advantage of Environmental Management* (Delray Beach, Florida: St. Lucie Press, 1996), p. 100.

2. Stephen E. Whicher, Robert E. Spiller, and Wallace E. Williams, eds., *The Early Lectures of Ralph Waldo Emerson,* 3 vols. (Cambridge, Massachusetts: Harvard University Press, 1959–72), in Robert D. Richardson Jr., *Emerson: The Mind on Fire* (Berkeley, California: University of California Press, 1995), p. 271.

3. William H. Gilman, et al., eds., *The Journals and Miscellaneous Notebooks of Ralph Waldo Emerson,* 16 vols. (Cambridge, Massachusetts: Harvard University Press, 1960–82), in Richardson, *Emerson: The Mind on Fire,* p. 335.

4. John F. Avedon and Donald S. Lopez Jr., eds. *The Way to Freedom by His Holiness the Dalai Lama* (San Francisco: HarperCollins, 1998), throughout.

5. Tom Schuller, "Social Capital, Human Capital, and Sustainable Development," in *Frameworks to Measure Sustainable Development* (Paris: OECD, 2000), p. 63.

6. Board on Sustainable Development, National Research Council *Our Common Journey: A Transition Toward Sustainability* (Washington, D.C.: National Academy Press, 1999), p. 3.

7. Jonathan Rose & Companies, *Developing Times*, newsletter 5 (Winter 2001), pp. 7–8.

8. Ernst Mayr, *This Is Biology* (Cambridge, Massachusetts: Belknap Press, 1998), pp. 17–20.

9. Carl Zimmer, "Is This Chip Educable?" *New York Times Book Review*, 9 March 2002, p. 25.

10. Alvin Toffler, *Future Shock* (New York: Random House, 1970).

11. Ralph Waldo Emerson, "Politics," in *Essays*, second series (Boston: Houghton, Osgood & Co., 1879), pp. 163–80, excerpted in Bernard E. Brown, *Great American Political Thinkers, Vol. 2* (New York: Avon Books, 1983), p. 133.

12. Henry David Thoreau, *A Yankee in Canada with Anti-Slavery and Reform Papers* (Boston: Ticknor and Fields, 1866), pp. 123–51, excerpted in Bernard E. Brown, p. 150.

13. For more on this issue see Friends of the Earth, et al., *Green Scissors 2000: Cutting Wasteful and Environmentally Harmful Spending* (Washington, D.C.: Friends of the Earth, 2000).

14. Mayr, *This Is Biology*, p. xiv.

15. Henry David Thoreau, *Walden; or: Life in the Woods* (Boston and New York: Houghton Mifflin Co., 1893).

16. Edward O. Wilson, "The Solution," *Conservation in Practice*, Vol. 3, No. 2 (Spring 2002), pp. 3–4.

7. Forming Partnerships: Moving Past the Roadblocks

> Each man of thought is surrounded by
> wiser men than he: Cannot they combine?
>
> —Ralph Waldo Emerson

INDUSTRIAL DEVELOPMENT as it is currently practiced is a highly exclusive undertaking. It is generally initiated, guided, and developed by a few senior corporate managers, marketing strategists, and financiers working within a single firm, with support from consultants drawn from within the industrial field. Industrial development is rarely born and implemented as an inclusive venture, out of a collaboration with community interests or sustainability advocates in the environmental world. However, as should be obvious by now, the design and development of a successful, sustainable industrial-ecology project acceptable to the local community requires cooperation among a diverse set of interests including industrial managers, community interests, environmentalists, financiers, construction executives, engineers, lawyers, government bureaucrats, and politicians. All of these participants bring their own valuable perspective, political influence, resources, and information, which can helpfully define and advance sustainable practices in the local community, for the firm, and for the planet. The trick is to get them to work together supportively and effectively.

Everything is pregnant with its contrary, and as chapter 5 has detailed, even once-progressive interests such as unions, community groups, and grassroots environmentalists can now pose retrograde obstacles to sustainable industrial development. In part this is a result of self-interest on the part of unions and community groups, and environmentalists' aversion to collaborations with industry, out of a concern about being perceived as "selling out," when in fact all they might be doing is trying to find an effective path to resolve a problem.

I personally was present at a high-level meeting among some of the world's most influential environmental activists where even using the term *collaboration* with business was frowned upon. Instead, euphemisms such as *engagement* and other terms were sought. Collaboration somehow seemed, well, too friendly a term. It made me think of the ancient religious rivalries: Must we have a five-thousand-year war between environmentalists and industry before we see the devastating futility of such antagonistic behavior? Future generations require that we identify and design policy and actions to overcome all barriers to sustainability. If we leave them burdened with the consequences of this animosity between environmentalists and industry, will they praise us for such "principled" behavior?

If there is a foundation to the new environmentalism, to eco-realism, its cornerstone is collaboration—the forming of strategic partnerships, even with erstwhile adversaries. Collaboration is the key to clearing the social market, as well as to advancing the development project through its many financial and technical stages. Collaboration should rightfully be viewed as having the lion sit down with the lamb—an ethical obligation. Dialogue is essential for developing accurate science and engineering, and dialogue is essential for promoting peace and social harmony, both of which are essential to a sustainable economy. Peace is an objective of, if not a prerequisite for, a sustainable society, and it is worth mentioning again that angry people—those who approach industrial developers, government officials, or environmentalists as adversaries—cannot create a peaceful world. Collaboration can help promote understanding, and thus reduce the anger and promote peace and socially sustainable behavior, all by fostering dialogue.

Collaboration also inspires innovation. As the great biologist Ernst Mayr has pointed out, "Often it is feedback from outside one's narrow domain that is decisive for a conceptual advance."[1] And an observer of the medical profession has commented that "[a]lthough physicians are reluctant to concede it, during the past twenty years the most significant reforms in medicine have been brought about by outsiders."[2] Commenting on this phenomenon, Dr. Dahlia Zaidel, a professor of neuropsychology at the University of California, Los Angeles, has noted that

> [t]here's no question that specialists in a particular field of science can sometimes be less enlightened than newcomers to the same field. . . . All scientists who have any sense at all know that it's good to listen and learn from people who are not directly in their field. Open-mindedness, it's called. And throughout the history of ideas it was always known that to be open-minded always leads to good things, to progress, always breaks "group think," the latter being detrimental to progress. . . . So science is not different from all other human endeavors, be they in politics, philosophy, child rearing, and so on. Open-mindedness is what leads to progress or, in our case here, [the BCPC] to innovation."[3]

Examples of scholars who have made important discoveries outside their field of training include the Nobel Laureate Max Delbruck, who was trained in physics and then moved onto genetics research, and Seymour Benzer, an extremely influential biologist who came from physics. James Watson—of the famed Watson-and-Crick team that discovered DNA—was a physicist, not an evolutionary biologist. Indeed, the master himself, Charles Darwin, was formally trained as a minister and had every expectation of becoming a country parson, not a biologist.[4] And, as is well-known, he credited his intellectual breakthrough in evolutionary biology to his readings in geology. Other examples include Leibniz, Hodgkin, Huxley, Newton, Descartes, and Einstein.

Industry therefore ought to recognize that it does have an interest in bringing in people from outside the traditional pool of narrow, industry-specific development experts to encourage more creative thinking and increase an industrial project's prospects for success, as well as its potential ecological and social value. And environmentalists ought to recognize that they too can benefit from collaborating with knowledgeable specialists outside *their* traditional pool of expert advocates.

From an environmentalist's point of view, the chronic absence of the kinds of collaborations needed to inform industrial developers about the environmental and social pitfalls raised by an industrial investment strategy is a primary reason why industry imposes so many inequitable ecological, social, and economic burdens on our planet. Without environmental representatives or local community representatives at the development table, is it any wonder that avoiding these burdens gets less authentic attention, or that adversarial relationships evolve between industry and the community during an industrial project's development phase?

When I launched the BCPC, I did so with a fact-finding mission to Sweden to visit recycling mills, regulators, and community groups there. This took place well before a site for the BCPC was selected, since I expected that the information the group acquired would guide us—collectively—to identify the most technically and socially suitable site. Mission participants included paper-company officials, environmental activists, community activists, local politicians, financiers, wastepaper processors, the borough president of the Bronx—which was the area likely to host the mill—and commissioners of three New York City agencies serving under the mayor's jurisdiction: the Sanitation Department, the Department of Consumer Affairs, and the Economic Development Corporation. As I previously noted, there is no doubt that the collaborative nature of the BCPC's development approach was responsible, perhaps more than any other factor, for the project getting through its environmental permitting and development-financing phases.[5] The collaborative composition of the development team may have been even more influential in getting the project its permits than its technology design. Why was this so? The reasons are several.

- By having members of the community involved from the beginning, and by having the project invited into the community by them, we were legitimately able to avoid the charge that we were merely clearing the way for investors to come in and burden a community with a locally undesirable land use (also known as a LULU) scheme.

- By having environmentalists involved from the very inception of the project's design, we were able to assuage concerns about the project's potential ecological impacts. Indeed, together with our community and industry partners we were able to design a project that would remedy many local environmental and social problems.

- By bringing in local political representatives at the beginning, we were able to more easily acquire state grants to spur the initial development phase of the project.

- By having paper companies on the team and involved in the design and development of the project, we were taken seriously by the governmental, investment, engineering, and construction communities, which are all obviously essential for any industrial-development project—sustainable or otherwise—to succeed.

- The local political support we brought to the project from its inception was able to help us obtain labor-union support for the project, which was critical in getting initial commitments of support from City Hall, the governor, and the White House.

- Finally, having all these diverse interests supporting the BCPC facilitated media relations and public outreach, because there were very few credible (politically supported, fact-based) voices in positions to raise authentic technical or political objections to the project.

Indeed, because the BCPC was a true collaboration, the interests of the community, environmentalists, and politicians were designed into the project's objectives from the start, so it was hard for anyone with credibility to oppose the project, although, as mentioned in chapter 5, a few people—but very few—still tried.

It is ironic that in a country like the United States, where public-opinion polls regularly show that 80 percent of the population consider themselves to be committed to environmental protection, it remains so difficult to get the major stakeholders needed to advance sustainability to work in partnerships to promote ecologically positive industrial development. As the National Research Council has observed, "the difficulties of actually delivering on the hopes that people around the world have attached to the idea of sustainable development have become increasingly evident. In part, these difficulties reflect political problems, grounded in questions of financial resources [and] equity. . . . [S]ome critical dimensions—assumptions about culture, values, lifestyles, and social institutions—require qualitative description."[6] It is these cultural and lifestyle barriers to which I am referring here. I believe nonquantifiable social and cultural barriers, more than any other obstacles, interfere with the collaborations needed to overcome most issues related to sustainable industrial development, including the technical issues.

When collaboration between industry, environmental NGOs, and community groups does take place, it is likely to be the most successful approach to industrial development. In the case of the BCPC, we were confident of the environmental and social value of the project because it had been openly and collaboratively designed and reviewed by many environmental, corporate, and community interests. With an understanding of—and wide agreement about—the BCPC's ecological and social value, we were able to make our requests for development funding and regulatory approval with more confidence than we could have done had we not known the project was sound and widely supported. Because our project had many participants from various fields, there was always someone on our team who had the technical expertise or political contact we needed—just when we needed it—to assist our engineering team with a regulatory issue, our permitting team with a technical issue, and our political team with a community-relations or media issue. Indeed, because we were a broad collaboration, we were able to tackle virtually anything the project initially needed to move forward more effectively than had only one sector been working alone.

If environmentalists seek a fuller partnership with business and community interests, there are ways to most effectively organize ourselves to achieve this.

CREATING A DEVELOPMENT PARTNERSHIP

Large private-sector corporations usually require little assistance to initiate, define, and finance a nonsustainable project. Because sustainable development projects incorporate many more social and technical issues than do traditional nonsustainable and exclusively bottom-line–driven industrial projects, they are more complicated to design and implement, and require a more technically and culturally diverse design and development team. Consequently, those of us promoting sustainability projects must act not only as project catalysts but as "cultural brokers,"[7] getting stakeholders with different objectives and different operating procedures to work together effectively. This demands, among other things, sensitivity to the disproportionate power and resources held by some stakeholders working on the development team relative to others. In other words, we must anticipate early on that there are professional and cultural tensions inherent in bringing together diverse interests that don't usually work together but must if sustainability is to advance to any meaningful extent. We must recognize, and help the team navigate around, each stakeholder's resource limits and worldview biases, including our own. And we must be capable of guiding stakeholders, including ourselves, beyond these limits.

There are two predominant types of approaches to industrial development. One involves working with a corporate sponsor from the outset; this is known as a corporate-sponsored deal. The second type is a developer-sponsored project. These are generally initiated by entities affiliated with the industry but are often independent of the large industrial corporations that dominate any market (in the paper industry these affiliated entities have included wastepaper collectors and equipment vendors).

The BCPC was originally designed as a corporate-sponsored deal. After deciding to help stimulate investments for a large-scale paper-recycling mill, I reviewed information about paper companies to try and identify the most environmentally and socially responsible firms with whom we might consider working. Originally I toyed with taking the opposite approach, thinking perhaps I should find the worst actor in the paper industry and try to build bridges with it, start a dialogue to try and turn it around. After all, if a company is already a good actor, does it need help from environmentalists? As it turns out, the most egregiously bad actors had no interest in even discussing the idea of collaboration—they mirror the angriest environmentalists—and, I discovered, even pro-environmental paper-company actors need help developing complex, world-scale industrial-ecology projects at hard-to-develop urban brownfields. Thus, I decided to try and find a firm that might be philosophically inclined toward locating a recycling project at a brownfield in an underprivileged urban area. To assist us in this endeavor, NRDC hired as a consultant a pulp-and-paper–industry expert who worked at Greenpeace. His name is Tim Martin, and when we brought him on board at NRDC, he was told to make no compromises in his evaluation of any paper company. We assigned him to work on assessing the pros and cons of collaborating with various paper-production firms. At the same time Martin was investigating paper-industry firms, I sounded out NRDC staff to learn who might have information on potentially progressive paper companies. I discovered that some of my colleagues in NRDC's Washington, D.C., office who were fighting to limit the industry's use of chlorine bleaching were relying on information provided by the MoDo Paper company, based in Sweden. In response to research findings that related chlorine bleaching at paper mills to dioxin contamination in rivers, Swedish firms long ago began a program to phase out the use of chlorine bleaching to eliminate the discharge of dioxins and other organic-chloride effluents from their paper mills. Moreover, Scandinavian companies also abandoned forest clear-cutting practices in response to documented impacts on resident species, habitat, and biodiversity more generally.

It just so happened that MoDo in 1992 was strategically interested in expanding its production of de-inked, recycled paper in North America. After a few months of due diligence and meetings with senior MoDo executives, including the fact-finding mission to Sweden I led for New York City government, business, and community-group officials, we agreed to collaborate—and take not one penny in profit for doing so— with MoDo to try and develop a model ecologically oriented, socially beneficial recycled-paper mill. Later, MoDo brought in an American firm, the S. D. Warren Company, as a partner in the endeavor. But by 1995 the ownership of both firms had changed hands and we sought a new project sponsor.

A corporate-sponsored deal is more financially attractive to investors than an independent-developer–sponsored arrangement because it has a corporate balance sheet—its publicly known creditworthiness—and proven marketing know-how backing the deal. There is more financial confidence in projects structured as a corporate-sponsored deals because there is less investor risk.

We were unable to find a suitable new industrial sponsor willing to financially guarantee the entire project the way MoDo and S. D. Warren were, so we shifted the financial structure of the BCPC deal from a corporate-sponsored project to a developer-sponsored one, with the BCPC owned by Banana Kelly and with NRDC as the project coordinator.

In a developer-sponsored project, no single stakeholder provides the full credit and market guarantees desired by the financial community to ensure that all the bonds issued to finance a deal will be paid off whether this particular project is profitable or not. A developer-sponsored deal obtains the performance guarantees the project requires from a combination of the equipment vendors, engineers, construction firms, financiers, facility operators, or marketing brokers brought into the deal. But such guarantees come—like any type of insurance—at a price, so developer-sponsored deals struggle more to keep development and operational costs down.

The nature of any collaboration formed to advance an industrial-development project will vary depending on whether the project is corporate sponsored or developer sponsored. Developer-sponsored deals, because they tend *not* to have a large corporation financially backing the project, will generally require more effort and resources from the not-for-profit collaborators throughout the life of the project's development—and possibly during operation as well—than may be necessary with a corporate-sponsored deal. Given the credible financial and technical resources it can bring to bear, and the credibility it almost immediately establishes with political interests, enticing a corporate sponsor to collaborate in an industrial-ecology initiative is the ideal approach. Corporations, in addition to having sizable financial resources, bring development experience, smart technical teams, political clout, a known market reputation, and a marketing track record, plus a large, often publicly traded balance sheet—subject to SEC scrutiny—that can help identify for investors the project's downside financial risks. However, the primary negative aspect of launching an industrial-ecology project with a corporate partner is that corporations have shown little interest in advancing environmentally or socially valuable investments unless they are somehow pressured to do so, and without effective counter-leverage, they can easily overwhelm—perhaps subvert—the NGO participants' input and objectives.

Although a corporate sponsor greatly strengthens a project's prospects for success, a corporate sponsor is not absolutely necessary to develop an industrial project. This is critical to remember, because in many industrial circumstances—especially in the slow-to-change paper industry—it is unlikely that corporate sponsors will be willing to partner with environmental and community groups to add new production capacity, regardless of how much more environmentally superior a new industrial-ecology facility might be. The paper industry, for example, views new production capacity as a threat to its cartel-propped-up commodity prices. Moreover, environmental enhancements alone will certainly not be enough of an incentive for any large corporation and, in fact, environmental enhancements may actually keep a paper company out of the deal: During a meeting I had with the CEO of the now-defunct Scott Paper Company (which was the parent owner of S. D. Warren, with whom we were working), I was told outright that the BCPC's socially and environmentally progressive features were a negative as far as the firm was concerned, because they built up expectations that, if unfulfilled, would subject the company to ridicule. We promised the Scott CEO that should his firm remain in the project and should it fail, we would publicly applaud the firm for at least trying to do a good thing, rather than sit idly by, allowing it to receive bad press for being part of an innovative failure. With that, the Scott CEO agreed to stay in the project and contributed $250,000 toward its development—until his firm was sold and taken over by Al Dunlap, a notorious deconstructer of corporate assets whose ignominious nickname is Chainsaw, which he bizarrely views as a compliment.

In cases like the paper industry, where corporate participation is hard to come by, it might actually be better to begin the project development as a developer-sponsored deal and define its progressive attributes without a corporate partner watering down the project's goals. This strategy would involve bringing together a development team under the coordination of a lead developer. The objective of this approach could be to develop a project to such an advanced stage that a major corporate player will take it over—with most of the design attributes set by the initial (environmental) developer. Alternatively, the developer sponsor can take the project through to financial closing, raising equity, and financing the deal as a "project-finance" (single-asset) off–balance-sheet deal, and operate the mill or factory as an independent player in the market, not affiliated with the transnational firms that dominate most industries. This latter approach would advance the movement toward having environmentalists own industrial-production facilities and also help to garner the political influence that economic position offers.

After the departure of our initial paper-company sponsors, MoDo and S. D. Warren, my objective with the BCPC was to either (1) have the project taken over by a paper-manufacturing firm that saw a strategic advantage in the deal or saw it as a strategic threat to its market, which it wanted to maintain control over, or (2) otherwise see the project through to completion and run the mill as an independent paper-production facility with an operating and marketing agreement between the BCPC and financially creditworthy firms in the paper industry.

CHOOSING CONSTRUCTION AND ENGINEERING PARTNERS

With any industrial-development project, whether it is corporate sponsored or developer sponsored, working with a financially strong and technically capable construction and engineering team is essential to success. To provide the performance guarantees against technology design and operations failures that bond underwriters and other investors require, the construction and engineering consortium must have substantial financial and technical resources. The Wall Street requirement that a construction firm have deep pockets is a major reason why outside firms, instead of locally based ones, are so often brought into even the most impoverished communities to build industrial facilities. Local, small-scale construction firms that community-development groups may use to rehabilitate housing are not suitable for the job. Given the fact that many of these firms have local political relationships, their exclusion from a large industrial-development project—totaling hundreds of millions of dollars in work—may cause political problems within the host community for the local-project sponsors. But beware: Financiers and transnational corporations require financially larger construction firms and world-class precision engineers with experience building these types of plants. And environmentalists have to heed this, whether we like it or not, or these projects won't get the backing of Wall Street or corporate participants. I learned this firsthand when I went to our community group as well as the National Minority Supplier Development Council (NMSDC) to find engineering and construction firms that might best represent local residents. After one round of engineering plans was drafted for the project by a Latino-owned engineering firm I found through the NMSDC and hoped the BCPC could use to design the mill, I was told in no uncertain terms by the paper-company officials with whom we were working that there were only a few firms in the world that built projects like what we had in mind, and if we didn't use one of those firms, the paper-company partners couldn't participate. Only a few firms could build mills that produced the high-quality product they marketed. Nor would equipment vendors guarantee the performance of their equipment unless qualified— read: big, experienced, with deep pockets—firms were doing the engineering and constructing the project. The absence of support from unions to my pleas for bringing locals residents into the union, which I discussed in chapter 5, only exacerbated my frustration at not being able to maximize local construction-employment opportunities in a community that so desperately needed jobs.

A construction firm that will provide the financial markets with confidence must obviously have excellent working relationships with a variety of engineering firms—for example, specialists in water systems, product manufacture, energy systems, and site preparation. And it must have excellent working relationships with equipment vendors, banks, unions, and politicians. A construction company must engender respect and influence with local unionized labor, must have experience in constructing the types of facilities being developed—preferably North American expertise if the project is to be in North America, in Asia if the project will be in Asia, etc.—and ideally should have a history of building complex industrial projects in cities, which have unique labor-practice regulations and higher costing obstacles. The industry representatives and financial team will help any environmental NGO or community-group developer identify the list of suitable firms to interview for the job, which is how I did it for the BCPC project.

Construction-company programs to *authentically* incorporate local community-based laborers into a project's construction job are especially valuable but regrettably rare. In part this is due to the closed door to new laborers that unions slam in the face of many local labor pools. However, an appropriate construction company can, and must, inspire confidence in the project's other participants, including environmentalists and, above all, the facility operator and investors committing equity and buying the project-related bonds. The construction firm's experience and performance guarantees must also inspire confidence in equipment suppliers, city and state officials who are being asked to supply critical resources, regulators, the surrounding community, and potential customers. It is always useful to bear in mind, though, that construction companies—like other industrial participants—are not known for their commitment to sustainable development or other socially progressive objectives and need to be overseen very conscientiously to prevent the project's larger, ecologically essential goals from being undermined under the guise of "cost containment."

Some large construction firms are so financially and technically strong that if they chose to do so they could by themselves initiate and bring to fruition a world-class industrial-development project. A construction and engineering consortium can develop a viable industrial-development idea, refine it, engineer it, get it sited, get political support and permits for it, finance it, build it, and solicit competition for an operator to run it and market the product it produces. Construction companies can be a one-stop shop for industrial development, for better or worse. Influencing the decisions made by large construction firms is one of the most important activities an environmental reformer can engage in.

Morse Diesel International, the construction firm working with us on the BCPC, was instrumental both in helping us advance the project as far as we got it and, I believe, in causing the project to fail. When we lost our initial paper-company partners to mergers, and were rejected by other paper companies (who saw a threat to their commodity prices if the BCPC's new paper-production capacity came on-line), our construction company stepped forward to help. In exchange for the right to build the half-billion-dollar mill, it offered to pay for all the construction costing and engineering work needed to design the facility, assist with negotiating the union agreements needed to build it, help sell the project to other potentially interested paper companies, hire apprentice laborers from the local community, and try to mobilize political support from influential politicians and other local, state, or federal officials. These efforts were of great strategic value for the project, helping to bring it to the verge of financing. Unfortunately, Morse Diesel became so influential in the BCPC that it was able to override both my protests (once the project was on the verge of financing, NRDC had withdrawn from its coordination role) and those of others in the project and tried unsuccessfully to work with a different paper-company investor/operator than the one we obtained to replace MoDo and S. D. Warren. (Earlier, after MoDo and S. D. Warren were out of the project, the BCPC had managed to obtain an agreement, which Morse Diesel failed to hold onto, with the Kruger Paper Company.) Plus, Morse Diesel designed the mill to so large a production capacity that it became impossible to raise the needed equity and state financial support for it. Why did it insist on such a large and ultimately untenable production capacity? Could it be because larger projects offer more profits to construction companies?

Nonetheless, suffice it to say that in big cities, large locally influential construction firms are sine qua non for large, complex, industrial construction projects that involve political decision makers and require union support, community and environmental scrutiny, and Wall Street financing in the hundreds of millions of dollars.

WORKING WITH INVESTMENT-BANKING FIRMS

It is essential to have an energetic and supportive working relationship with a financial-investment firm to successfully develop a large industrial project. There is no way around this, hence the central importance of financial firms, and knowledge of investment banking, to sustainable development. Needless to say, financiers are quite sophisticated about what it takes to get an industrial project to clear the financial market. In fact, as opposed to many in the corporate world, they are more likely to understand the effects of both types of market forces—financial and social—on a project, because protecting their clients from risks (investor risks are bank risks) is what investment banking is about. Although investment-banking firms appreciate the value of clearing the social market, in my estimation they are not particularly ethical about how to precisely do so most legitimately: I often felt that paying off an opponent would suit them just fine. Financiers are very attentive to the value of having environmental permits in hand. However, while they are good at managing elected officials and bureaucrats in behalf of a project's interests—often by making political contributions and hinting at the prospect of post-government employment—financiers, in my experience, don't typically display the most politically savvy and effective insights about how to best address the local grassroots obstacles industrial projects typically encounter. These social obstacles usually arise at the local-community level, and investment bankers seem to have few clues, other than co-optation through financial payments, about how to engage in (indeed, they seem to abhor) that level of politics.

Wall Street investment banks provide vital services for industrial projects. They can

- help identify equity investors in a project and bring lenders and borrowers together,

- issue the bonds (either tax exempt or taxable) that supplement equity investments at financing,

- review the pro-forma financials to help assess whether a project is financially viable,

- help arrange for supplemental financial support through hedge deals or other types of financial products,

- provide assessments about the market viability of a project within the prevailing market context, and

- provide confidence to politicians about whether a project can ultimately succeed.

Like construction firms, investment banks currently tend to have an inhibiting effect when it comes to incorporating sustainability objectives into a project. Because broader and longer-term ecological and social impacts are not priced into industrial-development projects, they are not factored into investment decisions, and it is well-known "that short-term profit maximization impedes the attainment of a sustainable society."[8]

On the other hand, if investment banks are responding to development conditions created by environmentalists, they can also serve to facilitate sustainability. Alas, it depends on who is the development master: If environmentalists owned more production facilities, or otherwise became more substantial forces in the industrial-development world, we could harness the enormous market influence—hence, political influence—of investment banks to our cause. Three things are required to get a major Wall Street investment house on board to finance a sustainable industrial-development project: (1) a site, (2) environmental and development permits, and (3) some form of corporate backing.

The BCPC initially choose Merrill Lynch and, later, during the last 18 months of the project, a smaller firm that was comprised of former Goldman Sachs officials as its investment banker. We were able to attract their interest only after we had our site, our permits, and a paper-company partner on board. With those tangible project attributes in hand we were able to conduct a series of interviews with various Wall Street firms, including Bear Stearns, J. P. Morgan, Goldman Sachs, and Merrill Lynch. In fact, after our paper-company partner withdrew from participation in the project, our investment bank tried to help locate another paper company to replace it.

Despite their clumsy relationship with grassroots community groups, financiers—more than most stakeholders involved in an industrial development deal—understand the broad range of details that contribute to or detract from a project's potential success, both in the financial markets and the global–commodity-market context. Merrill Lynch and, eventually, the firm that replaced it, which had each signed on as the BCPC's bond underwriter, provided valuable assistance in defining what was needed from a facility operator and investors as well as the construction team. Our investment bankers were involved in evaluating the critical engineering and design abilities of the construction teams vying for our project, helped craft the investment and operating agreement with the paper-company the mill attracted, and assessed as well the paper company's ability to financially guarantee the production performance of a half-billion-dollar facility. Because, as previously mentioned, client risks and project risks are ultimately bank risks, the investment bank's participation in reviewing and shaping the details of the project help inspire confidence on Wall Street so the bonds and other financial products related to an industrial financing can be efficiently sold.

Investment banks that finance large industrial projects also have lobbying teams dedicated to acquiring political intelligence and influence at the local (invariably above the community level), state, and federal levels. Because, as I have discussed, they can and do donate to political parties and campaigns—and offer the prospect of post-government employment to the individuals they're trying to influence—they and their cohorts in the construction industry and in unions have enormous clout with politicians and regulators, which environmental or community groups can never obtain alone, or obtain without being owners of or otherwise controlling the industrial project. Should a development team manage to attract an investment-banking firm as a project-development ally, it can use the influence of that financial firm to great advantage.

However, while developing the BCPC I learned how extraordinarily difficult it is to influence the investment-banking sector in behalf of environmental or social causes. Few professional activities are motivated by such self-interest as is investment banking, and few are as insulated by social class. But if environmentalists do not begin to mix more substantially with these powerful sectors, we will be stuck with a government-dependent approach to environmental reform that is plainly not effective enough to remedy the diverse, severe, and global ecological burdens humanity faces. Gaining more control over industrial capital is indisputably the next necessary step.

Clearly, having a world-class investment firm on your team greatly increases the prospects for seeing an industrial project to fruition. But because market forces are social as well as financial, having a construction company, corporate participants, and an investment firm are not enough to achieve this. Without a supportive community component and an environmental component, the project is much less likely to succeed and, if history is any guide, would be of questionable value as an industrial-ecology project. And also, obviously, it is essential to be savvy about the fields of industrial-project development and investment banking in order to advance industrial-ecology projects but, alas, these are the social-policy arenas where the expertise of environmental advocates remains weakest and where we must learn to operate more skillfully.

ENCOURAGING COMMUNITY- AND ENVIRONMENTAL-GROUP PARTICIPATION

A mantra in the sustainable-development movement argues for environmentally friendly and community-based development. Indeed, for quite some time the field of sustainable development has included an appropriate emphasis on promoting sustainable communities.

While this sounds good, no one has yet specified what *community-based* development actually means in practice when it comes to large-scale industrial-development projects. Obviously, virtually all industrial projects are situated in someone's community,[9] and this couldn't occur unless some group of interests in that community—whatever their motivation—supported the project. Although some may argue that larger-scale industrial projects are inherently incompatible with sustainable communities, emphasizing the inspiring "Small is beautiful" and "human scale" approach to economic development, my experience and research in communities throughout the world suggests that larger-scale industry and sustainable communities are not incompatible. A larger industrial project can often achieve higher resource productivity than a smaller-scale project and, if it is developed with effective community participation, it can more effectively advance social benefits and industrial-ecology objectives. Moreover, if our objective is to develop projects that have a meaningful impact on the global ecological problems we face, then large, sustainable industrial-ecology initiatives must be developed to compete with the large nonsustainable industrial projects that now dominate the economy. With few exceptions, smaller projects just won't be as cost competitive, however much we ideologically wish they would be. And if they're not cost competitive, they won't get built, so where would that leave us? Right in the ecologically dire place we are.

Without question, it was only because of NRDC's involvement that an inclusive, community-participation approach was investigated at all. That said, I can state categorically that no one on the BCPC development team, whether they were industrialists from the paper industry or financiers from Wall Street or construction-company officials, had any objections to having community interests play a legitimate and influential role in the project. Indeed, the lawyers working on the project's environmental-permitting process saw our efforts to incorporate community interests as valuable and likely to increase our chances of obtaining the permits we required. Unfortunately, too few environmental advocates have experience trying to obtain permits, and their experience of regulatory approvals is skewed toward stopping the process rather than refining it to advance sustainability. Frankly, even though I often relied on my environmentalist "instincts," based on what I've observed during twenty years of advocacy, perhaps none of the permits we needed could have been obtained without the presence and assistance of our community-group partner. This underscores the value of grassroots collaborations to industrial developers as well as advocates for industrial-ecology projects.

A model that environmentalists might use to develop these projects is based on the work of community development corporations (CDCs). CDCs, launched by community activists during the 1960s and thriving afterward, evolved to help channel public- and private-sector funds toward the rehabilitation of aging or abandoned housing in poor communities throughout the United States. When local activists recognized they could no longer count on government assistance to develop the type of housing infrastructure they desired, they developed CDCs to stimulate these investments directly. In effect, CDCs engage in direct market intervention in a fashion not dissimilar to land trusts: Both of these entities bring capital to the table to help advance their objectives.

The kinds of industries environmentalists want—the industries our planet requires—do not yet exist. Conceivably, we might follow the model offered by CDCs and develop our own version of these industries. This, rather than taking the more difficult approach of trying to stimulate an out-of-political-fashion (in the United States) government-owned public-works recycled mill, was the logic behind my effort to develop the Bronx paper mill. Perhaps if New York City had had a mayor with a more progressive political philosophy, I would have tried a different industrial-development path, one that relied more on the government as a developer and owner. Perhaps someday this will happen. Certainly government-owned industrial-ecology mills could happen—and I believe are likely to happen—in countries less ideologically driven against government ownership than is the United States. Perhaps, if industry doesn't reform its ways, government development and ownership of ecologically healing factories will *have* to happen, even in the United States.

In addition to working with CDCs and similar types of local groups that focus on economic rehabilitation, it is useful to collaborate with grassroots environmental community groups in the development of industrial-ecology projects. The BCPC had only one CDC as its community partner. However, it is without a doubt preferable to get at least both types of community groups—environmental and economic development—as stakeholders in the collaboration. Preferably, there should be numerous CDCs and environmental groups involved.

Inclusion of an important CDC from the local neighborhood was critical in getting the BCPC project launched and through the permitting process. And with a community group involved as a partner in the project—with authentic, legally enforceable ownership rights, instead of a merely symbolic role—it was easier to obtain development grants from state agencies and to get political support from local, state, and federal elected officials.

My approach to choosing the BCPC paper-mill site highlighted the value of having an environmental group join with a community-development group as lead collaborators in the development team. Above all, the participation of NRDC and Banana Kelly emphasized to the world at large—and, more important, to the local host community—the project's potential to be an environmentally positive and socially useful development. Based on more than three decades of environmental advocacy and twenty years of development work in the South Bronx, respectively, NRDC and Banana Kelly brought a recognition that many communities may not view a paper mill in their neighborhood in a positive light, either ecologically or socially. Industrial ecologists should do better than typical industrial developers, and shouldn't consider proposing a development unless technical investigations and community meetings reveal that the project will help improve environmental and social conditions in the host community (and the planet at large). My colleagues and I spent months, in addition to many years of previous research, meeting with community interests and locally elected officials, and reviewing site options, community needs, and technical features associated with making recycled paper at high-volume, world-scale mills.

How the BCPC Found Its CDC

I originally intended to prepare a short "white paper" outlining NRDC's conclusions on the potential social and technical value and risks of recycled paper mills at urban brownfields. The white paper was to be circulated to all fifty-nine community boards in New York City—the city where I decided the mill should be built, perhaps prematurely, without considering other cities as options—with a cover letter explaining that NRDC viewed paper recycling as something valuable for the city, the environment at large, and possibly for certain communities in the city. The letter would ask if any community thought hosting such a project was in line with its development plans and needs, and if it did, we were interested in working with it to develop such a project in the most environmentally superior and economically beneficial fashion. Essentially, our intention, as I've noted before, was to locate the mill where it was *invited.*

As it turned out, a legal intern working at NRDC at the time was a former economic-development planner at the Banana Kelly Community Improvement Association. That intern felt that a recycled-paper–mill project was in line with the development interests of Banana Kelly and other development groups in the South Bronx, and he arranged for a meeting with Banana Kelly to discuss the possibility of working together on the mill's development. During our meeting, the executive director of Banana Kelly, Yolanda Rivera, made it clear her community was in dire need of livable-wage jobs, that the only so-called economic-development proposals the neighborhood ever received were for garbage-transfer stations or incinerators, and that while the burned-out buildings characteristic of the 1980s South Bronx had been rehabilitated, there was still a great need for jobs.

At the time of Banana Kelly's visit to NRDC's offices to discuss collaborating on the development of a paper mill, no similar industrial-development collaboration had ever been tried anywhere. (And to the best of my knowledge, none has been tried since.) To the extent that suggestions have been offered on how to advance so-called "community-based sustainable-development projects," they have been offered more or less abstractly, without the benefit of on-the-ground experience, and with inadequate sensitivity to the needs and concerns of the private-capital interests who are putting financial capital at risk, are seeking a competitive return on their investment, and need to develop a cost-competitive project to achieve this. Indeed, some of the ethically motivated approaches to community-based development, while admirable in their broader objectives, are perceived by private-capital interests as misguided efforts to rewrite the definition of private-property rights, by arguing for nothing less than equal control over the private capital brought to the investment by private investors. However much these concepts are motivated by ethical impulses to remedy historic abuses, officials in the for-profit sector, less cognizant of such abuses, might view them as disregarding the interests or prerogatives of private investors—who are the ones who will ultimately make sustainable investments possible.

On this issue I again made critical mistakes in developing the BCPC: Given my sympathy for community groups, their central place in the theories promoting sustainable communities, and my project-related concern about clearing the permitting process and gaining political support, I convinced the BCPC board of directors to give complete ownership of the project to our CDC partner. This subsequently caused complex problems in the project's evolution, with both potential investors and with politicians. Not-for-profit organizations are not structured correctly for a large industrial financing. Moreover, although the BCPC's CDC partner helped during the permitting process, it was able to contribute very few financial and technical resources. In fact, the management of our CDC collaborator turned out to be less than reliable. Consequently, other participants in the project who were making substantial financial investments and who were contributing essential staffing and analytical resources resented the fact that the BCPC's CDC owner didn't bring them in as ownership partners. It caused great resentments within the project team, because permitting, the stage of the project where our CDC was useful, took less than two years and many others were doing the majority of the work during the five years of project development that followed permitting. Because of this, all the project participants were obligated to respect a decision-making authority—including the allocation of financial rewards—controlled by our CDC partner that did not correspond fairly to the allocation of labor, technical resources, or investments upon which the project's ultimate success depended. Even though I initially defined that structure, I grew to resent it myself, as some new officials at our community-group partner took gross advantage of the legal rights bestowed on the group early on in the project before they arrived.

At the same time, with the CDC suddenly owning the largest industrial development project in the history of New York City, local politicians, who are more comfortable accepting financial support from traditional businesses without a community presence, felt that by assisting the project they were being asked to elevate a local community group to an economic and political stature beyond their own position.

The predominant ownership position I gave to the BCPC's CDC partner further complicated the project's development progress because our community group was a weak one in terms of the financial resources, technical capabilities, and personnel attributes it brought to the effort. Initially I was thrilled just to have a community-group partner progressive enough to see the value of having, in its own community, a world-scale recycled-paper mill. Since no one had ever before attempted to "empower" a community group so substantially with the ownership of such a large-scale industrial project, I had no idea how to judge the strengths or weaknesses of any potential community-group partner. I simply asked an official at a philanthropic foundation that had supported the CDC for a few years what she thought. But the management of Banana Kelly had recently changed, and the foundation official didn't understand how unreliable a manager the CDC's new executive director would turn out to be. None of us did. And, of course, at the time I had no idea that the project I was launching would become as large as it did. It never occurred to me that I would have to anticipate how Banana Kelly's ever-evolving management would behave personally when confronted with the financial upside of legally owning a half-billion-dollar business deal. But the lesson to remember is that everything associated with an industrial-development project evolves and tends to grow, especially after environmental permits are obtained.

Evaluating Community Partners

When NRDC first met with Banana Kelly, there was no guidebook to the institutional traits and resources one should look for when seeking community-group partners with whom to collaborate in advancing an industrial-ecology project. With the exception of the few words written about the subject in this book, none exists to this day. Bearing that in mind, we regrettably learned firsthand that cultural obstacles to sustainability do not merely afflict officials in the industrial and governmental sectors. Anti-collaborative behavior, self-interest, ego-driven greed, and prejudicial biases that lead to an inability to successfully work together with other types of institutions characterize some influential people in the not-for-profit world as well as some influential people in for-profit industry. Indeed, my experience with the BCPC suggests that it is often more difficult to get community groups to work with others than it is to get various private-sector firms to do so. With private-sector firms, everything gets smoothed over if people get paid. With community groups, money is certainly a factor, but because there is less money available to compensate and soothe damaged psyches, turf wars, anger, and ego-driven identity politics are more likely to interfere with collaborations than I personally found to be the case in the for-profit world.

How does one evaluate a community group's current and future ability to participate in an industrial-development collaboration?

For collaborations to work, each stakeholder in the partnership obviously has to add value to the project's development and ultimate success. If any participant in the collaboration is deemed to be there merely for ideological or symbolic reasons, but not actually to contribute value to the project's day-to-day needs or longer-term prospects for success, resentments will justifiably develop, and the basis for the collaboration may collapse. Industrial-ecology–development projects may be seen as socially progressive, but their success is earned by meritocratic, hard work.

The key skills community groups must maintain as partners in industrial-ecology projects are, above all, an ability to adapt to the complex technical and financial pressures to which these projects inevitably give rise; a sense of respect and inclusion toward other partners' objectives and managerial skills; and good political relationships. The ability of a community group to raise development funds and manage them effectively in behalf of the project—to inspire confidence in potential funders and investors, and not submit to the temptation to channel such funds away for other organizational needs—is another necessary community-group skill that potential collaborators should assess carefully.

Keeping community groups actively involved and supportive is among the most valuable aspects of an industrial-development collaboration. Getting community groups and grassroots environmental organizations to support an industrial-development project, having them help define the plans for it so it best suits the needs of the community, and helping them to see the wealth-enhancing potential of such investments—and the need to build new sustainable factories to replace the older polluting ones—will strengthen the project and make it most appropriate for the community's long-term interests.

However, while community groups are very valuable at the outset of a project—when it is first being defined and political relationships and permitting issues are in the forefront and need to be developed—their lack of financial and technical expertise and resources relative to the corporate-sector participants may lead some to view their role in the latter stages of the project as less valuable and less clear. After community groups have coordinated early-stage neighborhood input, helped obtain the necessary permits and approvals to develop the project, and helped to obtain the early development funding that not-for-profits are sometimes uniquely situated to acquire, industrial interests and financiers mistakenly tend to see little value in keeping community interests actively involved in the project's ongoing development and evolution. This is a mistake. All parties need to recognize that industrial-development projects always suffer setbacks, that political and economic winds can change abruptly, and that continued community support will help the project weather those storms. If we are truly interested in sustainable communities, the bridges that development collaborations build should not be temporary. Moreover, many grant programs and financing ventures give priority to projects that incorporate community participation, so the potential to get a project financed is enhanced if community groups remain active throughout. Decisions on hiring workers to build and, later, operate the project are also made more locally appropriate if community interests remain actively involved throughout a project's financing. Indeed, ideally not only community participation but also some level of community-based ownership should be designed into the project. For example, I had hoped to develop a financial product that would allow investments in the mill as low as one hundred dollars so local residents could be equity beneficiaries of the project.

It is tempting, and to some degree necessary, to allocate roles and potential rewards to stakeholders early in the project's evolution. Specifying early in a project's life what the potential upside is for each stakeholder certainly helps encourage and focus the participation and enthusiasm among members of the development team. While an early allocation of tasks makes sense, there is the danger that longer-term rewards and decision-making responsibilities will be allocated based on the project's early needs or the anticipated—not proven—capabilities of each stakeholder. Care must be taken to make sure that decisions about who is responsible for what can be reviewed periodically to allow any weak link to be strengthened or replaced. In the latter stages of a project's development, for instance, when financing, high-level politics, engineering, construction, operations, and marketing are paramount, community interests are likely to have less to contribute.

The management of an industrial development project is a fast-paced multifaceted endeavor that requires quick turnover of many documents, both legal and financial. Unfortunately, I was to learn after I made critical legal decisions about the project's ownership that the community-group partner I was working with (1) had little appreciation of this fact and (2) had few resources to effectively participate in the quick review and turnover of pertinent materials. Earlier I mentioned that there are cultural barriers to sustainability, and nowhere did these emerge more prominently than when our business partners needed the quick and full attention of our community-group partner. Meetings were often scheduled and the community group representative would not show up, would show up very late, or would show up with staff members—in some cases with relatives—who weren't invited to the meeting and had not agreed to any of the confidentiality protocols that every industrial-development project inevitably requires. It is vital to remember that these projects require a high degree of trust among the collaborators, since literally hundreds of millions of dollars in investments are at stake. In some cases the success or failure of such a project can actually determine the future of a career. Consequently, being tardy or remiss when critical participation is required undermines the confidence needed to bring the project to the finish line.

Alliances with Grassroots Environmental Groups

Whether or not a local environmental group is actually a participant in the collaboration, the environmental group will in fact be a player in one way or another in the project—either as an active supporter, an active opponent, or a potential supporter or opponent that must be carefully, if not constantly, attended to. Obviously, it is preferable to have grassroots environmentalists supporting the project. Getting their support is complicated but eminently doable.

If there is any sector of the environmental community that remains largely disinclined to collaborate with industry, it is likely to be the grassroots sector. Indeed, the extent of grassroots participation in market-based environmentalism is generally limited to promoting boycotts of certain products that are deemed to be manufactured or used in an environmentally irresponsible fashion. Grassroots opposition to industry is certainly understandable, given the fact that each polluting factory that is a part of the global industrial economy is located in someone's neighborhood. Because grassroots environmentalists by definition focus on local issues, and given that virtually all the factories in the global industrial economy are polluting and damaging to local habitat and ecosystems, the adversarial relationship between grassroots environmentalists and industry is understandable. What's more, industrial development, however well-intentioned it currently pretends to be, never authentically incorporates a meaningful role for grassroots environmental groups, and that is wrong and understandably generates antagonistic relationships.

To obtain the valuable political support and locally informed ecological information that grassroots environmental groups have to offer an industrial-ecology initiative requires an ethically high-minded, environmentally focused, community-friendly, technically honest approach. Rarely do we find these traits among middle management in the corporate world. As one savvy banker more tactfully put it: "The degree to which sustainability makes it onto a corporate agenda depends to a large extent on the board of directors or chief executive officer (CEO). . . . [T]op-down legitimacy must exist for the business to really get involved in the sustainability issue. . . ."[10] Incorporating community interests and grassroots environmental groups authentically into an industrial development initiative is indisputably the type of transitional behavior needed to usher in a more sustainable society.

To gain the support of a grassroots environmental group, an industrial project must, as its first step, demonstrate environmental integrity. If the grassroots group is understandably suspicious of industry, then the most effective way to begin a dialogue is to present, for the group's review and modification, a positive vision of environmental remedies having community-wide economic value. The approach to this aspect of the collaboration, best mediated by an environmentally progressive third party, must be politically and substantively authentic.

After mutually defining the project with the grassroots group to assure that it has authentic environmental value and economic potential, it is then possible to take the budding dialogue to the next strategic level. Numerous other community interests—such as those working on economic development or housing or seniors' issues; religious institutions; or other agencies promoting community development—must be informed and consulted with meaningfully on a regular basis. This is one of the most important catalytic cultural-brokering roles the professional staff at larger national environmental groups might play. I know from firsthand experience that it is high-risk, nuanced, intellectually challenging, and logistically exhausting work.

At this stage, because community interests should be given authentic—but not unilateral controlling—rights related to the project's design and community-development benefits, some adjustments to the project will obviously take place, both in terms of its potential operational design and its ultimate economic structure. Unfortunately, as discussed in chapter 4, environmental-permitting procedures currently make it more costly and risky to publicly undertake technical adjustments to industrial-development plans, even those that are environmentally valuable, because antagonistic community interests, or competing businesses, have the right to initiate lawsuits when technical designs are modified from their original specifications in the environmental-impact statement or permit application. This discourages innovation and, because many technical and economic modifications are essential for the project to actually succeed, it also encourages a less than open relationship between the industrial developer and the community.

All this is complicated by the fact that, among the participants in an industrial-ecology–development collaboration, community interests and grassroots groups will bring to the table the least amount of technical and financial information, expertise, and resources, even while they hold great influence within the neighborhood. An experience gap or information gap between the community interests and the private-sector participants, who are endowed with better resources, can cause suspicion and other types of friction, although it is certainly not a reflection on the ability of community interests to ultimately learn and acquire many private-sector skills and resources—in fact, I argue that part of a sustainable-development project's objectives is to strengthen the skills of these valuable local groups. It is important to remember that the integrity of the project and its ability to succeed depends on no single interest obtaining inappropriate powers and responsibilities before they are properly earned.

Some level of project ownership and a share of other financial benefits should be offered to the community and environmental groups participating in the collaboration. This is politically sensible and economically valuable for both the community and the project. To diversify local support and guard against turf battles, as many local groups as possible should be involved as project stakeholders, not just one community group.

The Input of State and National Environmental Groups

If industrialists will not develop the ecologically valuable projects the planet needs, it is the job of the environmental community to reduce the entry risks and costs associated with doing this. To be the catalysts for sustainability that we must be, early on it is critical to establish the political and technical legitimacy of industrial-ecology projects. To help do so it is important to test the project's design and objectives with a variety of technically informed and environmentally interested organizations, including other statewide and national environmental groups. Since grassroots environmental groups and CDCs often have few resources, they will ultimately welcome technical assessments by other environmental groups. I say they will "ultimately welcome" such help because local environmental groups and community-development groups not infrequently express resentments toward their conventionally attired, sometimes more well-to-do colleagues in the national movement, feeling—inappropriately, counterproductively—that the national groups don't pay enough attention to their local concerns. This is not the place for me to offer corrections to this gross fiction, but suffice it to say that there is no doubt that alliances forged between local environmental interests and national and statewide groups are beneficial. Moreover, because input and assessments from diverse interests increase the chances that both flaws and opportunities in a development project will be identified, the project's design and long-term viability are likely to gain from this type of varied and informed input. Having environmental and community stakeholders in the project lead collaborative technical reviews—supported with the substantial technical resources, from the government or for-profit stakeholders, that these projects require—will give all parties in the endeavor confidence that the effort will produce an environmentally and socially sustainable factory. It will help boost belief in the project's potential with community activists, politicians, regulators, and financiers alike.

If the local community or grassroots environmental groups initially had suspicions about pursuing a market-based collaboration with for-profit interests to build an industrial project, this collaborative initial–project-design stage can help give all stakeholders confidence in the reform potential inherent in market-based advocacy.

The involvement of community-grassroots and national environmental groups in a project gives it enormous momentum. Community interests can help a project succeed or, as is well-known and much more common, cause it to fail. Few issues related to industrial ecology are as important to understand and pay attention to as is the fact that the usually overlooked—or avoided—social market must be cleared. The degree to which a community group can be helpful depends on its resources, its institutional strengths, and personnel attributes as these relate to a variety of project needs.

Above all, if a not-for-profit group wants to be a partner in a major industrial-development project, it needs four critical attributes: (1) excellent managerial skills, (2) good relations with other community and political interests in the area, (3) at least a modicum of financial and technical resources, and (4) a willingness and confidence to learn.

FOSTERING MUTUAL RESPECT AMONG COLLABORATORS

The logistical demands of managing and participating in a large industrial-development project are many and complex. Multidimensional doesn't begin to express how varied, resource intensive and frequently evolving the effort is. Other stakeholder organizations involved in the development effort will not appreciate a community-group partner or any project participant unable to meet the demands of the incessant work necessary to achieve success: community outreach; environmental evaluations; political networking; fund-raising; financial management; meetings with regulators; technical assessments; financial pro-forma reviews; negotiations with equipment vendors, construction companies, and engineering firms; progress reports to senior industrial officials; presentations to potential investors; and relations with the media. As just mentioned, in all likelihood community-group participants will be at a resource disadvantage relative to the other stakeholders in the project. The corporations, financiers, and large environmental groups will not only have more capital and staff expertise but also better managerial capabilities. Learning to respond to the demands of the project's development tasks can help refine and strengthen a community group or, as in the BCPC situation, it can reveal the group's weaknesses, ultimately exacerbate the institution's managerial problems and bring a project down.

Collaboration enhances a project because it brings the various strengths of different partners to focus on a common objective. It does not mean that other partners should have to pick up and carry out the tasks or adopt the interests of any other stakeholder when that stakeholder consistently fails to perform responsibly.

When Banana Kelly petitioned NRDC to become the community-group stakeholder in the BCPC, I understood virtually none of these things. Having an incompetent community-group partner makes it much harder to convince the project's industrial and financial partners that community interests are worth embracing: If the community group itself can't get it together to represent and carry out the needs of the project adequately and in that way advance the community's interests, why should the corporate interests be expected to do so? These issues relating to professional comportment should not be underestimated; they are important signifiers of confidence and commitment.

Every institution has its own standard operating procedures based on its organizational needs and historical experiences. As discussed, community and environmental groups' history of fighting for local economic development and environmental protection has often placed them in opposition to industry and Wall Street financiers. Essentially, it has made all parties—community and grassroots environmental organizations, industry, and government—suspicious at best, and often outright hostile, toward one another. For community and environmental groups to helpfully participate in a much-needed industrial-ecology–development collaboration, each organization must reveal an ability to trust institutions and people they traditionally considered adversaries when they have an established common goal. Just imagine how much more would be accomplished if environmentalists and industry worked side by side, respecting and trusting one another. In part this means learning a new language: The language of collaboration is very different from the language of opposition. An environmental activist's language is often viewed by industry as presumptuous, moralistic, tendentious, and insensitive to the legal rights of private property. In an industrial-ecology collaboration a substantial degree of cultural brokering is needed to bridge the gaps among the diverse stakeholders. This means community groups must be both sophisticated and generous in their patience and willingness to reach out and understand the needs of fellow collaborators who are focused on technical efficiency and clearing the financial market. Conversely, industrialists and financiers must ultimately acknowledge that worsening ecological trends and grossly inequitable social and economic realities are not figments in the imagination of environmentalists and community groups.

Examples that show how developing this new, more inclusive language played a role in shaping the BCPC collaboration abound. To cite one recurring instance: The emphasis on making the project not merely profitable but making it more profitable than other mills and other competing investment opportunities required a huge conceptual shift from the way environmentalists and community groups customarily evaluated technology or policy options. Usually, we are not especially sympathetic to those seeking huge profits (20 or 30 percent and higher), as opposed to just making typical profits (under 20 percent). However, whether those of us working on the project liked it or not, investors considering the BCPC had opportunities to place their money in stocks or mutual funds that at the time were more attractive than investing in a more risky industrial development, regardless of our project's broader ecological or social value. (Remember, the BCPC was being developed during the 1990s high-technology stock bubble, when returns of even 40 percent or 50 percent were not uncommon to institutional and individual investors alike.) To make the project work, the project's environmental participants had to adopt (or at least acquiesce to) the same enthusiasm for extremely high profits as our for-profit partners, even though those profits weren't going to be ours. In the same way, we expected our for-profit partners to adopt our enthusiasm for environmental issues, because addressing these environmental issues was critical to the project's purpose as well as its political success and social acceptance. As one construction-company official told me, "Allen, you've turned me into a tree hugger." (I would be dissembling if I did not report I am convinced he said that not because he had a new appreciation for the adverse global effects of deforestation, but rather because understanding the environmental angle of the project helped him sell it to investors and government alike.)

Community groups typically bring political resources to the table, and while these are critical for a project to clear the social market, they are meaningless without the financial and technical resources brought in by the project's other stakeholders. If environmentalists and community-development reformers want society to realize the potential betterment that an industrial-ecology project offers, if they truly want to build bridges with traditional adversaries, they will try to learn about their partners' needs and help them advance those needs in the same way they expect their own needs to be fostered. To a great degree, the NGO community needs corporate participation to make strides in sustainability more than the corporate sector needs or wants our participation: The corporate sector has done quite well developing its interests all around the world—often destructively, yes, but also profitably, and that is what that sector cares about.

CONCLUSION

Collaborations must be designed to not only overcome the barriers that get in the way of developing new industrial-ecology projects but to enhance the prospects of financial return for investors, the sustainability of host communities, and the ecological health of the planet. Their success depends entirely on the skills and the resources brought to the effort by the diverse stakeholders involved. Good intentions and lofty ideology cannot substitute for intelligent, skillful, well-resourced, and diplomatic implementation. In a well-designed collaboration, participants would bring needed resources and cover the spectrum of knowledge about, and be sensitive to, the social- and financial-market obstacles industrial-ecology projects face, as well as these projects' economic and technical issues. Such participants might logically include:

- a national environmental group,
- a local grassroots environmental group,
- local community-development groups,
- philanthropic supporters,
- political champions,
- a corporate sponsor,
- an investment bank,
- various law firms (that specialize in real estate, zoning, environmental permitting, etc.),
- labor unions, and
- construction and engineering firms.

This type of collaboration would then be able to design advanced technical features, promote authentic political support from the local, state, and federal government, gain confidence from Wall Street and the relevant industry, and establish beneficial media relationships. Having all these different players in place still doesn't guarantee that the process will be without error and smooth. Complications are inherent in a diverse, multistakeholder development deal, especially an innovative industrial-ecology approach that, while admirable, is still subject to potent, countersustainable competitive pressures. But without such collaborations, developing sustainable industrial-ecology projects in the locations that need them most will *never* happen. And, in ecological terms, the world just can't afford another century like the past one.

NOTES

1. Ernst Mayr, *This Is Biology* (Cambridge, Massachusetts: Belknap Press, 1998), p. xiv.
2. David J. Rothman, "What Doctors Don't Tell Us," *New York Review of Books,* 29 February 1996, p. 31.
3. Dr. Dahlia Zaidel, professor of neuropsychology, University of California, Los Angeles, personal communication, 20 August 2001, excerpted with permission.
4. Darwin's only formal academic credential was a B.A. from Christ's College, University of Cambridge, which he was awarded in 1831 after abandoning his medical studies at the University of Edinburgh. See Charles Darwin, *The Voyage of the Beagle* (New York: Random House, 2001), p. v.
5. Interestingly, when I was working on the National Recycling Act—which I described in the Introduction of this book—I led a similarly inclusive collaboration of government officials, environmentalists, and business-people on a fact-finding mission to Europe to study recycling policies and try to end the adversarial battles that characterized the lobbying on the bill. Together we saw the same technologies, met the same regulators, and agreed, while we were in Europe, that government policies of the sort that the National Recycling Act was trying to promote did in fact work economically and environmentally. When we returned, the congressional members of our trip were effectively paid by the virgin-based industries to forget what they saw and learned in Europe, so the benefits of that collaborative initiative were undermined.
6. Board on Sustainable Development, National Research Council, *Our Common Journey: A Transition Toward Sustainability* (Washington, D.C.: National Academy Press, 1999), pp. 2 and 6.
7. I am indebted to Anne Fadiman for teaching me this term, which helped me make sense of my most important role in the BCPC collaboration while I participated in it. See her extraordinary book, *The Spirit Catches You and You Fall Down: A Hmong Child, Her American Doctors, and the Collision of Two Cultures* (New York: Farrar, Straus and Giroux, 1997).

8. Marcel Jeucken, *Sustainable Finance and Banking: The Financial Sector and the Future of the Planet* (London: Earthscan Publications, Ltd., 2001), p. 68.

9. Offshore oil-drilling rigs, remote energy-production facilities, and remote timber harvesting and paper mills are a few exceptions, although they are indisputably located in some species' habitat.

10. Jeucken, *Sustainable Finance and Banking*, p. 67.

8.   Getting Started: What Is to Be Done?

> You can't go around criticizing something you're not part
> of and hope to make it better. It ain't gonna work.
>
> —Bob Dylan

WHEN ONE THINKS of the South Bronx, the local area I
hoped the BCPC would help remediate, one thinks of New York City's
poorest borough,[1] of a district with the city's lowest recycling rate and
highest childhood asthma rate, of abandoned industrial sites and of social
dysfunction: Unemployment,[2] economic underdevelopment, political
shakedowns, racial and ethnic tensions, apartments in disrepair, pollution, stress on families. It is the inverse of the sustainable society. The
issues the South Bronx faces are nothing less than a catalog of the barriers to sustainability, all of them must be overcome, and, sadly, none of
them are unique to the South Bronx.

Can there be a better future for places like the South Bronx and,
indeed, for us all? This of course is an open question. I'm convinced that
if there is to be a cleaner, richer, and safer future for *all* species, environmentally committed activists—better trained, out from behind our desks,
and using all the financial, technical, and legal resources we can muster—
must be the catalysts. Although we can partner with other potentially

progressive forces like community groups, we must substantially increase our decision-making influence over business. Ever-increasing and larger mergers and consolidation in the global corporate sector add more urgency to our need to do so: Mergers do not result in new industrial-ecology–oriented factories being built; instead, they allow ever larger and remote firms to increase their control over more and more industrial capacity, even though the factories they are buying are ecologically obsolete. Environmentalists on corporate boards or in ownership positions will not only add a very much needed public-interest perspective to these currently non–public-interested entities, but will also provide more green influence over government, to offset the influence corporations now hold over it. On corporate boards, environmentalists can serve as ombudsmen for the public interest. As owners or developers, they can more fundamentally reorient their firm's or factory's relationship to the global ecosystem and society. But even if environmentalists do begin to own and control more industrial firms, the barriers to sustainable development described throughout this book still must be overcome, and these barriers are great.

Beyond describing the obstacles to sustainable industrial development, this book has attempted to reveal some of the ways businesses, community groups, and environmental reformers might begin to navigate around barriers to sustainability. What follows is a set of fourteen principles for industrial-ecology developers. Respecting these fourteen principles will help guide future industrial developers as they try to make a difference.

1. *Outcompete the bad: Always keep in mind that a development project has to be profitable to be sustainable.* Sustainable development projects, whether developed by government or the private for-profit sector, must be able to clear the market, i.e., be cost competitive and produce a high profit to investors. If a project or an idea does not get financed, is not cost competitive and cannot clear the market; it is always at risk of either not justifying the interest of investors or, if it is government owned or assisted, of being undermined by a change in the political winds. Respect the for-profit sector's need for profit. Moreover, creating environmentally beneficial jobs must be a goal that industrial ecologists should strive to develop. If a company is not

cost competitive and profitable, its long-term ecological value and its employees' jobs are at a greater risk. Unemployment is among the greatest threats to sustainability.

2. *Use recycled waste.* Choose raw materials—such as agricultural wastes, recovered municipal waste, industrial or commercial wastes, etc.— that offer the best environmental remedies or, at worst, produce the least environmental burdens. The world is being overrun with billions of tons of wastes each year, and industrial ecologists must urgently focus on remedying this potentially disastrous environmental and economic threat.

3. *Choose a brownfield. Avoid greenfields.* The best way to preserve habitat and terrestrial biodiversity, prevent sprawl, protect freshwater, and reduce transportation-related pollution is to avoid conversion of forests, meadows, prairies, wetlands, and other types of green spaces. The most environmentally responsible location in which to site a factory is a brownfield. Locating an industrial project in an urban brownfield is one of the most important decisions any industrial developer can make. Moreover, because locating at a brownfield implies that the site has been previously used by a commercial or industrial facility, there is likely to be some type of preexisting transportation and sewage infrastructure there. Other potential benefits associated with locating a project at a brownfield include avoiding freshwater use (allowing for sewage-effluent recycling) and avoiding the development impacts associated with building and maintaining new roads. Brownfield redevelopment could also allow for the rehabilitation of underutilized transportation infrastructures like barge and rail; thus, should one form of transportation be interrupted—by a truckers' strike or a railroad accident, for example—other transportation options would be available.

4. *Opt for ecological water use.* Instead of relying on potable water, industrial ecologists should design their industrial process to rely on cleaned sewage effluents that would otherwise be released into waterways. It is a sad and threatening fact that the vast majority of scarce potable water used in the world is used only once and then discharged, sometimes to a septic or sewage-treatment plant, often

directly into a waterway. Although freshwater is safest for drinking and cooking, most industrial processes can be run without fresh–drinking-water supplies. Industrial ecology requires that sewage-treatment–plant effluent be considered a useful supply of water, not a waste product.

5. *Diminish energy impacts.* Industrial projects engender energy impacts when (1) workers commute to the plant, (2) raw materials, water, and chemicals are acquired and delivered, (3) machinery is operated, (4) finished products are transported, and (5) solid and liquid wastes are disposed of. High-efficiency production technologies that integrate the use of non–fossil-fueled energy supplies as much as economically possible are essential. Also, by locating at a brownfield, there is a greater range of options available to reduce a factory's transportation-related energy impacts. Reducing energy impacts is among the most widely analyzed industrial options, and usually among the most cost-effective.

6. *Attend to social barriers.* Along with engineering analyses of material flows, industrial ecologists have to pay attention to the social barriers—social, political, and regulatory obstacles—which ultimately determine whether innovative ecological improvements will get developed. Though often overlooked by environmentalists and industrial developers alike, obtaining permits, navigating among regulators, maintaining good media relations, and contending with the conflicting attitudes and mind-sets of the diverse participants in an industrial-ecology project are the most critical, and often most difficult, barriers to overcome.

7. *Cultivate community support and partners.* Projects that are inclusive of community interests are more likely to succeed. Such inclusion will provide ecological, political, and logistical value during the permitting and development phase. An inclusive approach to development is more likely to respect and seek to address past burdens imposed in certain regions, is more appropriate from the perspective of democratic processes and community-development interests, and the project itself will benefit in many ways from community input.

8. *Collaborate with the private sector.* Collaboration helps a project devel-

opment team overcome the diverse technical, financial, and social barriers every industrial-ecology project will face. Collaboration, versus having adversarial relationships, also leads to discovery of the truth more expeditiously. Unlike government-dependent advocacy—which often subverts environmental sciences or economics in the name of getting legislation enacted or, more often, stopped—direct dialogue with corporate engineers, financiers, and CEOs tends to enhance scientific accuracy and economic understanding. Dialogue and collaboration are essential to advance knowledge and sustainability.

9. *Respect scientific evidence.* Making progress with sustainability is dependent on a respect for the facts. Legislative processes, on the other hand, have a different motivation. Reforming any industry to make it more sustainable requires an honest and thorough consideration of all relevant biological, physical, sociological, and economic facts and options in order to design an ecologically and socially integrated solution.

10. *Advance the spirit underlying environmental laws.* The motivations of the industrialists who implement government regulations are fundamentally different from the spirit and intention that prompted the legislative and regulatory requirements to begin with. For industrial ecologists implementation is supposed to foster biological diversity, public-health protections, habitat preservation, or some other biological—and social—need related to sustainability. By contrast, unless there is a healthy profit to be made, corporations tend to view implementation of environmental regulations merely as a compliance issue, to be achieved at the least possible cost, not as a call to usher in a new sustainable era. If the private sector wants to obtain the benefits that collaboration with environmentalists offers (e.g., faster permitting and help with development financing), it must authentically buy into the environmentalist ethic.

11. *Avoid shortcuts during permitting.* A developer who seeks the best environmental technologies for cleaning up a brownfield site to the highest standards, and who also relies on a community-input approach, is more likely to benefit from local goodwill and government support, including cleanup subsidies. On the other hand,

cleanup shortcuts always seem to become known, and when they do, they throw a development initiative into turmoil. While many industrial-project developers who take shortcuts do succeed and environmentally inferior projects are often developed, these are equally likely to face delays because of government investigations and community opposition. Local interests are obviously more likely to try and postpone implementation of a compromised cleanup plan they did not help design than to stymie a superb one they were involved with defining.

12. *Focus your efforts.* Although the most high-risk ecological problems are global—for example, loss of habitat and biodiversity, climate change, deforestation, and ozone depletion—solving these problems must be accomplished through local and industry-specific investments, a strategy that the National Research Council's Board on Sustainable Development has referred to as *place-based action.*

13. *Heal ecological problems: Don't just generate fewer of them.* Developing a "less bad" project ultimately still moves us in an ecologically negative direction. The guide all industrial ecologists should use is: What type of industry can I develop that will heal an ecological problem? Innovate. Doing "better" and trial and error are essential attributes of sustainable development. The pathways to sustainability depend on innovation and cannot be precisely mapped in advance. Instead, as the National Research Council has confirmed, "they will have to be navigated adaptively."[3] Too often, technical adjustments and strategic compromises elicit the charge that progressive principles are being abandoned. In fact, such adjustments and compromises may in practice mean achieving what is achievable at the time, with an eye toward building a better foundation from which to move forward in the future.

14. *Choose industries with impact.* Industrial ecologists should choose to develop industries that can have a positive environmental impact. In contrast to the interests of financiers, eco-realism demands that deciding what type of factory to develop is foremost an ecological decision. If possible, opt to build better factories in those industries causing the greatest environmental destruction, especially forest-

based and climate-changing energy-related industries. Beware of supporting the development of industries, even if located at urban brownfields, that may have ecologically incongruous consequences—for instance, certain hazardous synthetic-chemical-based–pesticide plants, generically known as synthetic organic chemical manufacturing industry (SOCMI) plants. While rehabilitating a brownfield for a SOCMI plant may be useful if it stops the development of a new plant at a sprawl-inducing site and instead leads to the cleanup of a contaminated site, and creating additional wealth in the surrounding community has merit, it is doubtful that helping chemical manufacturers produce pesticides more efficiently is something environmentalists should assist, given the adverse habitat impacts and public-health threats these products cause.

WHAT ENVIRONMENTALISTS CAN DO

Markets are tough to change. Even with twenty-first-century regulations, markets are ruthless in their self-interest. Without regulations, they are often deadly: In unregulated markets men, women, and children have been sold into forced labor and prostitution, wealth is so disproportionately distributed that a majority of humanity lives on less than two dollars per day, and there is a global proliferation of open hazardous-waste dumps. The absence of regulations, or ineffective regulations, has allowed humans to instigate the mass extinction of a substantial fraction of the world's species, without even having known they existed. Despite centuries' worth of intervention by government, charities, philanthropies, international agencies, and NGOs, the reality of the marketplace is, for most of humankind, more like the medieval times that Thomas Hobbes described as being in "continuall feare, [sic] and in danger of violent death . . . solitary, poore, [sic] nasty, brutish, and short,"[4] than the picture of harmony and efficiency so often painted by modern free-trade ideologues.

Today, the dominant market influence in the world is the corporation. Consequently, whatever else environmentalists do, we must above all acquire greater leverage over corporate decision making. That is why I advocate that environmentalists actually push ahead and become the developers of better industrial facilities. But that is not the only role environmentalists can take on. If we must use more than legislative and judicial strategies to gain greater influence over corporate behavior, specifically how might we do this? Trying to instigate even a marginal market transformation requires years of work by influential, smart, well-funded, and broad-based collaborators. And successfully instigating market transformations in behalf of ecological preservation or social betterment has been even more rare.

That so many diverse sectors need to adjust their thinking, and must come together to collaborate on advancing meaningful solutions, underscores how daunting the challenge is. In chapter 1, I argued that environmentalists must evolve away from an ideologically rigid anti-industrial posture and develop a reform movement that helps stimulate the construction of new industrial-ecology projects. The only way to achieve this is to take anti-industrial ideologies out of the mix. Actually, all ideology— intellectually rigid, usually untested ideas to which we revert when we have had no experience to fall back on—should be taken out of the mix. National environmental organizations should lead the way in rebuffing ideological zealots as well as corporate green-washing—public relations designed to present a company as environmentally responsible when it is in fact not—and should expose any self-interested tactics that some local groups occasionally employ under the pretext of ecological protection or vague references to community-based control.

To advance sustainability, environmentalists must complement their technical and legal arsenal with a more sophisticated and influential approach designed to develop and promote sustainability-oriented financial products. They have to think more like M.B.A.'s. Environmentalists are needed on Wall Street, in the corporate boardroom, and as CEOs. As I discussed in chapter 1, investment-banking decisions are environmental and social decision making under a different, more complex, and less accountable guise, so the time is long overdue for environmentalists and social reformers to infiltrate that sector. Activists and graduate students with degrees in environmental sciences should think about careers in investment banks and at corporations, and absolutely insist on promoting investment and operational decisions at their firms that advance sustainability rather than undermine it. When they get there, they will learn that it is not just profit that rules, it is an incessant, almost pathological desire for *very high profits.* Turning down more than a 30 percent return, as one paper company, Stone Consolidated, did when it rejected the BCPC project for a 40 percent return in a Korean investment, suggests there is an enormous amount of work to do on Wall Street to make industrial-ecology investments financially competitive and strategically attractive.

Decisions by corporations about whether to invest in a new production facility—whether it is a sustainable project or not—is more complicated than simply assessing a project's anticipated rate of return, of course. Marketing relationships, strategic assessments about industry-wide production capacity, tax issues, corporate culture, the personal biases of the CEO, individual talent, industry trends, anticipated support from the host community, etc., all affect corporate decision making. While corporate decisions are almost always an environmental decision in one form or another, explicit ecological assessments are usually not factored into the industrial-development decision-making mix. Invariably, these environmental decisions are made behind closed doors without input from environmentalists. This must change. To effectively advance sustainability in the global-industrial sector—the political-economic sector most critically in need of environmental reform—environmental advocates must proceed with a Wall Street–oriented strategy comparable to the government-oriented strategy we've refined over the past thirty years. Infiltrating the world of investment banking, transforming it into a sustainable banking sector, is critical to further progress.

As we pursue this potentially more ecologically effective and strategically aggressive advocacy strategy, environmentalists must also recommit ourselves to building peaceful and respectful relationships among currently antagonistic sectors. The ecologically harmonious vision of sustainability that we teach our children to dream of has no role for a raised middle finger, racial or ethnic biases, or class-based prejudices. Indeed, the name Greenpeace itself—arguably the most successfully branded name in the history of the environmental movement—derives so much of its international appeal precisely because it conjures up an image of collaborative, ego-free love as well as habitat preservation.

Much of the progress in sustainable development, industrial ecology, and sustainable banking and finance is originating in Europe. Based on my eight-year experience working with European businesspeople on the

BCPC project, and almost twenty years of international environmental research, I have observed a decisive difference in perspectives on environmental and technological matters between officials at European firms—for example, Swedish paper-company executives—and their counterparts in the United States. It is an open secret among industrial observers that corporate officials in the United States show much less interest in, and less knowledge of, more technically innovative and socially progressive approaches to business management and the social impacts of business than do many of their European counterparts. During the past twenty years European nations have adopted more thoughtful and progressive environmental practices and regulations, in large part because the companies that operate there have been more collaborative than adversarial when it comes to global ecological protection. Just look at the difference in attitudes between the much more supportive European firms and adversarial American firms on the Kyoto climate-change treaty. In fact, some of the greatest differences relate to paper-company practices: European firms long ago began phasing out toxic chlorine bleaching—something American firms continue to resist—and in Germany all domestic paper mills rely mostly (more than 70 percent) on recycled wastepaper, and the small fraction of virgin pulp that German mills do use is imported not from endangered forests, but from sustainably managed forests in Scandinavia.[5]

My own social theory on why this is so has to do with the historical size of the market opportunities a European businessperson has confronted compared with the market available to a U.S. businessperson, and the implications this has had for efficiency and considerations of social impacts. Historically, in the United States an industrialist could anticipate making profits on volume. Given the size of the U.S. market, and the government's export subsidies and subsidies for using virgin raw materials, freshwater, and energy, there could be—and has been—less emphasis on promoting industrial efficiency. On average, American factories use more water and energy and produce twice as much waste per unit of GDP than factories in Japan and every European nation except Hungary.[6] Produce a widget in the United States and a market of 260 million consumers awaits. In Europe, by contrast, each country's market is much smaller, freshwater is less easily obtainable, and energy is more costly and much less subsidized, so profits have to be made through the realization of greater efficiency and the ability to compete in the international export market, also more competitive. In this context, high-efficiency innovations make more sense. Moreover, since European nations are much smaller, it is much more likely that a corporate CEO or official will live among his or her workers than it is in the spread-out United States, with its huge pay-scale disparities. Justifying no action on climate change or other environmental concerns is socially, if not psychologically, more difficult for European CEOs.

Another critical task the environmental community must embrace to facilitate industrial-ecology growth is assisting good projects in the acquisition of environmental permits and approvals. Stopping bad projects does not automatically lead to good projects being developed. More often it means the bad projects will move to less contentious or less regulated environments, to the detriment of both the local and the global environment. As Rajeswari Kanniah, a consumer and environmental advocate from Malaysia, has stated, "The very same companies that are being forced to clean up your countries in the developed world are poisoning more and more of our countries in the developing world."[7]

Current permitting regimes can allow for less time-consuming and more public-spirited consideration of industrial projects, but this can happen only with the active support of environmentalists and community groups. When environmentalist and community interests weigh in in behalf of a good industrial-ecology project, with an advanced technical design and a beneficial social approach to development, this can lead to a collaborative, rather than an adversarial, relationship with permitting agencies. This can also help overcome length of time it takes to obtain permits, a penalty that causes so many industrial-project developers not to consider locating at urban brownfields.

ALLIES WHO CAN HELP

The responsibility for industrial-ecology reform falls on others as well as environmentalists, especially on those who are proponents of ecological causes in the not-for-profit world. Nongovernmental sustainability stakeholders logically include philanthropies, unions, and community groups. And government still has a key role to play.

Philanthropies Have to Act

Besides activist organizations themselves, no sector has been as influential in behalf of environmental reform as philanthropic foundations. Virtually all forms of environmental activism have been supported at one time or another, in one way or another, by these distinguished institutions. By intensifying two market-based advocacy approaches, foundations can increase their leverage in the sector they've been trying to reform for decades. First, foundations that haven't already done so should try to use their endowments to influence corporations in their role as stockholders, something environmental groups should also do. Admittedly, for most foundations this is more of a symbolic than a truly effective strategy—most corporations do as they please on environmental and social issues, regardless of shareholder positions—but foundations, just like environmental groups, must see to it that their investments correspond with their program goals. For some very large foundations with huge invested endowments, this strategy could be meaningfully influential.

Second, philanthropic foundations can—but rarely do—help provide early-stage development funding to environmental groups and community-development groups to help these NGOs entice corporations to work with them on industrial-ecology projects, or to allow these NGOs to develop their own industrial-ecology projects to the point where corporations take an investment interest in them. As the BCPC effort has shown, this can be one of the most valuable reform-oriented actions a foundation can perform.

Union Laborers Should Consider Creative Ways to Garner Profits

Unions can adopt many market-based advocacy strategies, including mobilizing consumer action, partnering with corporations to help them enhance their environmental and social performance, partnering with trade groups to create standards that will help reduce industry's environmental impacts, and participating as partners in an industrial-ecology development project. Unfortunately, as discussed in chapter 5, certain work rules and prohibitively high wages make unions now more of an obstacle than an asset to sustainable urban-brownfield redevelopment. This can change, and should change, in a way that benefits both union members and the cost competitiveness of urban industrial-ecology projects. Union members can and should diversity their base wages by becoming owners instead of merely wage laborers. Taking ownership positions may ultimately be more financially rewarding and will not raise a project's capital-construction costs. Moreover, union pension funds can be used to facilitate ownership positions and provide a project with a valuable equity investment. As Professor Heide Pfarr, a German sustainability theorist, has written, "unions are particularly well placed and able to face up to the challenge of formulating a process for the transition toward a sustainable society. Given the processes of change required to move toward sustainability in the workplace, their participation is essential. Alongside companies, they are the central players, whose task it will be to integrate the work of the future into sustainable development."[8] It is critical that union rules and wages no longer be barriers to developing industrial-ecology projects.

Community Groups Must Diversify Their Skills and Influence

Community groups are obviously essential to advance sustainability. One of the principle measures of success for sustainable development is how effectively a project involves local people in both the planning and action phases of the endeavor, and how extensively the community's wealth is enhanced. As mentioned previously, community groups can provide technical, political, and financial support—by strategically using grants from foundations and government, as Banana Kelly and NRDC did with the BCPC—to assist industrial-ecology developers. It is virtually unheard of for community groups to actively promote industrial projects, so when they do this, it has a big impact with regulators and politicians, who are already politically biased toward promoting business activities. The community-development movement must move beyond affordable-housing initiatives and the provision of social services and elevate sustainable industrial development to a much higher priority.

Community development groups typically engage in small-scale housing projects. The BCPC was the only world-scale manufacturing-based sustainability project I know of anywhere to be initiated, defined, initially financed, and developed with ownership by community interests and development direction by environmental activists. But community groups can—indeed, they must—play this important role in helping to jump-start industrial-ecology projects. Obviously, approaching corporate interests with plans for collaboration on a development project is more complicated than simply picking up the phone and requesting a meeting with the company president. It requires high-level corporate access, which most community-development groups don't have, as well as tolerance of and sensitivity to the corporate worldview, plus sensitivity to the corporation's market and longer-term strategic interests. Few community-development advocates hold this worldview.

Also, industrial-ecology projects require highly effective negotiating skills and an ability to develop and coordinate close working relationships with the major institutional players in government and the private sector, including large investment banks, bond underwriters, and engineering and legal firms. Few community groups have the staff, resources, and orientation needed to develop and sustain all of these relationships simultaneously. Also, and perhaps most critical, larger development initiatives are very resource intensive, requiring not only deep financial assets but highly sophisticated technical know-how, which are usually undeveloped—by the standards of global corporations—in most community groups. By collaborating with national or statewide environmental groups and industrial ecologists in the business sector, community groups have a better chance of acquiring more resources and refining the skills they need.

Community groups are best positioned to help industrial projects navigate around the bevy of potent social barriers any industrial development faces. But first, however, community groups, together with businesses and environmental groups, must confront and overcome the cultural obstacles to sustainability. This adjustment in worldviews is the factor that, perhaps most of all, must evolve if community-based environmental development is to become a meaningful economic sector.

How Government Can Participate

There are different pragmatic ways for an industrial-ecology collaboration to get off the ground. Local, state, and provincial governments can perform many of the advocacy tasks needed to launch an industrial-ecology project. But in the United States, government has shied away from doing so, because it is so thoroughly controlled by business interests that do not want the competition, however ecologically essential it is. The U.S. government's investment in civic planning and nonmilitary public-works projects has declined steadily throughout the twentieth century. Environmental proponents outside government can form partnerships with those within it in an attempt to overcome business's control of government and to initiate the building of industrial-ecology projects in a fashion similar to the great civic-minded public-works projects of times long gone. These can then either be operated by the government as a public-works project—necessary to preserve our public health and environment—or sold to the private sector in the same way this has been done for landfills, incinerators, stadiums, prisons, schools, defense establishments, and government buildings. In the United States it is not politically fashionable to discuss "government ownership" approaches these days, but there is no objective reason this shouldn't be considered. Moreover, in much of the developing world—where deforestation problems are the worst—and throughout Europe and Asia the ideological bias against government ownership of factories is not as intense. Since industry is now so thoroughly a global affair, it might be just as influential to begin building the industrial-ecology projects encouraged by this book in parts of the world other than the United States. The need to respond to the global ecological crisis makes this approach more necessary to consider, especially if industry doesn't change its deadly course on its own initiative.

If industry doesn't respond to overtures to help build a new industrial-ecology infrastructure, environmentalists should certainly lobby government to develop industrial-ecology public-works projects. Local, state, and provincial governments can help plan and finance industrial-ecology mills in the same way they help plan and build solid-waste– and water-treatment establishments. In fact, cities and provincial governments, even more than environmental and community groups, are well suited to design incentive programs to attract clean production. Along with environmental and community groups they can and should develop approval processes that distinguish between a bad industrial proposal and a good one. Perhaps to do so, cities should establish sustainability siting boards, run by environmentalists and community interests and designed to facilitate the development, permitting, and financing of industrial-ecology projects. In the past—actually, to this day—many government-owned facilities instigated huge ecological disasters and were by no means accountable to the public interest. Consequently, even if in the very unlikely event that some level of government does develop an industrial-ecology project, the oversight and influence of environmentalists must remain strong and vigilant.

Government can also reward good industrial proposals with lower-risk permitting processes and lower-cost capital. Credit guarantees backing these projects, especially for those projects that promote innovative environmental technologies and hold the potential to generate many jobs, should be offered. Currently, the opposite situation prevails: The financial sector penalizes environmentally innovative investments, and virtually the same regulatory hurdles one has to go through to build a waste incinerator apply to a green industrial project. This obviously needs to change.

ESTABLISHING MUTUAL RESPECT AND TRUST

Think of how much more effective we in the environmental movement could be if we trusted our counterparts in industry and if they trusted us. Sustainable industrial development provides great opportunities to build this trust. Green industrial projects can simultaneously promote species preservation and economic development, and even strengthen democratic institutions. To environmentalists, it seems like a winning approach for all concerned. Practically, though, the market is biased against it in profoundly strong ways—ways that we have only just begun to document.

Only by moving out from behind our desks and into the industrial fray can we understand how truly enormous these obstacles are. And only then can we authentically begin to overcome them. My experience, based on lecturing throughout the world to college and graduate students as well as to many businesspeople and regulators, is that there is an excitement about the idea of investing our way to sustainability. The idea of being able to provide or earn a livable wage and at the same time heal the planet is an enormously attractive one. It is a testament to the essential interest people have in self-preservation. Perhaps it confirms Edward O.

Wilson's "biophilia" argument, that an attraction to nature is one of the few instincts humans have.[9] And perhaps as well it is a testament to the fact that most people are also essentially good, however much the marketplace—and, sometimes, ideological or religious fanaticism—forces them to struggle against one other.

Compassion and science, money and hard-knuckled political work, are all needed to make progress on the industrial-ecology front. Breaking down presumptions about who is good and who is bad—or, indeed, who is right and who is wrong—is the necessary first step in promoting the dialogue among traditional adversaries, who must come together if the world and all its glorious species are to survive through the twenty-first century. The Bronx Community Paper Company was a first and important step designed to accelerate that movement. Though the project didn't get built, it almost did, and because of the progress we made on it, many lessons were learned. Many more still need to be learned. If we are really serious about preserving our children's habitat, and the habitat for the 30 million species with which we share the Earth, we have to take more control of the business and governmental decisions that determine our future. And we will.

NOTES

1. Residents of the Bronx have the lowest average household income of any borough in New York City, as well as a lower average household income than the average in New York State and the United States.
2. As of this writing the unemployment rate in the Bronx is higher than that in any other borough in New York City, higher than the city's overall average, higher than the New York State average, and higher than the average for the country as a whole. The data are as follows: the Bronx, 8.8 percent; Brooklyn, 8.3 percent; Manhattan, 7.5 percent; Queens, 6.6 percent; Staten Island, 5.8 percent; New York City, 7.5 percent; New York State, 6.3 percent; and United States, 6.3 percent. Source: New York City Department of Employment, 20 March 2002.
3. Board on Sustainable Development, National Research Council *Our Common Journey: A Transition Toward Sustainability* (Washington, D.C.: National Academy Press, 1999), p. 3.
4. Thomas Hobbes, *Leviathan* (first published 1651, reprinted London: Penguin Books, 1981), part. 1, chapter 13, p. 186.

5. Dr. Markus Kollar, director, Plastics Industry, Pulp and Paper, Timber and Packaging. Federal Environmental Agency, Berlin, Germany, personal interview, 12 March 2001.

6. *OECD Environmental Indicators: Towards Sustainable Development* (Paris: OECD, 2001), pp. 39, 50.

7. Speech before the "UNEP's 7th International High-Level Seminar on Cleaner Production," Prague, 29 April 2002.

8. Heide Pfarr, *Pathways to a Sustainable Future* (Düsseldorf, Germany: Hans Bockler Stiftung, 2001), p. 3.

9. See Edward O. Wilson, *Biophilia: The Human Bond With Other Species* (Cambridge, Massachusetts and London: Harvard University Press, 1984).

INDEX

Absorbable organic halides (AOX), 67
Accidents and permitting process, major
    industrial, 130
Adversarial *vs.* collaborative approach,
    211
AFL-CIO, 146, 187
Africa, 62, 68, 70, 80, 107
Agenda 21, 37
Agriculture, United States Department of
    (USDA), 71, 74, 78
Air quality/pollution:
    electrical power plants, 113
    gas boilers, 113–14
    landfills, methane-generating, 76–77
    research and analysis, 63–64, 67,
        76–77
    science/truth ignored in favor of
        political expediency, 32
    selective-catalytic-dentrification
        equipment, 20
    transportation-related energy impacts,
        76
    volatile organic compounds, 64, 67
Allied Waste Industries, 22, 165
Amazon, Brazilian, 69
American Forest and Paper Association,
    14
American Gas Association, 35
American Petroleum, 35
Amtrak, 157
Analysis, need, *see* Research and analysis
Arctic National Wildlife, 187
Army Corps of Engineers, U.S., 145, 157
Arthur Andersen, 47
A/S Bioteknisk Jordrens, 43
Asia, 68, 70, 80, 148

Asnaes Power Station, 43
Austria, 89
Automobiles and fuel issues, 10–11,
    16–17, 32, 187

Background extinctions, 59
Balkanized approach to policy making, 31
Banana Kelly Community Improvement
    Association, 101, 179, 187, 234,
    235–37, 245, 263
Banking firms, investment, 228–31
Baucus, Max, 9
BCPC, *see* Bronx Community Paper
    Company
Bear Stearns, 230
Belize, 31
Benzer, Seymour, 217
Berry, Wendell, 39
Beverage-container deposit requirements,
    10, 11
BFI, 22
Biochemical oxygen demand (BOD), 110
Biodiversity, forests and global, 67–72, 94
Biophilia argument, 266–67
Bleaching, paper manufacturing and
    chlorine-based, 63–64, 76, 222, 260
Blueprint for change, a new:
    boards of directors, environmentalists
        serving on, 47–49
    conclusions/chapter summary, 51–52
    eco-realism, 46–51
    government-dependent advocacy,
        inadequacy of, 30–31
    green strategies, the prevailing, 37–40
    idealism, practical side to, 29
    industrial-ecological approach, 40–46

269

Blueprint for change, a new (*continued*):
owners/developers of corporations, environmentalists as, 49–51
private sector crucial to building a sustainable economy, 28–29
traditional environmental strategies, inadequacy of, 27–29
Board on Sustainable Development, 203, 256
Boards of directors, environmentalists serving on, 47–49
Bond, Christopher, 32
Bottle-deposit requirements, 10, 11
Boundaries, government action limited by political/economic, 31
Brazil, 67, 69
Bronx, south, 251
see also Bronx Community Paper Company
Bronx Community Paper Company (BCPC):
Banana Kelly Community Improvement Association, 235–37
board of directors, 48–49
complicated project development issues, 21–22
construction companies suing to be part of project, 23–24
contracts with New York City, 22–23
corruption, 22
design of, 142–43, 190
energy efficiency/issues, 20–21
failure of, three decisive blows leading to, 22–24
forestry/forests, 19
Goldstein's (Eric) reservations about creating, 16–17
industrial ecology, 41
innovative features, 18–21
lessons learned from endeavor, 23–24
model for future development, 1, 4
partnerships, forming, 218–20
permitting process, 139–46, 236
politics/political issues, 180–83
reasons driving the creation of, 4–6
research and analysis, 57–59
water pollution/issues, 107–13, 154–59
see also individual subject headings
Bronx Kill landfill, 125, 145, 157
Bronx Museum of the Arts, 20
Brownfields, siting factories at urban: cleanup, 97–98, 124–29

community participation, 100–102
conclusions/chapter summary, 117–18
electricity and steam, 113–14
future, hope for the, 253
infrastructure and operational issues, 99, 102–3, 116
International Organization for Standardization management standards, 200
jobs/employment, 98, 99
sewage-treatment-plant wastewater, use of reclaimed, 104–13
Small Business Liability Relief and Brownfields Revitalization Act, 101
training, worker, 99
transportation energy use, 115–17
water issues, 103–7
see also Bronx Community Paper Company; Economic/technical obstacles to urban industrial-ecology development; Social-market obstacles to urban industrial-ecology development
Bruckner Expressway, 101, 125
Bush, George W., 35
Business-environmental community relationship:
culture of business as obstacle to industrial-ecology development, 188–91
environmentalists in business, old-guard resistance to, 191–93
industrial-ecological approach, existing businesses challenging, 174–76
see also Blueprint for change, a new; Community participation; Industrial-ecological approach

Cadmium yellow, 42
California, 107
Canada, 80
Carbon dioxide, 32, 75, 76, 114
Cardona, Aureo, 22
Catalytic-dentrification equipment, selective, 20
Cellulose, 4
Central America, 68, 70
Central Labor Council, New York City, 146
Champion International, 68
Chlorides, 110, 155–56
Chlorine, 42, 63–64, 76, 222, 260

Chloroform, 67
City Planning Commission (CPC), 143
Classifications/grades of paper, 61
Cleanup, brownfield, 97–98, 101,
    124–29
Clinton, Bill, 1, 4, 14, 22–24, 38–39
Clinton, Hillary, 22–23, 165
Coca-Cola, 11
Collaboration, the power of, 209–12
    see also Partnerships, forming
Commoner, Barry, 46–47
Community-based development,
    defining, 232
Community-development corporations
    (CDCs), 18–19, 101, 233–37
Community Health Institute (CHI),
    19–20
Community participation:
    BCPC project, 18, 21
    brownfield-reclamation approach,
        100–102, 128
    cleanup, brownfield, 128
    community-development corporations,
        18–19, 101, 233–37
    construction companies, 226–27
    defining community-based
        development, 232
    evaluating community partners,
        237–40
    future, hope for the, 254–55, 263–64
    infighting as obstacle to industrial-
        ecology development, 172
    partnerships, forming, 232–40
    permitting process, 135–37, 232–33
    social-market obstacles to urban
        industrial-ecology development,
        176–78
    unions, 150, 226
Commuting, energy-efficient forms of,
    115
Comprehensive Environmental Response,
    Compensation, and Liability
    Information System (CERCLIS),
    125
Compromises, strategic, 201–4
    see also Partnerships, forming
Congo, Democratic Republic of, 70
Congressional Research Service (CRS),
    8–9
Conrail, 157
Consciousness, need for change in
    human, 207–8

Construction companies, litigation
    intimidation from, 23–24, 183–84
Construction/engineering partners,
    choosing, 225–28
Construction-labor costs, 146–51
Consultants and biases in global
    industrial system, 206
Consumer Affairs Department, 218
Consumer decisions based on
    price/performance/style, 39–41
Consumption issues, 37–38, 40, 61–62,
    64, 68
Contracts with New York City and failure
    of BCPC, 22–23, 163–65
Corporate and cultural/social values,
    disjunction between, 45
Corporate-sponsored deals, 221–24
Corruption, 22, 177–78
Costa Rica, 68
Cost-effectiveness and legislative process,
    34
    see also Economic listings
Council of Economic Advisors (CEA), 34
Council of Environmental Quality, 14
Cram-down behavior, 189
Cultural and corporate values, disjunction
    between, 45
Cultural brokers and forming
    partnerships, 221
Cuomo, Mario, 182

DaimlerChrysler, 40
Dalai Lama, 203
Darwin, Charles, 217
"Death of Permanence" (Toffler), 207
Deforestation, 67–72
Delbruck, Max, 217
Denmark, 43, 89
Department of Environmental
    Conservation (DEC), 140, 144
Department of Environmental Protection
    (DEP), 144, 145, 154
Developer-sponsored projects, 221,
    223–25
Developing countries:
    consumption, paper, 62
    deforestation, 70–71
    forests and biodiversity, 68
    future, hope for the, 265
    globalization impacting negatively on, 5
    government ownership of factories, 265
    permitting process, 129

Developing countries (*continued*):
  rich/poor, sustainable development and
    gap between, 5–6
Development, sustainable/people-
  centered, *see* Sustainability
Development tasks, lack of knowledge
  about industrial, 45–46
Diesel fuel, 200
Dinkins, David, 154, 182
Dioxins, 8, 63, 67, 76, 222
Disposable practices, markets built on,
  207–8
Domestic Policy Council (DPC), 34
Duke University, 75
Dunlap, Al, 224
Dylan, Bob, 251

"Early Detection of Decay Will Extend
  the Service Life of Wood," 79
"Early Detection of Forest Health
  Stressors," 79
Earth Summit (1992), 39
East River, 108–11, 155
Economic Development Corporation,
  182, 218
Economic Development Zone, New York
  State, 101, 102
Economic issues:
  compromises, strategic, 203–4
  consciousness, need for a change in
    human, 207–8
  disposable practices, markets built on,
    207–8
  engineering/construction partners,
    choosing, 225–26
  feasibility assessments, 58
  financing practices, 156–57, 173, 207,
    228–31
  future, hope for the, 252–53, 258–59
  incentives promoting nonsustainable
    production/consumption, 77–80,
    205, 207–9
  legislative process, cost-effectiveness
    and, 34
  marketplace, change must happen in
    the, 208–9, 258
  partnerships, forming, 246–47
  political action and fragmentation of,
    33
  poverty alleviation essential to a
    sustainable society, 5–6, 98, 102

  profits, 229–30, 246–47, 252–53,
    258–59
  recycling and revenue generation, 95
  see also Research and analysis
Economic/technical obstacles to urban
  industrial-ecology development:
  cleanup, 124–29
  clearing the market, 201
  conclusions/chapter summary, 167
  construction-labor costs, 146–51
  energy expenses, 159–62
  permitting, 129–37
  recycled raw materials, difficulties of
    using, 162–67
  rural greenfields compared to urban
    brownfields, 122–24
  water issues, 151–54
  wealth-creation potential of projects,
    spreading, 198
  zoning, 137–39
Eco-realism, 46–51, 216
Electricity and brownfield-reclamation
  approach, 113, 161
Elemental chlorine free (ECF) mills, 64
El Niño/Southern Oscillation (ENSO),
  67
Emergence, life-sciences concept of,
  204–5
Emerson, Ralph W., 37, 202, 203
Employment and brownfield-reclamation
  approach, 98, 99
Employment opportunities essential to
  sustainable development, 5–6
Empowerment Zone Board, New York
  City Federal, 101, 181
Energy efficiency/issues:
  Bronx Community Paper Company,
    19–20
  commuting, 115
  economic/technical obstacles to urban
    industrial-ecology development,
    159–62
  electricity and steam, 113–14, 161
  future, hope for the, 254
  recycling, 91, 92
  transportation, 115–17
Engineering/construction partners,
  choosing, 225–28
Enron, 47
Environmental Assessment Statement
  (EAS), 140, 141

Environmental Conservation,
    Department of, 140, 144
Environmental Defense, 6–7, 102
Environmental Impact Statement (EIS),
    136, 140–43, 146, 157
Environmentalism:
  boards of directors, environmentalists
      serving on, 47–49
  consumer decisions based on
      price/performance/style, 39–41
  damaging impacts, dreadful record of
      industries', 59–61
  development tasks, lack of knowledge
      about, 45–46
  environmentalists in business,
      old-guard resistance to,
      191–93
  future, hope for the, 255, 257–61
  marketplace, change must happen in
      the, 208–9
  owners/developers of corporations,
      environmentalists as, 49–51, 166,
      230, 257–59
  partnerships, forming, 241–44
  permitting process, 134–35
  technology penalized by financing
      practices, innovative, 156–57
  traditional strategies, inadequacy of,
      27–29
  see also Blueprint for change, a new;
      Recycling; Research and analysis
Environmental Protection, Department
    of, 144, 145, 154
Environmental Protection Agency (EPA),
    63–64, 130, 144
Environmental Protection Department,
    192
European Union (EU), 8, 259–61
Executive Order 12873, 14, 38–39
Exploitation over conservation, global
    industrial system supporting,
    205–9
Extinctions, mass/background, 59

Feasibility assessments, 58
  see also Economic listings; Research and
      analysis
Federal Register, 98
Ferrer, Fernando, 22, 165, 181
Financing practices, 156–57, 173, 207,
    228–31

Flooding and tree plantations, 75–76
Food and Agriculture Organization
    (FAO), 61
Forest Products Laboratory (FPL), 74,
    78–79
Forestry/forests:
  BCPC, forestry practices impacted by, 18
  biodiversity, global, 67–72, 94
  future, hope for the, 256–57
  guidelines for the new industrial
      developer, 198
  recycling and tree harvesting, 93
  Scandinavian companies, 222
  southeastern forests, U.S., 93–94
  subsidies to timber industry, 77–80
  tree plantations, 71, 72–76
Forest Service, U.S., 71
Fortis, Inc., 31
Forums, international, 36–37
Fragmentation, see Habitat fragmentation
France, 89
Fresh Kills landfill, 7, 90
Fuel-efficiency standards, 10–11, 32, 187
Furans, 63, 67
Future, hope for the:
  Bronx, south, 251
  brownfields, 253
  community participation, 254–55,
      263–64
  developing countries, 265
  economic issues, 258–59
  energy issues, 254
  environmentalism, 255, 257–61
  European Union, 259–61
  forestry/forests, 256–57
  government participation, 264–66
  overview, 251–52
  partnerships, forming, 261–66
  permitting process, 255–56, 261
  philanthropic foundations, 262
  pollution issues, 257
  principles to help guide industrial
      developers, 252–57
  profits, 252–53
  recycling, 253
  respect/trust, establishing mutual, 266–67
  social-market obstacles to urban
      industrial-ecology development, 254
  technology, 255
  unions, 262–63
  Wall Street-oriented strategy, 259

Future, hope for the (*continued*):
    water issues, 253–54
Future Shock (Toffler), 207

Galesi Group Inc., The, 127
Garbage generation, paper's percentage of,
    76
Gas boilers, 113–14
Gasoline, lead in, 15–16
Georgia-Pacific, 68
Germany, 89, 260
Giuliani, Rudolph, 22–23, 154, 158,
    182, 183
Global Crossing, 47
Globalization:
    developing countries bearing brunt of,
      5
    exploitation over conservation, 205–9
Goldman Sachs, 230
Goldstein, Eric, 16–17
Gore, Al, 14, 22, 80
Government involvement, 30–31, 77–80,
    264–66
    see also Blueprint for change, a new;
      Regulations/legislation, government
Grades/classifications of paper, 61
Green Building Council, 199
Green Development, 121
Greene, Graham, 171
Greenfields, *see* Rural greenfields
Greenhouse gases (GHGs), 64, 74,
    76–77, 110–12, 114
Greenpeace, 259
Green strategies, the prevailing, 37–40
Guatemala, 31

Habitat fragmentation:
    roads, 63, 67, 78
    subsidies to timer industry,
      government, 78
    tree plantations, 75
Hardwoods, 71
Harlem River, 101, 102, 125
Harvard Business Review, 50
Hawken, Paul, 50
Hazardous air pollutants (HAPs), 64, 67
Health issues and waste-management
    practices, 7–8
Heilbroner, Robert, 37
Homelessness, 5–6
Hugo, Victor, 24, 143, 176, 190

Hydrogen peroxide, 63

Idealism, practical side to, 29
    see also Blueprint for change, a new;
      Industrial-ecological approach
ImClone, 47
Imposed-from-outside approach, 100
Incentives promoting nonsustainable
    production/consumption, 77–80,
    205, 207–9
Incinerators, 7–8, 41–42, 60, 76
"Increasing the Demand for Small-
    Diameter Material," 78
Indonesia, 70, 80
Industrial-ecological approach:
    barriers to sustainability, understanding
      systemic, 205–9
    BCPC's beginnings in, 41
    businesses challenging, existing,
      174–76
    clearing the market, 201
    collaboration, the power of, 209–12
    compromises, strategic, 201–4
    conclusions/chapter summary, 212–13
    design-for-recycling movement, 42
    development tasks, need to become
      knowledgeable about, 45–46
    examples of, 43–44
    future, hope for the, 265
    guidelines for the new industrial
      developer, 197–205
    life-cycle assessments, 42–43
    marketplace, change must happen in
      the, 208–9
    overview, 40–41
    politics as obstacle to, 157–59, 172
    precautionary principle, 204–5
    product policy, 42
    public-works projects, government
      sponsored, 265
    recycling fundamental component
      underlying, 44–45
    standards, no universally accepted,
      199–201
    sustainable business practices leading
      to, 41–42
    transportation impacts, 115
    wealth-creation potential of projects,
      spreading, 198
    see also Economic/technical obstacles to
      urban industrial-ecology

development; Social-market obstacles to urban industrial-ecology development

Industrialized countries:
consumption, increases in overall, 38
paper consumption, 62
permitting process, 129–31
rich/poor, sustainable development and gap between, 5–6
see also Organization for Economic Cooperation and Development

Industry-environmental community relationship, see Blueprint for change, a new; Industrial-ecological approach

Informed-consumer approach to ecological reform, 40

Infrastructure/operational issues and brownfield-reclamation approach, 99, 102–3, 116

Innovation, collaboration inspiring, 217
see also Technology

Internal Revenue Service (IRS), 77–78

International bodies, growing influence of, 36–37

International Fact and Price Book, 77

International Institute for Environment and Development (IIED), 61

International Organization for Standardization (ISO) management standards, 199–200

International Paper, 68

Investors in industrial projects, 156–57, 173, 207, 228–31

J. P. Morgan, 230

Japan, 8, 89, 260

Jeffords, Jim, 11

Jobs and brownfield-reclamation approach, 98, 99

Jurisdictions, government action limited by political, 31

Kanniah, Rajeswari, 261

Kirk, Ken, 105

Korea, 89

Labor-construction costs, 146–51

Landfills, 4, 6–8, 41–42, 60, 76–77, 90

Landmarks Preservation Commission, 157

Latin America, 68, 80

Latitudinal diversity gradients and species concentration/diversity, 71

Lawyers and biases in global industrial system, 206

Leadership in Energy and Environmental Design (LEED), 199

Lead in gasoline, 15–16

Legal/litigation issues, 21–23, 135–37, 183–84, 191–92

Legislation:
Clean Air Act of 1970, 113, 156
Comprehensive Environmental Response, Compensation, and Liabilities Act (CERCLA) of 1980, 127
Resource Conservation and Recovery Act (RCRA) of 1976, 41
Rivers and Harbors Act of 1899, 145
Small Business Liability Relief and Brownfields Revitalization Act, 101
see also Regulations/legislation, government

Les Misérables (Hugo), 190

Life-cycle assessments (LCAs):
purpose of, 62–63
tree plantations, 74
weaknesses of, 42–43

Lin, Maya, 20, 142, 143, 190

Lindenthal, Gustav, 157

Litigation issues, 21–23, 135–37, 183–84, 191–92

Little Hell Gate Bridge, 157

Lobbyists/experts and legislative process, 9–14, 34

Local industrial corrections, investing in and building, 27

Locally undesirable land use (LULU), 218

Location decisions, 87–88
see also Brownfields, siting factories at urban; Economic/technical obstacles to urban industrial-ecology development; Social-market obstacles to urban industrial-ecology development

Logrolling, 12

Long Island Sound, 108

Lovins, Amory, 50

Lovins, Hunter, 50

Macaws, 31
Major Degan Expressway, 101, 125
"Making the Most of Small-Diameter
    Western Softwoods," 79
Manufacturing:
    exploitation over conservation, global
        industrial system supporting, 205–9
    job declines, 5, 6
    social context, recognizing the, 44
Market-based environmentalism/issues,
    6–7, 172–74, 208–9, 258
    see also Blueprint for change, a new;
        Economic listings; Industrial-
        ecological approach
Markup stage in legislative process, 9–14
Mass extinctions, 59
Mayr, Ernst, 1, 211
McDonald's, 29
Medicinal plants and tree plantations, 75
Mercury, 42
Merrill Lynch, 230
Methane, 76–77
Methoxychlor, 74
Methylene chloride, 67
Mexico, 70
Microfiltration, 110–12
Middle East, 107
Mitchell, George, 15
Mobro barge, 7–8
Modlin, Reg, 40
MoDo Paper Company, 146, 222, 223,
    225, 228
Moosa, Mohammed V., 5
Morse Diesel International, 227–28
Muir, John, 37
Muschamp, Herbert, 143

National Audubon Society, 102
National Economic Council (NEC), 34
National Minority Business Development
    Council (NMBDC), 226
National Priorities List (NPL), 125
National Research Council, 27, 87, 203,
    219, 256
National Spill Reports, 126
Natural Resources Defense Council
    (NRDC):
    community participation, 232
    construction companies suing BCPC,
        23
    environmentalists in business, old-
        guard resistance to, 193

future, hope for the, 263
National Recycling Act, rise and fall of,
    8–15
    partnerships, forming, 222, 234
    permitting process, 137, 146
    recycling, litigation concerning,
        191–92
    solid waste management project, 6
Netherlands, 89
New England, 130
New Jersey, 130
Newsprint, 4–5, 96
New York Post, 22, 117
New York Times, 16, 20, 23, 192
NIMBY (not in my back yard), 7
1980s as decade when solid-waste
    management matured, 7–8
Nitrogen, 110–12, 114
Nongovernmental organizations (NGOs),
    174, 185, 188, 190, 262
North American Free Trade Agreement
    (NAFTA), 36
North Carolina, 75
Norway, 89
Novo/Nordisk/Novozymes, 43

Office of Information and Regulatory
    Affairs (OIRA), 34
Office of Management and Budget
    (OMB), 14, 33–34
Office of Parks, Recreation/Historic
    Preservation, 145
Oil drilling, 187
Organization for Economic Cooperation
    and Development (OECD):
    consumption, increases in overall, 38
    deforestation, 69–70
    paper consumption, 61, 68
    permitting process, 130
    regulations/legislation, government,
        30–31
    tree plantations, 72, 73
    water consumption, 64
Organizations, international, 36–37
Organochlorines, 64
Owners/developers of corporations,
    environmentalists as, 49–51, 166,
    230, 257–59
Ozone, 114

Packaging, toxic/nonrecyclable, 6–8
    41–42

Paper waste/recycling/production, 4,
    14–15, 38–39, 74–77
    see also Bronx Community Paper
        Company
Parks Department, New York City, 145,
    157–58
Partnerships, forming:
    Bronx Community Paper Company,
        218–20
    community participation, encouraging,
        232–40
    compromises, strategic, 201–4
    conclusions/chapter summary, 248–49
    construction/engineering partners,
        choosing, 225–28
    corporate-sponsored deals, 221–24
    creating a development partnership,
        220–25
    developer-sponsored projects, 221,
        223–25
    environmental groups, 241–44
    evaluating community partners,
        237–40
    future, hope for the, 261–66
    innovation, collaboration inspiring, 217
    investment-banking firms, 228–31
    overview, 215–16
    power of collaboration, 209–12
    respect among collaborators, 245–47
    see also Community participation
Pataki, George, 158, 182, 183
Pentachlorophenols, 67
Permitting process:
    accidents, major industrial, 130
    Bronx Community Paper Company,
        139–46, 236
    community participation, 135–37,
        232–33
    environmental friendly/harmful
        projects, 134–35
    future, hope for the, 255–56, 261
    innovation stifled by, 136–37, 202, 242
    limits of, 131
    litigation issues, 135–37
    pollution impacts, reducing, 131
    rationale for, 129
    rural vs. urban areas, 131–34
    subversion of, 129–31
Pfarr, Heide, 263
Phenolics, chlorinated, 63
Philanthropic foundations, 262
Photovoltaics, 113

Pinewoods, deciduous hardwood trees
    converted into, 71
Place-based understanding of ecological
    threats, 27
Planning Commission, City, 143
Plantations, tree, 71, 72–76
Plastic bottle deposit requirements, 10, 11
Plastic vs. paper reforms, researching,
    57–58
PM analysis, 19
Politics/political issues:
    Bronx Community Paper Company,
        180–83
    contracts, 22–23, 163–65
    failure of projects, political opposition
        and, 100
    fragmentation of, 33
    industrial-ecology development
        hampered by, 157–59, 172
    investment banks, 231
    jurisdictions, government action
        limited by political, 31
    local leadership, interests of, 178–80
    obstacle to industrial-ecology
        development, 157–59, 172
    rural greenfields, 182
    social-market obstacles to urban
        industrial-ecology development,
        178–80
    waste hauling, corporate, 165–66
    wastewater, reclaimed, 157
    see also Regulations/legislation,
        government; Social-market
        obstacles to urban industrial-
        ecology development
Pollution issues:
    bleaching, paper manufacturing and
        chlorine-based, 63–64, 76, 222,
        264
    compromises, strategic, 202
    dioxins, 8, 63, 67, 76, 222
    electricity and steam power plants,
        113–14
    Fresh Kills landfill, 90
    future, hope for the, 257
    guidelines for the new industrial
        developer, 197–98
    packaging, toxic/nonrecyclable, 6–8,
        41–42
    paper products,
        consumption/disposal/production
        of, 74–77

Pollution issues (*continued*):
    permitting process, 131
    recycling and water pollution, 91, 93
    research and analysis, 63–67, 76–77
    sewage effluent, 105–6, 108–12,
        155–57
    tree plantations, 73–75
    see also Air quality/pollution; Research
        and analysis; Water pollution/issues
Polyaromatic-hydrocarbons (PAHs), 18
Polychlorinated biphenyls (PCBs), 126
Population growth, 38
Poverty alleviation essential to a
    sustainable society, 5–6, 98, 102
Precautionary principle, 203, 204–5
Private sector crucial to building a
    sustainable economy, 28–29
    see also Blueprint for change, a new;
        Industrial-ecological approach
Production processes and global industrial
    system supporting exploitation over
    conservation, 205–6
Production stage, environmental impacts
    occurring in, 46–47
Product policy, 42
Profits, 229–30, 246–47, 252–53,
    258–59
Property rights, 129
Public Authority Control Board, New
    Your State, 143
Public Interest Research Group, New
    York, 102
Publicly owned treatment works
    (POTWs), 104, 105

Racism, 177
Rail-freight development, 18
Raw materials, benefits of using recycled,
    89–96, 253
Raw materials, difficulties of using
    recycled, 162–67
Recycling:
    benefits of using recycled raw materials,
        89–96, 253
    Congressional Research Service (CRS),
        8–9
    design-for recycling movement, 42
    difficulties of using recycled raw
        materials, 162–67
    economic/technical obstacles to urban
        industrial-ecology development,
        162–67

energy savings, 91, 92
    Executive Order 12873, 14, 38–39
    future, hope for the, 253
    industrial-ecological approach, 44–45
    limited markets for recycled products,
        45
    litigation concerning, 191–92
    National Recycling Act, rise and fall of,
        8–15
    newsprint, pluses of producing, 96
    product policy, 42
    product yield per ton, 93
    regulations stimulating markets, 6–8
    research and analysis, 58–59
    revenue, potential to generate, 95
    sustainability, recycling as fundamental
        to, 44
    virgin material *vs.* recycled-based
        factories, 88
    water pollution, 91, 93
    wild ecosystems, reduced need to
        destroy, 93–95
    see also Bronx Community Paper
        Company
Reforestation, mistaking tree plantations
    for, 72–73
Regulations/legislation, government:
    adversarial *vs.* collaborative approach,
        211
    balkanized approach to policy making,
        31
    cost-effectiveness and legislative process,
        34
    Executive Order 12873, 13, 38–39
    exemptions to timber industry, 79
    inadequacy of government-dependent
        advocacy, 30–31
    limits of the legislative process, 33–36
    markup stage in legislative process,
        9–15
    National Recycling Act, rise and fall of,
        8–15
    recycled materials, stimulating broader
        markets for, 6–8
    social/economic issues, fragmentation
        of, 33
    timber industry, exemptions to, 79
    trade groups writing policy, 35–36
    treaties/forums/organizations,
        international, 36–37
    truths ignored in favor of political
        expediency, 31–32

zoning, 137–39
see also Legislation; Permitting process
Request-for-proposal (RFP), 164
Research and analysis:
air emissions/water effluent/solid
wastes, 63–67
conclusions/chapter summary, 80–81
consumption, surge in, 61–62
damaging ecological impacts,
industries', 59–61
downstream impacts, 76–77
economic-feasibility assessments, 58
extinctions, mass/background, 59
forests and global biodiversity, 67–72
life-cycle assessments, 42–43, 62–63, 74
plastics vs. paper reforms, 57–58
subsidies to timber industry, 77–80
upstream burdens, 62–72
see also Economic listings
Research Highlights of 1999, 78
Resource distortion and globalization, 5
Respect/trust, future hope and
establishing mutual, 266–67
Revenue generation, recycling and, 95
Reverse-osmosis system, 110–12, 155
Rich and poor, sustainable development
threatened by gap between, 5–6
Rivera, Yolanda, 22, 235
Roads and habitat fragmentation, 63, 67,
78
Rose, Jonathan F. P., 203–4
Rothschild, Emma, 40
Rural greenfields:
construction-labor rates, 147, 148
economics and urban brownfield
compared to, 122–24
energy expenses, 160–61
exploitation over conservation, global
industrial system supporting, 206
future, hope for the, 253
guidelines for the new industrial
developer, 198
permitting process, 131–34
politics/political issues, 182
virgin material vs. recycled-based
factories, 88
water acquisition costs, 151–53
zoning, 138
Russia, 70

S. D. Warren Company, 148, 222–25,
228

Sanitation Department (New York), 90,
102, 163, 182, 192, 218
Scandinavia, 80, 222
Science ignored in favor of political
expediency, 31–32
see also Technology
Scott Paper Company, 224
Sears, Phil, 100, 132
Securities and Exchange Commission
(SEC), 128
Selective-catalytic-dentrification
equipment, 20
Sentiments as objective of economic
striving/exchange, 40
Sewage-treatment-plant wastewater,
reclaimed, 19, 104–13, 154–59
Shabecoff, Philip, 23–24
Siting a factory/industry complex, 87–88
see also Brownfields, siting factories at
urban; Economic/technical
obstacles to urban industrial-
ecology development; Social-market
obstacles to urban industrial-
ecology development
Smith, Adam, 40
Smurfit-Stone, 68
Social-market obstacles to urban
industrial-ecology development:
businesses, challenges from existing,
174–76
community groups, difficulties working
with, 176–78
conclusions/chapter summary,
193–94
construction companies, litigation
intimidation from, 183–84
culture of business, 188–91
environmentalists in business,
old-guard resistance to, 191–93
examples of, 171–72
fragmentation of social issues, political
action and, 33
future, hope for the, 254
market forces, understanding social
forces shaping, 172–74
political leadership, 178–80
unions, 185–87
values, disjunction between corporate
and social, 45
Socrates, 37
Softwoods, 71
Soil and tree plantations, 75

Sole-source contracts, 164
Solid-waste management, 6–8, 41–42, 63–67
"Solution, The" (Wilson), 212
South America, 68, 70, 148
Southeastern forests, U.S., 93–94
Spain, 44, 89
Species diversity and latitudinal diversity gradients, 71
Stakeholders with different objectives forming partnerships, 221
Standards, no universally accepted sustainability, 199–201
Starbucks, 29
STATOIL refinery, 43
Steam/gas boilers and brownfield-reclamation approach, 113–14, 161–62
Stiglitz, Joseph E., 5
Stone Consolidated, 259
Stone Container, 68
Subsidies promoting nonsustainable production/consumption, 77–80, 207, 208–9
Sustainability:
    barriers to, understanding systemic, 205–9, 219–20, 251–52
    Board on Sustainable Development, 203, 256
    consumption, confusion over sustainable, 40
    dialogue and collaboration, 255
    poverty, sustainable development threatened by, 5–6, 98, 102
    private sector, importance of, 28–29
    recycling as fundamental to, 44
    standards, no universally accepted, 199–201
    top-down legitimacy, 241
    see also Industrial-ecological approach
Sweden, 89, 218, 260
Swift, Al, 9, 11
Switzerland, 89
Synthetic organic chemical manufacturing industry (SOCMI) plants, 257

Tax incentives for timber industry, 77–80
Technology:
    compromises, strategic, 202–3
    financing practices penalizing innovative, 156–57
    future, hope for the, 255

global industrial system, biases in, 205–7
    innovation, collaboration inspiring, 217
    permitting procedures stifling innovation, 136–37, 236, 242
Tennessee-Tombigbee Waterway, 80
Theory of Moral Sentiments (Smith), 40
"Things: The Throw-Away Society" (Toffler), 207
Thoreau, Henry D., 37, 211
Tierney, John, 4
Timber industry, see Forestry/forests
Toffler, Alvin, 207
Top-down legitimacy and sustainability, 241
Töpfer, Klaus, 40, 46, 67–68
Total suspended solids (TSS), 110
Trade groups writing government policy, 35–36
Training, brownfield-reclamation approach and worker, 99
Transportation Department, New York, 127, 141
Transportation-related energy impacts, 76, 115–17
"Treated Wood-Does More Preservative Mean a Better Product?", 79
Treaties, international, 36–37
Tree plantations, 71, 72–76
    see also Forestry/forests
Triborough Bridge, 101, 125
Triborough Bridge and Tunnel Authority, 145, 158
Trichlorophenols, 67
Trust/respect, future hope and establishing mutual, 266–67
Truths ignored in favor of political expediency, 31–32

Unemployment, 5–6
Unions:
    community-based laborers, hiring, 150, 226
    future, hope for the, 262–63
    obstacle to industrial-ecology development, 172, 173
    rules, work, 148–50
    social-market obstacles to urban industrial-ecology development, 185–87
    voting on unionization, 150–51

United Nations:
  Convention on the Elimination of
    Genocide, 177
  Convention on the Environment and
    Development (UNCED) in 1992,
    39
  Environment Program (UNEP), 156
  Food and Agriculture Organization,
    61
  Universal Declaration of Human Rights,
    177
"Updating the Standard Reference on
  Wood," 79
U.S. Trade Representative (USTR), 34

Values, disjunction between corporate and
  cultural/social, 45
Veblen, Thorstein, 37
Virgin-based approach to industrial
  production, 88, 205–8
  see also Industrial-ecological approach
Visy Paper, 22–23
Volatile organic compounds (VOCs), 18,
  64, 67

Walden (Thoreau), 211
Wall Street–oriented strategy as a hope for
  the future, 259
Wards Island Water Pollution Control
  Plant (WPCP), 108–11, 145, 154,
  157
Waste haulers, corporate, 165–66
Waste Management, 21–22, 47, 165
Wastepaper, 4
  see also Bronx Community Paper
    Company

Wastes from all sources, worldwide
  generation of, 30–31
Water pollution/issues:
  Bronx Community Paper Company,
    107–13, 154–59
  brownfield-reclamation approach,
    103–7
  economic/technical obstacles to urban
    industrial-ecology development,
    151–54
  future, hope for the, 253–54
  permitting process, 145
  recycling, 91, 93
  research and analysis, 63–67
  rural greenfields, 151–53
  sewage-treatment-plant wastewater,
    reclaimed, 19, 104–13, 154–59
  tree plantations, 75–76
Water vapors, 76
Watson, James, 217
Wetlands, 75
White House Council on Economic
  Advisors, 14
Wild ecosystems, recycling and reduced
  need to destroy, 93–95
Wilson, Edward O., 57, 212, 266–67
Wordsworth, William, 37
World Bank, 58
WorldCom, 47
World Health Organization, 62
World Trade Organization (WTO), 36
Worldwatch Institute, 38

Zaidel, Dahlia, 217
Zimmer, Carl, 204
Zoning issues, 133, 137–39

Allen Hershkowitz is a senior scientist at the Natural Resources Defense Council, specializing in issues related to sustainable development, industrial ecology, health risks, solid-waste management, recycling, the paper industry, medical wastes, and sludge. He frequently advises government, NGO, and corporate officials in the United States, Europe, Central America, and Japan and testifies regularly before federal agencies, House and Senate congressional committees, and state and local agencies. In 1989 Dr. Hershkowitz served as a delegate to the United Nations Treaty Convention on the Transboundary Movements of Hazardous Wastes, where he worked to prevent the dumping of hazardous wastes into less developed countries. He is the originator, former president, and cochairman of the board of the Bronx Community Paper Company, arguably the most ambitious world-scale industrial-ecology project conceived to date, the promise and demise of which is detailed in this book. In 2002 he was awarded a Special Citation by the American Institute of Architects for his work developing the BCPC. His work has been the subject of numerous profiles and articles, including a feature in *The New Yorker*. His own writings have appeared in *Technology Review*, the *New York Times*, *The Atlantic Monthly*, *Newsday*, and *The Nation*, among many other publications, and he is the author of *Garbage Management in Japan* (1986) and *Too Good to Throw Away: Recycling's Proven Record* (1997).

Maya Lin is an artist who has had a studio practice in New York City since 1985. She received a Master's in architecture from Yale University, where she also completed her undergraduate studies. Though best known for her monumental works, such as the Vietnam Veterans Memorial and the Civil Rights Memorial, she has created a body of art and architecture works throughout the country that focus on her concern for landscape, topography, and the environment.